D1832003

MEDIA
SOCIETY AND CULTURE

OM GUPTA

ISHA

ISHA BOOKS

DELHI - 110033

Media Society and Culture

ISBN: 81-8205-363-3

Rs. 690

© Om Gupta

All rights reserved. No part of this book may be reproduced in any manner without written permission.

Published in 2006 in India by
Isha Books
D-43, Prithviraj Road, Adarsh Nagar, Delhi-110033
E-mail : ishabooks@hotmail.com

Laser Typesetting at: Master Computers, Delhi
Printed at: Salasar Imaging System, Delhi

Contents

Preface

The media plays a very significant role in our society today. It is all around us. From the shows we watch on TV, the music we listen to on the radio, to the books, magazines, and newspapers we read each day. Without the media, people in societies would be isolated, not only from the rest of the world, but from governments, law-makers, and neighbouring towns and cities.

Media is a powerful socialising agent. It affect how we learn about our world and interact with one another. It mediate our relationship with social institutions. We are dependent on the media for what we know and how we relate to the world of politics because of the media-politics connection. Politicians rely on media to communicate their message. Similar dynamics are present in other mediated events such as televised sports and televangelism. Media is part of our routine relations with family and friends. They define our interaction with other people on a daily basis as a diversion, sources of conflict, or a unifying force.

Media often act as the bridge between our personal/ private lives and the public world. We see ourselves and our place in society through mass media. It is because of this connection that we need to pay special attention to mass media if we want to understand how society functions. Media play many different and maybe incompatible roles. For the audiences, it is a source of entertainment and information while for media workers, media is an industry that offer jobs and therefore income, prestige and professional identity. For the owners, the media is a source of profit and a source of political power. For society at larger, the media can be a way to transmit information and values. Therefore depending on whose perspective and which role we focus on we might see a different media picture.

As a healthy and objective media can prevent a society from many maladies, negative presentations in mass media can create and promote social trends as well. Media forms a society's outlook, if its impact is positive and media accomplishes its tasks and responsibilities in an outstanding manner and guides the new generations by imparting knowledge and awareness then the society has greater chances of being a pluralistic, just and democratic one. On the other hand, negative impacts of media might intensify hatred leading to violence and bloodshed forming all brutal conflicts. So the role of mass media has to be that of a guide or torchbearer showing right path.

This book examines the ways in which the media have become deeply entwined in our social life. It provides invaluable information in key areas such as theories of media and society; studies of media organisation; and studies of media, culture, and ideology. It will create an understanding of the processes through which the media are enabled and constrained by such factors as technology, industry structure, law and market. It uses sociological theories, contemporary industry data and several examples to give readers a better understanding of why they have certain media choices available to them and the possible effects of those choices. Besides students and teachers of journalism and mass communication, the contents of the book will be immensely useful for sociologists, communication and mass media specialists, film, music, and pop culture critics, and enthusiasts of these fields.

Editor

1

Power of Media

Media of communication are organised means of dissemination of fact, opinion, entertainment, and other information, such as newspapers, magazines, cinema films, radio, television, the world wide web, billboards, books, CDs, DVDs, videocassettes, computer games and other forms of publishing. Mass media are that section of the media specifically conceived and designed to reach a very large audience. The mass-media audience has been viewed by some commentators as forming a mass society with special characteristics, notably atomisation or lack of social connections, which render it especially susceptible to the influence of modern mass-media techniques such as advertising and propaganda. It is also gaining popularity in the blogosphere when referring to the mainstream media.

During the 20th century, the growth of mass media was driven by technology that allowed the massive duplication of material. Physical duplication technologies such as printing, record pressing and film duplication allowed the duplication of books, newspapers and movies at low prices to huge audiences. Radio and television allowed the electronic duplication of information for the first time. Mass media had the economics of linear replication: a single work could make money proportional to the number of copies sold, and as volumes went up, units costs went down, increasing profit margins further.

Vast fortunes were to be made in mass media. In a democratic society, independent media serve to educate the public/electorate about issues regarding government and corporate entities. Some consider the concentration of media ownership to be a grave threat to democracy.

Governments and political parties have focussed on the mass media as sources of powerful influence. More recently, businesses and organisations have recognised the importance of the media not only as channels for advertising, but for their perhaps even more influential editorial content. Editorial in leading mass media has been shown to significantly affect stock prices; lead to corporate collapses; cause falls in sales; result in the resignation of senior officeholders.

Effects of Mass Media

Early media research assumed direct effects, adopting a 'hypodermic' injection concept of mass media, also described as the 'transmissional' model based on the wellknown model of communication developed by Shannon and Weaver which simplistically described communication as transmitting a message from a sender to a receiver. In this view, power was thought to reside in texts and the producers; audiences were perceived as passive receivers of information.

Views of the media as powerful propaganda tools which were or could be unleashed on a hapless mass audience led to the Mass Manipulative Model of the media and underpinned later cultural hegemony and political economy views. In 1937, with the proliferation of radio, Antonio Gramsci proposed that 'ideological hegemony' created through powerful mass media was used by the ruling class to 'perpetuate their power, wealth and status'. Marxist and neo-Marxist scholars such as Adorno & Horkheimer saw the media as "managers of opinion at the behest of the powerful".

The transmissional or hypodermic injection model of mass media dominated thinking during the first half of the 20th century. Landmark research in the late 1950s and 1960s refuted many claimed effects of the media and showed media power was overestimated. Key studies were those of Katz & Lazarsfeld and Joseph Klapper. Klapper concluded that "mass communications ordinarily do not serve as a necessary and sufficient cause of audience effects". He concluded instead that mass media were more likely to reinforce existing attitudes than change them or create new attitudes. His findings became known as Klapper's 'law of minimal consequences' and triggered a 'limited effects' view of mass media.

Klapper drew on cognitive dissonance theory of the 1950s as espoused by psychologist Leon Festinger who found that people resisted messages that were dissonant with their existing attitudes and accepted information which was consonant with their existing views. Research into media violence and pornography supported Klapper's view. No clear correlations have been found between media violence and violent behaviour in 30 years of research.

Studies of pornography in Denmark found no link to sex crimes and violence against women. In fact, following repeal of Danish prohibitions against written pornography in 1967 and the ending of film censorship in 1969, the number of sex-related crimes in Denmark declined. Even today, the link between TV and film violence and actual violence in society remains a site of debate. Another approach which considered the influence of mass media to be limited was a pluralist view of society which emerged in the 1940s and was popular through the 1960s.

Proponents of pluralism considered that there are many different centres of power in society and that natural checks and balances are achieved through "countervailing forces". "Under pluralistic views, the power of the media was seen as limited and conditional, a power that was 'mediated' by an ever-extending range of factors". Another strain of media research which also rejected the direct effects thinking of earlier research and first introduced the notion of audience interpretation became known as the 'uses and gratifications' perspective.

Proponents of this theory claim that people use mass media to gratify human needs. "Instead of asking what the media do to people, uses and gratifications research turned the question around: what do people do with the media?"

'Uses and gratifications' thinking about mass media continues today, although it has lost some favour as it is linked to functionalist theory which assumes people willingly engage with mass media and benefit from the experience. Functionalist mass media theory was advanced by influential American political scientist, Harold Lasswell. He claimed that the media performed four basic functions for society: surveying the environment to provide news and information; correlating response to this information (editorial function); entertaining (diversion function); and transmitting culture to future generations.

American sociologist Charles R. Wright took Lasswell's view of media functions further by outlining manifest and latent (not apparent or unintended) functions as well as dysfunctions of mass media communication. Wright proposed that when the media alerted the public to a health risk, for instance, it was serving its news and information function, but if a public panic was created, this was a dysfunction of the media.

Direct Effects of Political Economy and Cultural Studies

Political economy thinking of mass media saw the dominant political, financial and industrial institutions of societies having a direct effect on the ideological forces maintaining control, including the media. Mosco defined political economy as the "study of the social relations, particularly the power relations, that influence the production, distribution, and consumption of resources, including communication resources". Like Marxist thinkers, "the radical political economy tradition continued to argue that the media were powerfully shaped by their political and economic organisation." This included media ownership, cross-ownership, monopolies, competition, public service broadcasting, and controls over quantity and content of advertising. In turn, political economy thinking argued that this political and economic structure influenced media audiences.

Political economy views on the media saw the media as having a moral purpose and aiming at social action. In this sense, political economy and later cultural studies views of the media reversed thinking that mass media had limited effects. However, they did not return to direct effects thinking. "Rather, political economy and cultural studies started from the premise that reinforcement was not neutral." Moreover, they took the concept of reinforcement further arguing that "reinforcement was the inevitable and contrived outcome of a system whose very purpose was to maintain order and to prevent change in societies that were riven by manifest inequalities".

Political economy theory saw mass media involved in 'the manufacture of consent'—a concept made famous by Naom Chomsky. McCombs in his 'agenda-setting theory' argued that the effect of mass media was less to do with "what people think" and more "what they think about" - ie. the media set the agenda of public debate and thinking. McCombs saw mass media as originators of influential messages rather than simply channels used by sources of information.

Marshall McLuhan's famous adage 'The Medium is the Message' built on this thinking and further focussed attention on the mass media. 'The medium is the message', often misunderstood in popular discourse, pointed to the production and representation processes of the mass media (eg. news selection, production techniques, etc) as fundamental in shaping the message. The weakness or Achilles Heel of political economy thinking about the media was exposed by the emerging fields of content analysis and audience research.

Whereas political economy theory focussed only on quantitative (often crude) mass media content methodology, assuming quantitative repetition was equivalent to semiotic or affective significance, new methods of qualitative content analysis began to consider the subtleties of narrative structure, characterisation and semiotics to determine likely meanings that audiences might take from texts. Cultural studies approaches to mass media borrowed from literary criticism and cinematic analysis and drew on linguistics and sociolinguistics. Cultural studies moved focus away from the structuralist traditions of Marx, Engels and Freud and introduced qualitative methods which examined how different readers interpreted texts differently. Even so, early neo-Marxist cultural studies saw mass media being used to influence or control audiences. However, they saw this as more subtle than direct control. Mass media, they argued, exerted influence through cultural hegemony.

Hegemony is summarised by Lull as "the power or dominance that one social group holds over others" gained through "a tacit willingness by people to be governed by principles, rules and laws which they believe operate in their best interests, even though in actual practice they may not". "Hegemony is a process of convergence, consent, and subordination. Ideas, social institutions, industries, and ways of living are synthesised into a mosaic which serves to preserve the economic, political, and cultural advantages of the already powerful". He adds: "The mass media play an extraordinary role in the process".

That people do not necessarily see the hegemonic power of mass media is not surprising when the subtle process of hegemony is understood. Lull points out: "The victims of hegemony don't realise they are being repressed through ideology". Habermas proposed a variation on political economy thinking with his concept of mass media as a 'public sphere' in which mass media function as a "forum of public communication: a forum in which individual citizens can come together as a public and confer freely about matters of general interest" . However, Habermas' concept of mass media as a 'public sphere' of debate where reason and logic would prevail has been widely dismissed and seen as flawed because of its "idealisation of public reason" —one could conclude naïve.

In short, with the advent of cultural studies, media effects thinking evolved from force, to coercion to consent (albeit an engineered consent). The 'ethnographic turn'— 'death of the author'; birth of the reader 'The ethnographic turn' in social and cultural studies research brought a major shift in thinking about mass media effects. Early cultural studies approaches to mass media drew on literary analysis, linguistics and socio-linguistics.

Early cultural studies ushered in what Curran terms "a reconceptualisation of the audience as an active producer of meaning". Socio-linguistic interpretations and semiological studies saw "meaning as mobile rather than fixed" and recognised "socially situated meaning systems". In simple terms, texts could mean different things to different people in different situations.

Post-Marxist cultural studies further turned attention to 'human agency', drawing from anthropological and social research to specifically examine how audiences interpret media texts. Building on Stuart Hall's important 'encoding-decoding' model, and his concept of the 'critical reader', sociologists and modern media scholars point out that audiences actively construct meanings of (decode) media texts within a matrix of influences, rather than passively absorb pre-determined meanings imposed on them.

Hall suggested that a media producer may 'encode' certain meanings into a text, based on a certain social context and understandings, but another person's reading ('decoding') of it will be based on their own social context and understandings, and they are likely to interpret it differently. McQuail "reversed the classic question of media effect from 'what effect do the media have on people' to 'how do people use the media' and thus helped turn around or modify previous assumptions of linearity and cause effect in thinking about media and audiences".

Cultural studies' main contribution to media studies was the identification of "intervening variables" that influence the relationship between text and audience. The 'new audience research' conducted in modern cultural studies of mass media found diversity of meanings drawn by people from the media they consume and revealed contradictions in how people consume mass media. For example, people were found in research to be "quite capable of conforming with prevalent social disapproval or depreciation of certain categories of text on one hand, while continuing to take pleasure from those same texts on the other".

In cultural studies approaches to mass media, texts are viewed as "polysemic, which is to say that they offer the possibility of a diversity of reading, even if a 'preferred reading' is inscribed within the text by its producers", Newbold, et al conclude. Curran and others agree saying: "... the media have fractured meanings". Audience 'reception analysis' carried out by David Morley advanced theory of audience power by focussing on textual meaning not as messages implanted by either media producers or influential institutions as proposed by earlier Marxist and Neo-Marxist theories, but in more sophisticated and complex ways drawing on semiology and ideology. New thinking proposed "interdiscursive processes in audience reception".

"The rediscovery of audience power in revisionist reception studies" was an important development in media effects theory and debunked media ideology leading to a "more cautious assessment of media influence". Fiske, one of the most outspoken cultural studies theorists, argued that it is the audience, not the, media, which has the most power However, more recently, scholars have put the view that Fiske "hopelessly romanticises the role of audience members". British sociologist, Keith Tester argues that "Fiske's work confuses the possibility that the audience might carry out oppositional readings of media texts with the claim that they actually do carry out such readings". Also, reception analysis, while seen as a major advance in understanding how mass media and audiences inter-relate, relied heavily-some say over-relied—on group discussions and rather loose concepts of 'decoding'.

Ethnographic methods of research such as discussion groups and participant observation, while widely acclaimed as a qualitative research method allowing direct first-hand data gathering, also contain inherent dangers through 'intervention' by the researcher (eg. respondents 'playing to the camera' or, in this case, the researcher) and through the researcher becoming 'too close' to the audience (colloquially termed 'going native' from early ethnographic studies of tribal cultures).

Contemporary Theory of Media Effects

Lull summarises what he calls "three zones of indeterminancy" of media effects which he identifies as (1) institutions which he claims are diverse; (2) technology which he holds is ultimately unmanageable; and (3) messages which he agrees are diverse and polysemic (open to multiple interpretations by different readers). Modern thinking on mass media recognises that "identities cannot be viewed as being constructed by media representations alone".

Curran adds that first-hand knowledge, word of-mouth relaying others' first-hand knowledge, sceptical dispositions towards the media and internal processes of logic also influence audiences' reading of media texts. However, there are flaws in 'limited effects' or 'minimal impact' theories of mass media. Mass media do have significant impact for a number of reasons.

"Throughout most of the 20th century the trend in culture industry ownership was toward concentration in the hands of fewer and fewer multinational corporations" Bagdikian notes. Lull says "the culture industries became part of a vast system of inter-related agencies". At the same time, globalisation of mass media has led to a small group of powerful, mainly western, publishers and broadcasters distributing increasingly homogenised media content worldwide.

Curran points out that audiences' ability individually and collectively to make oppositional readings or interpretations of mass media content depends on their access to oppositional discourses. A number of studies suggest that the influence of traditional sources for interpretation and meaning such as the family, the Church and work have declined in recent times . A clear indication of the decline of the Church as an influential institution in many societies is shown in an Australian report that religious orders have shrunk by one-third between 1981 and 1997. The 1996 Catholic Church Life Survey also reported that the number of Catholics attending mass weekly declined by 10% between 1991 and 1996 and found "less than half of 160,000 Catholics surveyed accepted without difficulty the Vatican's authority to teach certain doctrines".

International evidence of this trend was found in a Times Mirror Center for the People & the Press survey which reported that the Church had declined as a source of influence in the US, Canada, Britain, France and Germany and in all countries except the US it was rated lower than television and newspapers as a source of guiding and influential information.

"From the last quarter of the nineteenth century onwards, there was a cumulative process of de-Christianisation". Also, "during the same period" there was "decline of the factory, trade union, church, local neighbourhood and extended family . . ." media academic, James Curran notes.

Accompanying the decline in sources of alternative or oppositional discourse to mass media, modern mass media employ increasingly sophisticated methods (including 'docu-drama' and 'mockumentaries' which involve fiction made to look like factual presentations of information, Reality TV, etc) to maximise their semiotic efficacy. News media overtly claim to represent 'truth', facts and reality. These trends, when combined, result in substantial impact on media audiences.

There are some flaws can be identified in 'limited effects' thinking on mass media:

— *Reinforcement is an effect*: Media reinforcement is itself a powerful and significant effect. By reinforcing the status quo and/or selective discourses, mass media exert a major influence in society.

— *'Overspill' of meaning*: While audiences read their own meanings off media texts (including rejecting some media messages), researchers propose that some media-produced meanings get through. In other words, mass media representations are not fully absorbed by audiences, but 'seepage' occurs.

— *Lack of oppositional discourse*: Social and economic changes in the late 20th and early 21st centuries have resulted in many audiences having lack of access to oppositional discourse. Studies shows that the influence of family, Church and work have declined in many developed western societies. At the same time, globalisation of mass media and media monopolies or oligopolies have homogenised media content and reduced the number of independent media capable of representing alternative or opposing views.

Umberto Eco's concept of 'aberrant decoding' is informative. Eco describes texts as 'open' or 'closed' and says that 'aberrant decoding' is most likely to occur with 'open' texts. Exemplars of 'open' texts, which have a wide range of possible meanings are literary works which use metaphor, symbolism and poetic expression. Mass media texts tend to be 'closed' because they are written to formulaic journalistic styles and produced to programming standards which are widely followed. Eco believes 'aberrant decoding' is less likely or unlikely to occur with 'closed' texts. Furthermore, while he argues that diverse decodings can occur with mass media texts when they are broadcast to heterogeneous audiences, many media target specific demographic groups and package their content for those groups (eg. men's and women's magazines), resulting in homogenous audiences accessing increasingly homogenous content.

— *Short-term versus long-term effects*: Most media effects studies have examined only short-term impact of mass media content on audiences. Long-term cumulative effects have been little studied. Other fields of social and scientific research suggest that long-term exposure to influences results in cumulative effects. Long-term mass media representation, particularly repeated and consistent messages, may therefore have effects not detectable in short-term studies.

The notion of intertextuality discussed by J. Kristeva points to likely cumulative effects of mass media exposure. Kristeva refers to texts on two axes: a horizontal axis connecting the author and reader of a text, and a vertical axis on which the text is connected to other texts. Few if any audiences are exposed to only one media text. Most read one or more newspapers and several magazines, listen to radio, and watch several hours of television programming each day according to media research.

— *The blurred boundaries of mediation*: While TV drama, comedy and movies are prima facie identifiable by audiences as 'not real' because of canned laughter, music soundtracks, etc, news, current affairs, documentaries and, to some extent, talk-back radio programmes are presented as though they are 'real'. The advent of 'Reality TV' is an extreme example of the blurred boundaries between fact and fiction in mass media. Documentaries, 'mockumentaries' and 'docu-drama' are other media programming formats which present representation as fact or reality. The distinction between what is real and what is a mediated representation blurs for many audiences.

— *Media self-promotion*: Mass media widely promote themselves as providers of 'the truth' and some programmes and newspapers make specific claims to present 'how it is', 'the one you can trust', etc. This promotion further erodes audiences' critical abilities.

— *The 'vicious circle' of media influence*: While audiences turn to other sources of information and discourse such as interpersonal relationships or institutions such as political parties, government bodies, organisations, etc, these too are media consumers often reacting to mass media representation.

Most modern researchers accept that a synthesis of influences comprised of (a) the content mediated by the producers; (b) the semiotic complexity and efficacy of the medium; and (c) the reader shape meaning from media texts. The latter influence—the 'Ethnographic turn' in research—recognises both internal factors in the reader such as race, ethnicity, religion, gender, education level, socio-economic background, etc. and external factors such as influence of family, peer groups, the Church, etc. This evolution of media effects theory to a synthesis or integrated view is summarised in Figure 1.

Newbold et al summarise: "... the tradition of media effects has undergone a number of transformations ... in the past two decades. These transformations may be summarised as movements away from 'transmissional' models of effects towards a study of media within contexts of making of meaning, of culture, of texts and of literacy, in the interaction between media texts and media readers. Those who have asked how people make meaning from texts have had to look both at the ways in which texts are structured, and at the readers themselves". Newbold, et al conclude that "media texts, including representations, do not affect audiences in a simple and direct way, but rather that this process is complex, ambiguous and at times even contradictory".

McQuail summarises the evolution of mass media research as follows: "In the early days of mass communication research, the audience concept stood for the body of actual or intended receivers of messages at the end of a linear process of information transmission. This version has been gradually replaced by a view of the media receiver as more or less active, resistant to influence, and guided by his or her own concerns, depending on the particular social and cultural context".

Theory developed in public relations which is a sector with a vested interest in understanding the power of the media also sheds light on the likely effects of mass communication. While studies by Keith Stamm and others refute the 'domino' view of mass communication which suggests that messages lead to attitudes which, in turn, lead to behaviour, US academic, James Grunig has developed what he terms 'situational theory' of communication effects. Grunig has found that mass communication can have significant effects on audiences, but it is contingent on a

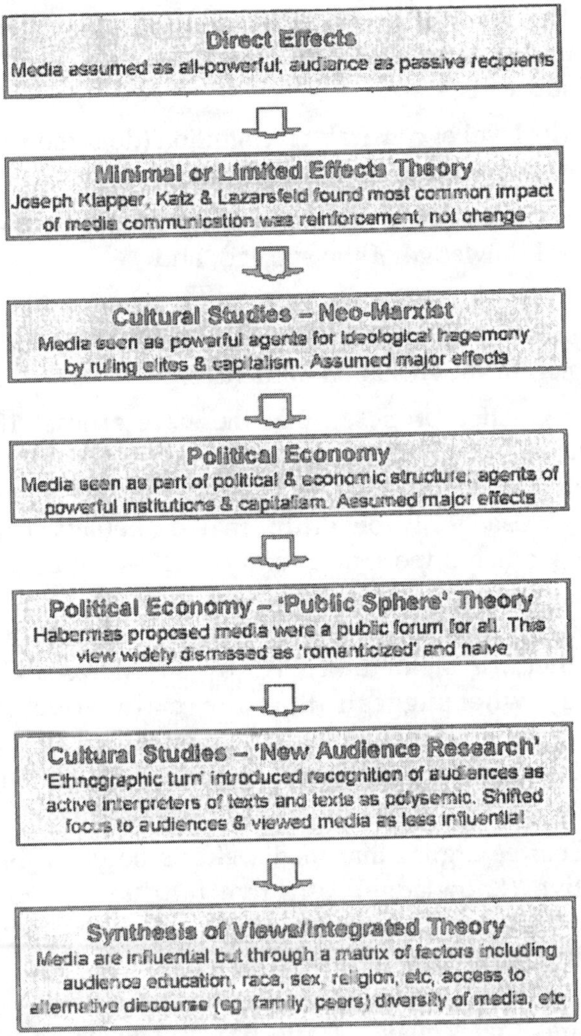

***Figure 1.** Summary of evolution of media effects theory*

number of situational factors. He presents four important factors that determine the likelihood of mass communication having effects:

1. The level of problem recognition (does the audience understand and perceive there is a problem to be addressed);
2. The level of constraint recognition (does the audience feel empowered to do anything about it);
3. The presence of a referent criterion (previous experience or knowledge of the subject); and
4. Level of involvement. If these situational factors are present, he argues that mass communication can have significant effects on audiences.

Steven Chaffee proposed that there are at least 18 kinds of media effects and he and other mass communication academics such as Grunig suggest that social researchers have focused only on attitudinal or behavioural change, missing other important effects. Chaffee argues that media effects occur for two reasons—because of specific content and simply because of the amount of time audiences spend with them, a factor taken up by social researcher Hugh Mackay who suggests that the main effect of media consumption is that it takes audiences away from other activities (eg. inter-personal relations) which might have affected them in other more constructive ways.

Chaffee argues that media effects occur at three levels: cognitive (knowledge); affective (attitudes) and conative (behaviour) and that these can have effects in three spheres: on individuals; on interpersonal relations, and on larger social systems such as communities or societies. Thus, he calculates that 2 ways of affecting × 3 levels of effects × 3 spheres of effect = 18 areas of media effects.

2

Theories of Human-Media Interaction

Mass communication occurs when a small number of people send messages to a large anonymous and usually heterogeneous audience through the use of specialised communication media. The units of analysis for mass communication are the messages, the mediums, and the audience. Mass communication represents the creation and sending of a homogeneous message to a large heterogeneous audience through the media. This chapter describes the mass communication theories which explain the relationship between media and society.

Agenda-setting Theory

According to the agenda-setting theory, propounded by Maxwell McCombs and Donald Shaw in the 1970s, mass media set the agenda for public opinion by highlighting certain issues. Studying the way political campaigns were covered in the media, Shaw and McCombs found the main effect of news media to be agenda-setting, telling people not what to think, but what to think of. Agenda setting is usually referred to as a function of mass media and not a theory.

The basic ideas of the theory can be traced back to the work of Walter Lippmann, a prominent American journalist. Lippmann proposed that people did not respond directly to events in the real world but lived in a pseudo-environment composed of "the pictures in our heads". The media would play an important part in the furnishing of these pictures and shaping of the pseudo-environment. The basic premise of the theory in its modern form, however, was first formulated by Bernard Cohen: "[The press] may not be successful much of the time in telling its readers what to think, but it is stunningly successful in telling its readers what to think about.

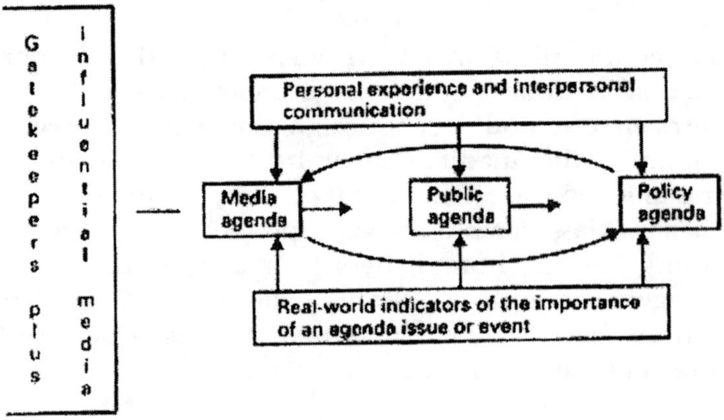

Figure 1. Conceptual model agenda-setting theory

The theory explains the correspondence between the rate at which media cover a story and the extent that people think that this story is important. This correspondence has repeateadly been shown to occur.

The agenda-setting function is a three part-process:

— *Media agenda:* issues discussed in the media.

— *Public agenda:* issues discussed and personally relevant to the public.

— *Policy agenda*: issues that policy makers consider important.

Agenda-setting is believed to occur because the press must be selective in reporting the news. News outlets act as gatekeepers of information and make choices about what to report and what not. What the public know and care at any given time is mostly a product of media-gatekeeping.

Cultural Imperialism Theory

The theory of cultural imperialism was developed in the 1970s by Herb Schiller to explain the media situation as it existed at that time. The nature of media (i.e., print, radio and television), at that time, promoted a one-way, top-down transmission system from dominant country to dominated country that theoretically gave rise to a passive audience and a powerful media. Advanced media, that are becoming widely available in the form of telecommunications, computers, and satellite technology, provide for greater interaction between sender and receiver than has ever before been possible. Therefore, the cultural imperialism argument that has been framed in terms of centre nations with power over disempowered periphery nations must be reevaluated as the advanced media slowly penetrate into developing nations.

The cultural imperialism theory states that Western nations dominate the media around the world which in return has a powerful effect on third world cultures by imposing them western views and therefore destroying their native cultures. Western civilisation produces the majority of the media (film, news, comics, etc.) because they have the money to do so. The rest of the world purchases those productions because it is cheaper for them to do so rather than produce their own. Therefore, third world countries are watching media filled with the western world's way of living, believing, and thinking. The third world cultures then start to want and do the same things in their countries and destroy their own culture.

The theory says that humans do not have the free will to chose how they feel, act, think, and live. They react to what they see on television because there is nothing else to compare it to besides their own lives, usually portrayed as less than what it should be. This theory explains that there is one truth and no matter what that truth never going to change. As long as third world countries continue to air western civilisation's programmes then the third world countries will always believe they should act, feel, think, and live as western civilisations act, feel, think, and live. This theory is value-neutral and objective. It does not matter what beliefs the people of third world may already hold the television programmes from the western world will communicate the same message and effect them in the same way.

Compared to other macroscopic theories of mass communication, one may conclude that cultural imperialism has broad scope. It has generated a lot of academic discourse. It has been used not only in the field of communication but also in other areas such as international relations, anthropology, education, sciences, history, literature, and sports. But this is not sufficient evidence to support the view that cultural imperialism may have broad scope. Like neomarxism, cultural imperialism is very specific to the time period in which it was being proposed. The Frankfurt School of neomarxism, for example, offers an explanation and critique of society and media that are particular to the time period, the early 1900s, in which it was proposed. Cultural imperialism, also, is probably very applicable to the time in which it was proposed, the 1970s; with the advent of advanced communication technologies that allow for a multi-directional as opposed to a uni-directional flow of information between countries, cultural imperialism is no longer a useful framework for explaining the same phenomena that it was applied to in the 1970s.

In this sense, it has limited scope as it cannot be used to explain media relations between nations at different points in time. Even though some may argue that it can still be applied to some situations today as the media of some periphery countries are even now dominated by western transnational media corporations, the theory does not hold true in all situations. There are periphery countries such as Brazil, India, Mexico that have media that are not dominated by foreign media organisations. Again, this proves that cultural imperialism does not have a broad scope. Other macroscopic theories such as symbolic interactionism and social construction of reality have more scope than cultural imperialism as they can be applied in different time periods across various cultural settings with different geographical backgrounds to describe and explain how a particular society create meaning and eventually their culture through the use of signs and symbols.

Diffusion of Innovation Theory

Diffusion research centres on the conditions which increase or decrease the likelihood that a new idea, product, or practice will be adopted by members of a given culture. Diffusion of innovation theory predicts that media as well as interpersonal contacts provide information and influence opinion and judgment. Studying how innovation occurs, E.M. Rogers argued that it consists of four stages: invention, diffusion (or communication) through the social system, time and consequences. The information flows through networks. The nature of networks and the roles opinion leaders play in them determine the likelihood that the innovation will be adopted.

Innovation diffusion research has attempted to explain the variables that influence how and why users adopt a new information medium, such as the internet. Opinion leaders exert influence on audience behaviour via their personal contact, but additional intermediaries called change agents and gatekeepers are also included in the process of diffusion. Five adopter categories are: (1) innovators, (2) early adopters, (3) early majority, (4) late majority, and (5) laggards. These categories follow a standard deviation-curve, very little innovators adopt the innovation in the beginning (2,5%), early adopters making up for 13,5% a short time later, the early majority 34%, the late majority 34% and after some time finally the laggards make up for 16%.

The process of the diffusion of innovation has been around since the first new idea popped into some ones head. The diffusion process is not a math equation or a chemical reaction but rather a natural progression of peoples' attitudes, opinions, and feelings towards accepting a new idea.

All four elements of diffusion of innovations have many different factors that affect the outcome of the process as well as act intimately to affect each other. It is also evident that the diffusion process holds constant for social system adopting an innovation no matter that filed it is in. When looking at the diffusion process it is hard not to see the importance to the advertising world. Learning the process an individual as well as a society goes through before they will accept an innovation is vital to the success of any company that plans to be on the frontier of innovation.

Functional Approach to Mass Communication

This theory was proposed by Harold Laswell and Charles Wright. According to the theory, there are five functional approaches the media serves users: surveillance, correlation, transmission, entertainment, and mobilisation.

The mass media serves many functions for our society. The five elements the theorists put together describe the audience's use for the media. Surveillance means that the media provides news and information. Correlation means that the media presents the information to us after they select, interpret, and criticise it. The cultural transmission function means that the media reflects our own beliefs, values, and norms. Media also entertains us in our free time and provides an escape from everyday life. Mobilisation refers to the media function of promoting society's interest especially in times of crisis.

This theory assumes that humans have a certain amount of free will. They can use mass communication for any variety of functions but they have to use it for something. Humans can make a choice in what to watch for any variety of reasons even if it is just for noise. The knowledge is universal and it is one truth that mass communication functions as a part of our society. It is a main source of surveillance, entertainment, correlation, transmission, and mobilisation.

This theory is objective and value-neutral. It does not matter what person is going to watch the television because everyone watches it for a reason.

Human Action Approach

According to the human action approach, proposed by P. Winch, human behaviour can be predicted because people make choices with a purpose about their actions. Behaviour is chosen by individuals to reach certain goals.

There is some fate concerning this theory, although free will does rule behaviour which can be predicted when goals are observed. Since there can be many different goals assessed for a person's behaviour, there are many truths that could be possible for this humanistic theory. Values definitely play a part in this humanistic theory, which ones are more important to an individual are the ones that goals will be modelled after and could be used to track behaviour. This theory is used as a measure to provide better understanding of behaviour that has already occurred, it says nothing about future behaviour.

The human action approach is useful to apply in situations when trying to explain behaviour that has already occurred. Studying historical events or known past experiences could use the human action approach. An applicable example to help illustrate the human action approach is a group of people listening to a persuasive speech about smoking and lung cancer. Fear appeals had nothing to do with changing people's minds. They were presented with new information—that stopping smoking increases life expectancy even for former smokers—that was what led the audience members to quit. There was a change in behaviour because the audience saw living longer as a goal.

Altercasting

According to the theory of altercasting, a tactic for persuading people by forcing them in a social role, so that they will be inclined to behave according to that role. Although the term altercasting is used quite frequently, it is not a very well-known or elaborated theory of persuasion.

According to the theory, when a person accepts a certain social role, a number of social pressures are brought to bear to insure that the role is enacted. The social environment expects the person to behave in a manner that is consistent with the role; the role also provides the person with selective exposure to information consistent with the role.

Altercasting means that we 'force' an audience to accept a particular role that make them behave in the way we want them to behave.

There are two basic forms of altercasting:

1. Manded altercasting means that we 'tell' people who they are (or are supposed to be) by making an existing role salient ('You as a Christian should....'), by placing others in a particular role ('You as a young abitious person

should....'), by attributing a new identity or role to someone, or by asking people to play a role.

2. Tact altercasting means that we put ourselves as senders in a role that 'evokes' a natural counter-role for the other. Some common role sets are for instance expert-unknowing public, fool—normal, helper—dependent, scapegoat—sinners, etc.

Altercasting is a powerful tactic because:

— the social role is a basic unit in people's everyday condition;

— presenting oneself in a social role that can be used to cast the alter (tact altercasting) is relatively easy

— constructing roles that trap others in a course of action is also relatively easy;

— people often accept easily the social roles offered to them.

The tactic is frequently used in advertising and health promotion.

The Domestication Approach

This theory sees households are seen as part of a transactional system of economic and social relations within the formal or more objective economy and society of the public sphere. Within this framework households are seen as being actively engaged with the products and meanings of this formal, commodity and individual based economy. This engagement involved the appropriation of the commodities into domestic culture—they are domesticated—and through that appropriation they are incorporated and redefined in different terms, in accordance with the household's own values and interests.

Domestication deals with the cultural, social and technological networks of the everyday life of households. The meanings and significance of all our media and information products depend on the participation of the user.

Four phases describe the concept of domestication.

1. *Appropriation*: When a technology leaves the world of commodity it is appropriated. Then it can be taken by an individual or a household and owned. From this perspective appropriation stands for the whole process of consumption as well as for that moment at which an object crosses the threshold between the formal and the moral economics.
2. *Objectification*: this is expressed in usage but also in psychical dispositions of objects in the spatial environment of the home (living room). It is also expressed in the construction as the environment as such. All technologies have the potential to be appropriated into an aesthetic environment. Many are purchased as much for their appearance of the home as for their functional significance.
3. *Incorporation*: The ways in which objects, especially technologies are used. Technologies are functional. They may be bought with other features in mind and indeed serve other cultural purposes in appropriation. They may indeed become functional in ways somewhat removed from the intentions of designers or marketers. Technologies also may have many functions.
4. *Conversion:* defines the relationship between the household and the outside world. It may happen that technologies pass the household defines and claims itself and it members in the wider society.

The domestication approach can be used to describe technological change in a wide range: from households to institutional settings. It provides a network for an understanding of the complex interrelationships of cultures and technologies as they emerge in institutions and individuals.

Cultivation Theory

Cultivation theory, sometimes referred to as the cultivation hypothesis or cultivation analysis, was an approach developed by Professor George Gerbner, dean of the Annenberg School of Communications at the University of Pennsylvania. He began the 'Cultural Indicators' research project in the mid-1960s, to study whether and how watching television may influence viewers' ideas of what the everyday world is like. Cultivation research is in the 'effects' tradition. Cultivation theorists argue that television has long-term effects which are small, gradual, indirect but cumulative and significant.

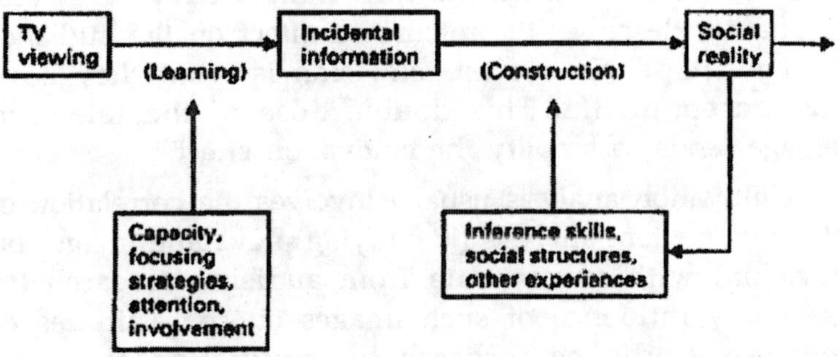

Figure 2. Conceptual model of cultivation theory

Cultivation theory in its most basic form, suggests that television is responsible for shaping, or 'cultivating' viewers' conceptions of social reality. The combined effect of massive television exposure by viewers over time subtly shapes the perception of social reality for individuals and, ultimately, for our culture as a whole.

Gerbner argues that the mass media cultivate attitudes and values which are already present in a culture: the media maintain and propagate these values amongst members of a culture, thus binding it together. He has argued that television tends to cultivate middle-of-the- road political perspectives. Gerbner called this effect 'mainstreaming'. Cultivation theorists distinguish between 'first order' effects (general beliefs about the everyday world, such as about the prevalence of violence) and 'second order' effects (specific attitudes, such as to law and order or to personal safety). There is also a distinction between two groups of television viewers: the heavy viewers and the light viewers. The focus is on 'heavy viewers'. People who watch a lot of television are likely to be more influenced by the ways in which the world is framed by television programmes than are individuals who watch less, especially regarding topics of which the viewer has little first-hand experience. Light viewers may have more sources of information than heavy viewers. 'Resonance' describes the intensified effect on the audience when what people see on television is what they have experienced in life. This double dose of the televised message tends to amplify the cultivation effect.

Cultivation analysis usually involves the correlation of data from content analysis (identifying prevailing images on television) with survey data from audience research (to assess any influence of such images on the attitudes of viewers). Audience research by cultivation theorists involves asking large-scale public opinion poll organisations to include in their national surveys questions regarding such issues as the amount of violence in everyday life. Answers are interpreted as reflecting either the world of television or that of everyday life. The answers are then related to the amount of television watched, other media habits and demographic data such as sex, age, income and education.

Cultivation research looks at the mass media as a socialising agent and investigates whether television viewers come to believe the television version of reality the more they watch it. In a survey of about 450 New Jersey schoolchildren, 73 percent of heavy viewers compared to 62 percent of light viewers gave the TV answer to a question asking them to estimate the number of people involved in violence in a typical week. The same survey showed that children who were heavy viewers were more fearful about walking alone in a city at night. They also overestimated the number of people who commit serious crimes. This effect is called 'mean world syndrome'. One controlled experiment addressed the issue of cause and effect, manipulating the viewing of American college students to create heavy- and light-viewing groups. After 6 weeks of controlled viewing, heavy viewers of action-adventure programmes were indeed found to be more fearful of life in the everyday world than were light viewers.

Dependency Theory

Dependency theory was originally proposed by Sandra Ball-Rokeach and Melvin DeFleur. This theory merged out of the communication discipline. Dependency theory integrates several perspectives: first, it combines perspectives from psychology with ingredients from social categories theory. Second, it integrates systems perspectives with elements from more causal approaches. Third, it combines elements of uses and gratifications research with those of media effects traditions, although its primary focus is less on effects per se than on rationales for why media effects typically are limited. Finally, a contextualist philosophy is incorporated into the theory, which also features traditional concerns with the content of media messages and their effects on audiences. Research generated by this model had tends to be more descriptive than explanatory or predictive.

Dependency theory proposes an integral relationship among audiences, media and the larger social system. This theory predicts that you depend on media information to meet certain needs and achieve certain goals, like uses-and-gratifications theory. But you do not depend on all media equally. Two factors influence the degree of media dependence. First, you will become more dependent on media that meet a number of your needs than on media that provide just a few. The second source of dependency is social stability. When social change and conflict are high, established institutions, beliefs, and practices are challenged, forcing you to reevaluate and make new choices. At such times your reliance on the media for information will increase. At other, more stable times your dependency on media may go way down.

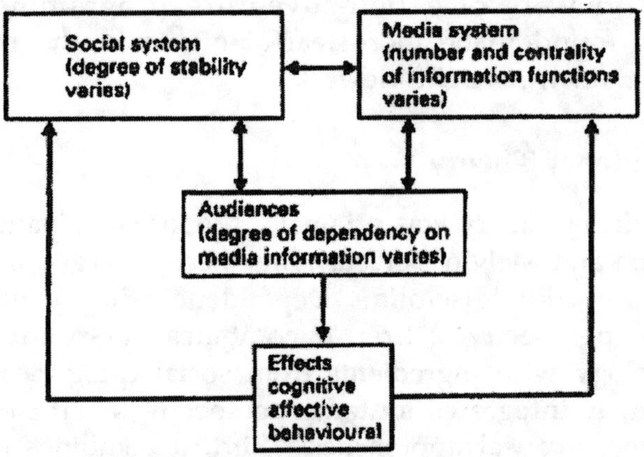

Figure 3. Conceptual model of dependency theory

One's needs are not always strictly personal but may be shaped by the culture or by various social conditions. In other words, individuals' needs, motives, and uses of media are contingent on outside factors that may not be in the individuals' control. These outside factors act as constraints on what and how media can be used and on the availability of other non-media alternatives. Furthermore, the more alternatives and individual had for gratifying needs, the less dependent he or she will become on any single medium. The number of functional alternatives, however, is not just a matter of individual choice or even of psychological traits but is limited also by factors such as availability of certain media.

One of the most powerful critiques of modernisation/ diffusion theories came from the dependency paradigm. Originally developed in Latin America, dependency analysis was informed by Marxist and critical theories according to which the problems of the Third World reflected the general dynamics of capitalist development. Development problems responded to the unequal distribution of resources created by the global expansion of Western capitalism.

Against modernisation theories, dependency theorists argued that the problems of underdevelopment were not internal to Third World countries but were determined by external factors and the way former colonies were integrated into the world economy. It forcefully stated that the problems of the underdeveloped world were political rather than the result of the lack of information. What kept Third World countries underdeveloped were social and economic factors, namely the dominated position that those countries had in the global order. Underdevelopment, they argued, was the flip side and the consequence of the development of the Western world. The latter concentrated economic power and political decisions that maintained underdevelopment and dependency. Third world countries were politically and culturally dependent on the West, particularly on the United States.

Asides from external problems, internal structures were also responsible for the problems of under-development. Dependency positions charged development programmes for failing to address structures of inequality and targeting individual rather than social factors. Unequal land distribution, lack of credit for peasants, and poor health care services strongly limited the possibilities for an overall improvement in social conditions. Interventions were doomed when basic conditions that could make it possible for people to adopt new attitudes and behaviours were missing. Also, innovations promoted by development programmes were adopted by individuals from higher socioeconomic strata living in cities rather than by rural and poor populations. In singling out the mass media as having a central role in introducing innovations, modernisation theories ignored the issue of media ownership and control. Urban and powerful interests controlled the media that was supposed to promote development. The media were not interested in championing social goals or helping underprivileged populations but in transmitting entertainment and trivial information. The relation between media structure and content was virtually ignored in modernisation theories. Only a small percentage of programming was devoted to development issues and in regions such as Latin America, the media were commercially run and their the central goal was profit-making not social change.

For dependency theorists, modernisation theories was driven by behaviourist, positivist and empiricist approaches in the mold of the "scientific model" that prevailed in U.S. universities and research centres. These particular biases accounted for why structural factors were ignored and for why interventions were focused on behaviour changes at the individual level rather than on social causes of poverty and marginalisation. Modernisation theories as applied in the third world featured, to quote Bolivian communication researcher Luis Ramiro Beltrán, "alien premises, objects and methods."

The solution to underdevelopment problems was essentially political, rather than merely informational. What was required was social change in order to transform the general distribution of power and resources. Information and media policies were necessary to deal with communication problems. Solutions to underdevelopment required major changes in media structures that were dominated by commercial principles and foreign interests. Policies needed to promote national and public goals that could put the media in the service of the people rather than as pipelines for capitalist ideologies. Such positions were expressed in a number of international fora, particularly during the UNESCO-sponsored debates about the New World Information and Communication Order in the 1970s and 1980s. Representatives from Third World countries proposed "national communication policies" that emphasised the need for governments to control media structures and oppose domestic and foreign elites and business interests.

Gatekeeping Theory

Kurt Lewin was apparently the first one to use the term "gatekeeping," which he used to describe a wife or mother as the person who decides which foods end up on the family's dinner table. The gatekeeper is the person who decides what shall pass through each gate section, of which, in any process, there are several. Although he applied it originally to the food chain, he then added that the gating process can include a news item winding through communication channels in a group. This is the point from which most gatekeeper studies in communication are launched. White was the person who seized upon Lewin's comments and turned it solidly toward journalism in 1950.

In the 1970s McCombs and Shaw took a different direction when they looked at the effects of gatekeepers' decisions. They found the audience learns how much importance to attach to a news item from the emphasis the media place on it. McCombs and Shaw pointed out that the gatekeeping concept is related to the newer concept, agenda-setting. The gatekeeper concept is now 50 years old and has slipped into the language of many disciplines, including gatekeeping in organisations.

The gatekeeper decides which information will go forward, and which will not. In other words a gatekeeper in a social system decides which of a certain commodity—

materials, goods, and information—may enter the system. Important to realise is that gatekeepers are able to control the public's knowledge of the actual events by letting some stories pass through the system but keeping others out. Gatekeepers can also be seen as institutions or organisations. In a political system there are gatekeepers, individuals or institutions which control access to positions of power and regulate the flow of information and political influence.

Gatekeepers exist in many jobs, and their choices hold the potential to colour mental pictures that are subsequently created in people's understanding of what is happening in the world around them. Media gatekeeping showed that decision making is based on principles of news values, organisational routines, input structure and common sense. Gatekeeping is vital in communication planning and almost all communication planning roles include some aspect of gatekeeping.

The gatekeeper's choices are a complex web of influences, preferences, motives and common values. Gatekeeping is inevitable and in some circumstances it can be useful. Gatekeeping can also be dangerous, since it can lead to an abuse of power by deciding what information to discard and what to let pass. Nevertheless, gatekeeping is often a routine, guided by some set of standard questions. This theory is related to the mass media and organisations. In the mass media the focus is on the organisational structure of newsrooms and events. Gatekeeping is also an important in organisations, since employees and management are using ways of influence.

Knowledge Gap Theory

The knowledge gap theory was first proposed by Tichenor, Donohue and Olien at the University of Minnesota in the 70s. They believe that the increase of information in society is not evenly acquired by every member of society: people with higher socioeconomic status tend to have better ability to acquire information. This leads to a division of two groups: a group of better-educated people who know more about most things, and those with low education who know less. Lower socio-economic status (SES) people, defined partly by educational level, have little or no knowledge about public affairs issues, are disconnected from news events and important new discoveries, and usually aren't concerned about their lack of knowledge.

The knowledge gap can result in an increased gap between people of lower and higher socioeconomic status. The attempt to improve people's life with information via the mass media might not always work the way this is planned. Mass media might have the effect of increasing the difference gap between members of social classes.

Tichenor, Donohue and Olien present five reasons for justifying the knowledge gap.

1. People of higher socioeconomic status have better communication skills, education, reading, comprehending and remembering information.
2. People of higher socioeconomic status can store information more easily or remember the topic form background knowledge
3. People of higher socioeconomic status might have a more relevant social context.
4. People of higher socioeconomic status are better in selective exposure, acceptance and retention.
5. The nature of the mass media itself is that it is geared toward persons of higher socioeconomic status.

Media presenting information should realise that people of higher socioeconomic status get their information in a different way than lower educated people. Furthermore, this hypothesis of the knowledge gap might help in understanding the increased gap between people of higher socioeconomic status and people of lower socioeconomic status. It can be used in various circumstances.

The knowledge gap was used in a research for presidential campaigns. The knowledge gap hypothesis holds that when new information enters a social system via a mass media campaign, it is likely to exacerbate underlying inequalities in previously held information.

Specifically, while people from all strata may learn new information as a result of a mass media campaign, those with higher levels of education are likely to learn more than those with low levels of education, and the informational gap between the two groups will expand. The results of the analysis show that knowledge gaps do not always grow over the course of presidential campaigns and that some events, such as debates, may actually reduce the level of information inequality in the electorate.

Medium Theory

McLuhan challenged conventional definitions when he claimed that the medium is the message. With this claim, he stressed how channels differ, not only in terms of their content, but also in regard to how they awaken and alter thoughts and senses. He distinguished media by the cognitive processes each required. McLuhan popularised the idea that channels are a dominant force that must be understood to know how the media influence society and culture.

Medium theory focuses on the medium characteristics itself (like in media richness theory) rather than on what it conveys or how information is received. In medium theory, a medium is not simply a newspaper, the Internet, a digital camera and so forth. Rather, it is the symbolic environment of any communicative act. Media, apart from whatever content is transmitted, impact individuals and society. McLuhan's thesis is that people adapt to their environment through a certain balance or ratio of the senses, and the primary medium of the age brings out a particular sense ratio, thereby affecting perception.

Medium theory is an analytical theory with few empirical model building. Some of the methods used are: analysis of media characteristics and historical analysis of human perception. It examines physical, psychological and social variables as the senses that are required to attend to the medium; whether the communication is bi-directional or uni-directional, how quickly messages can be disseminated, whether learning to encode and decode in the medium is difficult or simple, how many people can attend to the same message at the same moment, and so forth. Medium theorists argue that such variables influence the medium's use and its social, political, and psychological impact.

Mental Models

Boltzmann made a statement which refers in a way to the use of mental models today: "All our ideas and concepts are only internal pictures". Craik first thought and wrote about small scale models, to anticipate events. Mental models are representations of reality that people use to understand specific phenomena. Mental models are consistent with theories that postulate internal representations in thinking processes Johnson-Laird proposes mental models as the basic structure of cognition: "It is now plausibl‿ to suppose that mental models play a central and unifying role in representing objects, states of affairs". We can summarise the theory in terms of its three principal predictions, which have all been corroborated experimentally:

1. Reasoners normally build models of what is true, not what is false—a propensity that led to the discovery that people commit systematic fallacies in reasoning.
2. Reasoning is easier from one model than from multiple models.

3. Reasoners tend to focus on one of the possible models of multi-model problems, and are thereby led to erroneous conclusions and irrational decisions.

To build models of what is true is a sensible way to deal with limited processing capacity, but it does lead to illusions. Yet, it does not imply that people are irredeemably irrational. The fallacies can be alleviated with preventative methods. Without them, however, reasoners remain open to the illusion that they grasp what is in fact beyond them. We suspect that similar short-comings may underlie judgment and choice in game-theoretic settings.

The theory accounts for the informality of arguments in science and daily life, whereas logic is notoriously of little help in analysing them. If people base such arguments on mental models, then there is no reason to suppose that they will lay them out like the steps of a formal proof.

Modernisation Theory

A macro-theory with a historical and sociological inspiration. Developed in large-scale historical research investigating the effects of the modernisation process on human communication. Modernisation means the appearance of 'modes of social life or organisation which emerged in Europe from about the seventeenth century onwards and which subsequently became more or less worldwide in their influence'. Modernisation theories explain the changing ways of communication and media use in traditional and (post)modern societies.

Modernisation theory has evolved in three waves. The first wave appeared in the 1950s and 1960s. One made the attempt to explain the diffusion of Western styles of living, technological innovations and individualist types of communication (highly selective, addressing only particular persons) as the superiority of secular, materialist, Western, individualist culture and of individual motivation and achievement. This first wave of theory produced three variants:

1. *Economic development*: mass media promote the global diffusion of many technical and social innovations that are essential to modernisation.
2. *Literacy and cultural development:* mass media can teach literacy and other essential skills and techniques. They encourage a 'state of mind' favourable to modernity, e.g. the imagination of an alternative way of life beyond the traditional way.
3. *National identity development*: mass media could support national identities in new nations (colonies) and support attention to democratic policies (elections).

Most of these theories have been discredited because of their pro-Western bias.

The second wave of modernisation theory is a part of the critical theory that was popular in the 1970s and 1980s. It does not support but criticise the influence of Western modernisation. This is held to be a case of Western cultural and economic imperialism or dominance.

One of the theories concerned is media dependency theory. Peripheral (developing) countries are assumed to be dependant on mass media in the core (the Western world).

The third wave of modernisation theory rising in the 1990s is the theory of late-, high- or post modernity. It tries to be more neutral, being not in favour or against Western modernisation. Rather it attempts to unearth the contradictions in the modernisation process and to explain the consequences of modernity for individuals in contemporary society. Giddens showed that modern society is characterised by time-space distantiation and disembedding mechanisms. Traditional society is based on direct interaction between people living close to each other. Modern societies stretch further and further across space and time using mass media and interactive media.

Disembedding mechanisms such as money, symbolic means, English as the lingua franca and the Internet help to lift out and activities in an abstract or online form that were once embedded in particular material goods and in places.

Spiral of Silence

Elisabeth Noelle-Neumann introduced the "spiral of silence" as an attempt to explain in part how public opinion is formed. She wondered why the Germans supported wrong political positions that led to national defeat, humiliation and ruin in the 1930s-1940s.

The phrase "spiral of silence" actually refers to how people tend to remain silent when they feel that their views are in the minority. The model is based on three premises:

1. people have a "quasi-statistical organ," a sixth-sense if you will, which allows them to know the prevailing public opinion, even without access to polls,
2. people have a fear of isolation and know what behaviours will increase their likelihood of being socially isolated, and
3. people are reticent to express their minority views, primarily out of fear of being isolated.

Figure 4. Conceptual model of spiral of silence theory

The closer a person believes the opinion held is similar to the prevailing public opinion, the more they are willing to openly disclose that opinion in public. Then, if public sentiment changes, the person will recognise that the opinion is less in favour and will be less willing to express that opinion publicly. As the perceived distance between public opinion and a person's personal opinion grows, the more unlikely the person is to express their opinion.

It is related to the mass media, in such a way that mass media influences public opinion. Shifts in public opinion occur commonly and therefore this theory is used to search an explanation for behaviour (speak up or stay silent). The theory has also been criticised for ambiguity and methodological weakness, but the idea has persisted. Evidence of the spiral effect is usually small but significant.

Uses and Gratifications Approach

Uses and gratifications, also known as usage and gratifications or needs and gratifications, is not a single approach but a body of approaches to media analysis that developed out of many varied empirical studies, beginning in the mid 20th century. The basic theme of uses and gratifications is the idea that people use the media to get specific gratifications.

The basic tenet of uses and gratifications (called UG for short) is that people are not helpless victims of all powerful media, but use media to fulfil their various needs. These needs serve as motivations (gratifications sought) for using media. Gratifications obtained should correspond with gratifications sought for the media to be able to meet the needs of the users.

Jay G. Blumler and Elihu Katz devised their uses and gratifications model to highlight four areas of gratification in media texts for audiences. These include:

1. *Personal identity*—for example, characters in soap operas experiencing something the audience once did.
2. *Personal relationships*—a media text provides information for 'water-cooler talk' at work with colleagues, what's happening in the latest reality TV show?
3. *Surveillance*—lets the audience know what is happening in the world, for example print and broadcast news.
4. *Diversion*—a media text which provides escapism for the audience, for example a holiday programme.

Uses and gratifications theory attempts to explain the uses and functions of the media for individuals, groups, and society in general. There are three objectives in developing uses and gratifications theory:

1) To explain how individuals use mass communication to gratify their needs. "What do people do with the media".
2) To discover underlying motives for individuals' media use.
3) To identify the positive and the negative consequences of individual media use.

At the core of uses and gratifications theory lies the assumption that audience members actively seek out the mass media to satisfy individual needs.

3

Media Anthropology

Mass media-defined in the conventional sense as the electronic media of radio, television, film, and recorded music, and the print media of newspapers, magazines, and popular literature-are at once artifacts, experiences, practices, and processes. They are economically and politically driven, linked to developments in science and technology, and like most domains of human life, their existence is inextricably bound up with the use of language. Given these various modalities and spheres of operation, there are numerous angles for approaching mass media anthropologically: as institutions, as workplaces, as communicative practices, as cultural products, as social activities, as aesthetic forms, and as historical developments. But beyond approaching specific facets of mass media anthropologically, it seems that the greater challenge lies in integrating the study of mass media into our analyses of the "total social fact" of modem life.

The arena of media studies is a hotly contested and fragmented terrain, one that has been highly sensitive both to wider developments within contemporary social theory and to the particularities of changing media technologies and media uses. If there is any point of general consensus, it lies more in an acceptance of a common set of focal issues than in the theoretical frameworks or methodological techniques themselves. One enduring concern is "the power" of mass media, and in particular their roles as vehicles of culture. For example, in some approaches, mass media are analysed as forces that provide audiences with ways of seeing and interpreting the word, ways that ultimately shape their very existence and participation within a given society.

J.A. Anderson imagined community is a mass mediated collectivity where members may not all know each other, but where each shares the idea of a common belonging. Unfortunately, this conceptualisation of mass media as vehicles of culture, and as modes of imagining and imaging communities, has had limited empirical application to date. Until recently most studies of the ideological functions of mass media and the mass mediation of culture have focused primarily on media texts, with the common assumption that media's meanings are to be found in media's messages. Such textual analysis is important for establishing the possibility that mass media are sites of collective representations (and collective mediations) in modem societies, but a growing number of writers have argued that this picture is incomplete without an analysis of the culture of media production, the political economy and social history of media institutions, and the various practices of media consumption that exist in any given society.

Central to this theoretical reformulation of media power is the crucial problem of where to locate the production of meaning and ideology in the mass communication process, and how to characterise processes of agency and interpretation. The most pervasive paradigm of the mass communication process has been the linear model consisting of three discrete stages: message production, message transmission, and message reception. Quintessentially, "the message" is taken as the key unit of cultural meaning, and for some theorists, a powerful refraction or reproduction of a society's dominant ideologies.

For example, in Marxist and critical theory, the question of media power has been formulated in terms of how mass media serve the interests of a ruling class, e.g. in legitimising the authority of state institutions, building political and cultural consensus, and impeding the development of working class consciousness. Bennett studies in detail, these approaches have been informed greatly by earlier theories of "mass society", in which mass media are responsible for the emergence of a homogenised mass culture, the fragmentation of communities, and the erosion of cultural values and standards of artistic expression.

Within functionalist approaches-also called "positivist" and "liberal-pluralist" traditions—the dominant issue for :studies of media power has been their role in reinforcing or changing the attitudes, values, and behaviours of media audiences. Most prominent in this vein of analysis is Gerbner and colleagues' *Cultural Indicators Project,* which measures media "effects" in the statistical correlations between media exposure and people's perceptions of the world. Media exposure quantified as hours of television viewing time, and particularly exposure to certain kinds of media content units, e.g. violent scenes, while viewers' perceptions are assessed from scaled responses to formal questionnaires. Historically, this preoccupation with the political and cultural power of mass media and the drive to quantify media's effects on audiences has perpetuated the focus on isolatable media messages, and the related armchair analyses of media texts.

For the positivists, content units allow for easy quantification, and for the critical theorists, the function of mass media as a monolithic, and ultimately alienating, "culture industry" is best served if messages are understood to be unproblematically transmitted and absorbed. Media scholars have increasingly rejected these top-down, "hypodermic," or "magic bullet" models of media effects and media power, and have turned their attention to the interpretive practices of media audiences, the diversity of media audiences and media uses, and the multivocality and indeterminacy of media texts.

Especially in recent work stemming from British cultural studies, and in response to developments within critical theory, mass media are examined not so much as definers of "reality," but as dynamic sites of struggle over representation, and complex spaces in which subjectivities are constructed and identities are contested. For example, a number of researchers have examined the centrality of media stars, popular music, and magazines in youth cultures, and several have explored how relations with media figures form interpretive frameworks for personal decisions and entire lifestyles. A related line of research has begun document the integration of media use into the rhythms of daily life, the mass mediation of concepts of time, and the more general, but more elusive, experiential dimensions of media reception.

Paradoxically, for all their concern with the communication process, these widely differing approaches to audience reception and media texts tend to share a common inattention to linguistic form. The language of mass media, with its diverse textual structures, its relations with verbal art and other culturally-specific communication forms, and its claims to authoritatively represent social reality, is a vast topic that has been examined primarily through discourse analysis; most media researchers have yet to tap into recent developments within linguistic anthropology and the ethnography of communication.

Especially in examining the interpretive practices of media audiences, research would benefit from more critical analysis of how structures of reception and evaluation are established over the course of the communication event. Significantly, in some corners, the gradual erosion of the linear communication model began with an attempt to incorporate linguistic and semiotic approaches in the analysis of message transmission. In Hall's early encoding decoding model, audiences are seen as active decoders (instead of passive recipients) of media messages, who accept, reject, or resist what is conveyed based on their own class position within society.

Later amendments to the model grant even more active roles to audiences, recognising that they also negotiate, modify, and interpret media messages. While class positions may indeed structure people's responses to different media-e.g. P. Bourdieu has demonstrated that class distinctions in France are partly constructed and understood in such differential media use-the nature of what is reacted to, i.e. the so-called "message" remains under-analysed in the encoding-decoding model. In short, it borrows from semiotics the general notion of a code as a conventional meaning system, but at the same time assumes that language operates in a strictly referential function as a transparent means of conveying content.

If the form-substance dualism is absolute, the encoding-decoding model misses a major insight of contemporary linguistics (and semioties)—that linguistic forms both presuppose and create the contexts for their interpretation, as well as the relationships of participants to the event of communication. Applying this functional linguistic approach to mass communication would illuminate not just the propositional level of encoding and decoding ideologically loaded messages, but the semiotic construction of sender-receiver relations and evaluative frameworks for reception. Particularly in light of the recent debates over the problems of context and contextualisation, this approach would also move analysis beyond the individual communication event and the sender-receiver dyad, to consider how media forms are situated within broader social processes and in relation to specific understandings of the communication genres that they instantiate.

Since the early 1980s, one intriguing component of this move toward the "interpretive" audience has been the embracing of anthropology and the ethnographic method as empirical antidotes to the prevailing theoretical overload. As anthropologists have largely ignored mass media until recently, "the anthropological approach" to mass media has been rendered mainly through British cultural studies. In addition, with a few exceptions, this ethnographic turn seems to be occurring with little of the reflexivity that recent anthropologists have introduced into the understanding of ethnographic practice.

For example, people's self-report about their media practices and attitudes tends to be taken at face value, without examining how this discourse emerges and is structured, or how it relates to observable practices. Also, the position of the ethnographer is rarely factored into the analysis. Although not entirely ethnographic (though some would argue that no one can tightly lay claim to the word), these efforts have greatly enhanced our knowledge of the diversity of media practices, and they raise significant challenges for theorising mass media's relations to "reality" and the construction of social meaning. In supplanting the simple picture of media message transmission as a one-way communication from sender to receiver, one might say that these authors have moved into a "post-content" or "post-text" era, and toward a rethinking of the usefulness of the production-consumption dichotomy itself.

Within media studies, these recent developments have been criticised for being still too theory-driven, biased by populist agendas, and merely unknowing rediscoveries of earlier approaches in communication research. W.A. Evans, for example, argues that the ethnographic turn nothing new considering the substantial body of research since the 1940s on what people do with mass media. Significantly, the early practitioners of "on-the-ground" media studies, which later became the uses and gratifications approach to mass media, were part of developing ethnographic tradition in the Chicago school of urban sociology/ anthropology.

As literary theorists came to appropriate more of media studies, the disembodied text gained ascendancy as the main site of media's social and cultural significance. Now there is a return of the repressed (i.e. context and use) when the whole notion of the text has come under siege in that very discipline. Outside of literary criticism and film studies, the socially situated nature of people's engagements with and interpretations of mass media was not forgotten, The problem is, however, with the dominance of quantitative research methods throughout the social sciences, and especially as American media research became increasingly underwritten by commercial and political marketing interests, much of the pioneering ethnographic work of the 1940s and 1950s was replaced by audience measurement studies and statistical content analysis.

Anthropologists and "cross-over" communication scholars are beginning to fill this gap with studies of the use of newspapers, novels, television, video, radio, and recorded music in diverse societies. Also, the ethnographic study of media institutions and practitioners is relatively recent, and the emerging work on the recruitment of spectators and the imagining of audiences in media practice suggests new ways to understand how media consumption is embedded in the culture of media production.

Visual Media and Anthropology

To date, the most extensive attention to mass media within anthropology has been in the fields of visual anthropology and ethnographic film. There also has been a long standing concern with media coverage of anthropological activities and scholarship, including the publication of articles by anthropologists written for nonspecialist audiences. Such anthropological interest in the popularisation of anthropology has focused primarily on the fact that anthropology occasionally enters into the public eye, i.e. the eye of mainstream American media. This is useful and encouraging for anthropology practitioners because it highlights the wider application of anthropological research within American society, and assists with issues of publicity and scientific clarification.

However, except perhaps with the Mead-Freeman and Tasaday controversies, there has been little anthropological reflection on precisely what these popular renderings and appropriations of anthropology outside the discipline reveal about our own culture and the politics of mass media more generally. What indeed are the overall patterns of use and abuse (and omission) of anthropological findings and perspectives in mainstream mass media? For example, how do American media represent other societies and cultures, and does anthropology have any effect on this?

Certainly mainstream media patterns of cultural representation have implications for, and intersect with, wider debates in contemporary American society concerning multicultural curricula, the understanding of cultural difference, and the politics of media access. Inquiring into these processes would not only illuminate the meaning and positive potential of "anthropology" in the American public domain, but would also be a logical extension of recent work within critical anthropology. For example, analyses of orientalism and the "objectifying gaze" in colonial photography, travel literature, tourism, world fairs, and museums, apply equally well to the construction of "otherness," "the primitive," and "the exotic" in news reporting, photojournalism, comics, science fiction, and popular film.

Moreover, because many of these representational forms explicitly portray a gazing explorer amidst the gazed upon, this also allows a critical eye to be cast upon popular images of the anthropologist, including such notables as the archaeologist Indiana Jones from the Raiders of the Lost Ark film trilogy and the transgalactic ethnographers of the Star Trek television series and films. Unfortunately, a great deal of this recent work on such "objectifying discourses" is still limited by an overdependence on textual analysis and a presumption that the anthropologist as literary critic is qualified to single-handedly "read" the significance of films, museum displays, and popular novels. Less is known, for example, about the "everyday life" of such media representations, their contexts of production and circulation, and the practices and discourses of reception that envelop them.

Interestingly, the anthropologists are more concerned with "representation" (both imagistic and political) than are the filmmakers. For example, Weiner discusses how the real challenge in making ethnographic films for television lies in constructing multiple points of view within a single production, especially those that help to transcend any simple opposition between an "us" and a "them". Turton emphasises that such productions should strive to empower a diversity of "native voices", while Ginsburg suggests that series title *Disappearing World* itself is in need of radical rethinking.

Rather than focusing on cultural loss or the ahistorical "primitive," Ginsburg asserts that the series should explore the more positive fact that such people are actively drawing "upon their own cultures and social institutions as powerful resources in an increasingly interdependent world". Indeed, the differing visions of who and what is disappearing form the crux of the collaboration conflicts described by Turner. For example, Turner relates one editing room disaster where he found a carefully edited master version lying in pieces on the cutting room floor.

Finally, the various appearances of anthropology in the public eye also present rich opportunities for investigating more general questions about media authority and legitimacy. One major facet of this is the construction of truth and objectivity through specific linguistic forms, in established media genres. For example, in conjunction with analysing the semiotics of visual display and the politics of editorial decisions, it is also possible to interrogate the ideological implications of specific linguistic practices such as the use of "the ethnographic present", sentences that lack explicit agents or "voices", and the lexical and syntactic choices that structure discourses of scientific discovery and "live" narration.

The widespread use of "expert commentators" across a vast range of media genres (e.g. talk shows and regular columns) is often a major component of this linguistic construction of media authority, and represents still another aspect of the role anthropologists play as contributors in various media enterprises.

Development of Indigenous Media

One of the most exciting, extensive, and relatively unified anthropological approaches to mass media is represented by a newly emerging body of research on indigenous media that builds on Worth & Adair's pioneering work. The most general contribution of these recent studies is their sustained attention to the fact that mass media are at once cultural products and social processes, as well as extremely potent arenas of political struggle. This work has also begun to engage wider anthropological issues regarding race, ethnicity, symbolic processes, and the politics of the nation-state, and has been, for the most part, rooted in a strong interest in the possibilities of media advocacy and a politicised anthropology.

Indigenous media is a cover term for a broad spectrum of media phenomena, ranging from community owned and operated radio, television, and video operations to locally produced programmes that appear on national television. The precise definition of the term "indigenous" is a bit problematic, however, in both its scope of application and its political import, and this deserves some consideration.

The Aboriginal societies in Australia and the diverse Native American communities throughout North and South America are the inmost widely known representatives of indigenous people. The recent explosion of media use in some of these communities has come about largely because of the availability of inexpensive handicams and VCRs, and the installation of communication satellite down-links in areas previously untouched by large-scale media. In many situations, anthropologists and journalists have been the key mediators in the introduction of new media technology.

F. Ginsburg stresses that indigenous media should be distinguished from the national and independent media productions of Third World nations, as they have developed under distinct historical and political conditions. In terms of their politics, institutional structures, and types of intended audiences, Aboriginal community video productions are quite different from media such as Indian national television and Senegalese cinema. But numerous difficulties arise in the application of the label "indigenous media," and its isolation as a distinct area of study blurs its important connections with issues of media use across widely divergent social settings.

In the first instance, one finds that the adjective "indigenous" refers quite flexibly to the producers, owners, subjects, locales, and/or audiences of these various mass media. For example, in the case of the Aboriginally owned private television station, Imparja (which means "tracks" or "footprint" in the Arrernte language), roughly 90% of the staff is European and only 4% of the programming is produced locally. Nearly all of Imparja's programme material is obtained through its down-link from the national communications satellite AUSSAT, a large proportion of which is imported from the United States and is in the English language. In this case, the owners and audiences, but not the producers and products, are indigenous.

In this case, the producers and subjects are indigenous ("indigenes media experts"), but they are oriented toward a later stage of the mass communication process in which the producers and audiences are not indigenous. Other examples of the difficulty in specifying what is indigenous about indigenous media are found in ethnographic films and documentaries that are produced by and for Westerners, but that rely heavily on indigenous assistance in scriptwriting and set design.

In such cases, indigenous people are collaborators, but often have little editorial control. Their inclusion in the production process and their subsequent use of the final product may, however, have significant implications for the negotiation of their own identity, as Fienup-Riordan shows in a study of how Yup'ik traditions are recreated in response to a Western screenplay based on their historical narratives. These scenarios illustrate the substantial hybridity of indigenous media, and the multiple places within the mass communication circuit where a social group may be involved or indexed. In each case, the complex struggle over defining an authentic and politically correct version of indigenousness is foregrounded. This leads Michaels, positioned as a cultural analyst, to see the fundamental task as tracking these very debates over authenticity and the Aboriginality of Aboriginal media.

Declining to pinpoint it himself, he winds up with the tongue-in-cheek "Aboriginal content, who's got it-who needs it?". Ginsburg, on the other hand, grapples with analytic rather than culturally-specific definitions. She introduces the phrase "ethnographic media" to encompass both ethnographic film and indigenous media as they exhibit a common self-conscious engagement with topics of cultural identity and cultural dislocation. Unfortunately, this obscures the fact that all forms of mass media are potentially "ethnographic" in that they in various subtle ways negotiate and represent cultural identity. Some media genres explicitly signal a documentary or cingma *verite* mode more than others, and one critical issue is to investigate the cultural specificities of such evaluative frames (e.g. realism, factuality, historical truth) and their cross-cultural translatability.

Finally, the isolation of indigenous media as a separate area of study misses their vital connections with the more widespread phenomena of independent, alternative, or decentralised media production and consumption. Fundamental to all such alternative media forms and practices is the fact that their existence is intricately determined in relation to the dominant, "legitimate" media in the societies where they occur. There is thus a broad spectrum of different media and social settings where issues of control over self-representation and expression arise: pirate radio in Western Europe, "guerrilla television" the United States, community-based presses and radios operated by local labour unions in Latin America, small-scale private music cassette industries in India , mass mediated religious propaganda), and the newly emerging independent media throughout Eastern Europe.

Indicative of these connections, Sullivan uses the phrase "indigenous dramatic productions" to refer to independent films made by Papua New Guineans; this label does not indicate a "First Nation" people as much as an alternative to government produced or imported media products. Hamilton's study of pirated video cassettes in Thailand raises the related intriguing question of independent re-production (rather than production), and one might expand this even further to encompass alternative media uses as well. For example, researchers have documented oppositional forms of radio listening and film viewing in repressive media environments, as well as the creative appropriations and recyclings of various media forms within different subcultures.

Future Directions

In addition to the growing body of research on indigenous and alternative media, a number of new studies have begun to explore the sociocultural dynamics of national media. A significant part of this involves the intricate connection of media production and consumption with the wider processes of commoditisation and transnational culture. A major contribution these endeavours share with work on indigenous media is their insight into the culturally-specific dimensions of media production and reception, including culturally-based aesthetic evaluations innovative production styles, and the linkages with other forms of cultural knowledge and linguistic expression. In fact, although anthropologists have just begun to look at the various political, social, cultural, and linguistic dimensions of mass media, they have in some way already bypassed many of the debates within media studies.

Perhaps this is because they implicitly theorise media processes, products, and uses as complex parts of social reality, and expect to locate media power and value in more a diffuse, rather than direct and causal, sense. Certainly there is much more ground to traverse, and hopefully future work will contribute more directly to theoretical developments across these different disciplines and to a fuller understanding of modem life as we enter the twenty-first century.

4

Communication, Power and Social Order

Communications plays an important role in public thinking and public life. Establishing the relationships among communications, public opinion, and action on social issues, is an important step in developing a philanthropic stance toward communications. Prevailing theory in the field of communications posits close, but complicated, connections among these three phenomena. Whether in the form of music and the arts, entertainment, or the more recent trend toward Internet outlets, people learn about their world from an array of sources, and communications campaigns take advantage of these multiple sources of information.

Public opinion research over the past decade, however, confirms that news media constitute the main source of information about public affairs. What this means is that the real world is increasingly viewed through the lens of the news media. Social learning about race, family, poverty, etc., can be demonstrated to be highly influenced by the stories told to the public on the nightly news. This is not to say that movies and entertainment television, for instance, play an insignificant role in the construction of the average person's worldview; but, the news media should be accorded a central place in any thoughtful formulation of the role of communications in promoting the social good.

As issues rise and fall on the news media agenda, so does their potential for attracting the attention of the public and its policymakers. The ability of the news media to set the public agenda, in turn, determines to a large extent what issues policymakers will feel compelled to address. Indeed, media are often read by policymakers as the proxy for public opinion. Vincent Price expressed the relationship between the media and public opinion this way: "Public opinion-whether viewed in philosophical, political, sociological, or psychological terms-remains fundamentally a communication concept." This is important because too often public opinion is studied and addressed without reference to the way the culture's storytellers have framed public issues over time.

News media do more than tell us what to think about; they also direct how we think about particular social issues-whether, for example, we consider them to be individual problems necessitating better behaviours or whether they are collective, social problems requiring structural policy and programme solutions. Messages conveyed by mainstream media take on the value of public narratives about the ways of the world, and different types of stories produce different social learning. When news frames public issues narrowly, as problems of specific people or groups, support for policy proposals plummets. When a media story highlights conditions and trends, by contrast, public support for policies to address the problem increases dramatically.

Michael Pertschuk reports that, as long as smoking was covered as a story about individual behaviour choice, it was unlikely to galvanize a public following for more stringent tobacco control policies. Framed as a "defective product" that requires government intervention to protect the citizenry, however, tobacco control proposals gained supporters. How the media frame or present public issues is equally critical to the final resolution of public problems. Not only can framing affect whether the solution to any given social problem is judged by the public to be individual or collective, but the media's use of specific frames is an important influence on the way people judge the relevance and legitimacy of a communication's implicit or explicit call to action.

For example, if child abuse is portrayed as a criminal act perpetrated by evildoers, calls to action that ask people to befriend troubled parents before they become abusers, or even to support preventive treatment for stressed parents, are unlikely to meet with a positive public response. Thus, the concept of framing is important both to those campaigns that seek to move public opinion and to those that seek to change individual behaviour.

While many communications campaigns address the "public," they usually do so as an aggregate of individuals, not in the collective sense of seeking what is best for the society. Such campaigns seek to persuade individuals to change their beliefs, feelings, or behaviours, based on research about how individuals are affected by specific messages. In this sense, most communications campaigns pay more attention to the psychological orientation of the individual as a consumer who chooses between competing products than they do to the sociological or political roles people play in voting and expressing policy preferences about social issues. A key factor in determining the effectiveness of communications designed to achieve social good (is) whether the individual is the most appropriate or most effective agent to achieve social change.

Core Communications Concepts

What we know about how news media influence public opinion can be summed up in terms of three core communications concepts:

— *Agenda-setting*: The media influence which issues people think are important for government to address.

— *Framing*: The media influence how people think about and interpret ideas and issues, particularly how they think about solutions to problems.

— *Persuasion*: The media influence how people think about attitudes and behaviours they need to adopt in order to enhance their own well-being or prevent individual loss.

In order for foundations and their grantees to develop effective communications plans, they must be able to relate their challenges and their strategies to these core concepts.

Agenda-setting

Agenda-setting is the name given to the process of placing issues on the policy agenda for public consideration and intervention. News media are instrumental to the perceived salience of a particular social problem. Indeed, researchers view the policy agenda as the outcome of media influence on the public. As another communications scholar sees it, the media set the public agenda which, in turn, sets the policymaker agenda.

Experimental research over the last decade has demonstrated that even brief exposure to media coverage of a particular issue will increase public assessment of that issue's importance. Thus, an issue is by definition "a social problem that has received mass media coverage" and the agenda-setting process is defined as "an ongoing competition among issue proponents to gain the attention of media professionals, the public, and policy elites." The implications of these relationships are profound.

News media have the ability to place a high priority on issues that may, in fact, not be as important as others. Conversely, those issues that get relatively little media attention are unlikely to figure among the most important problems facing the nation. This essentially casts news media in the role of democracy's unelected gatekeepers. If a social problem does not conform to the needs and conventions of journalism, it is unlikely to get told and sold to the American public.

For example, in decrying "parachute journalism"-the media's tendency to move rapidly from crisis to crisis-David Gergen says, "It was as if the lights went out over El Salvador, and the country's subsequent struggle to preserve democracy disappeared from sight. Out of sight, it also passed out of mind for American viewers. Television loves sagas in which someone wins and someone loses. It abhors long, tedious, complex stories and will usually ignore them if possible." The important question of whether the United States' long-term policies toward El Salvador should figure more prominently in American concerns than, say, a dramatic story like an earthquake in Mexico, is muted by the media's uncontested demands for an entertaining narrative.

Foundations that labour to publish fact books without making parallel investments in translating these facts into public discourse ignore the function that the news media provide in the national public square, refining and rationalising the country's "to do" list. While the President and the major national newspapers, for instance, can have a powerful impact on an issue's salience, by contrast, "a real-world indicator is neither a necessary nor a sufficient cause for an issue to climb the agenda."

In a famous study of agenda-setting, Funkhouser compared the media agenda to real-world indicators-or descriptive statistics that demonstrate the extent or nature of a social problem-on 14 issues over the decade of the sixties and found little correlation. Other studies confirm that the issues salient in the media correlate to those expressed by public opinion. But what about those issues where people have first-hand experience? Are we still so susceptible to media's influence?

In fact, the evidence suggests that familiarity with an issue may make people more media attentive to that issue, and therefore more influenced by media coverage, not less. "Evidence from a half a century of polling in the United States supports the proposition that the more citizens know about politics and public affairs, the more firmly they are wedded to elite and media perspectives on foreign policy issues," says John Zaller.

> Elite and media influence is likely to be limited to those citizens who are sufficiently attentive to politics to be aware of what elites are saying...: and then the most politically aware citizens are most susceptible to influence because they are most heavily exposed to an elite consensus that they have no partisan basis for resisting.

Zaller further suggests that "as news issues come up, the public looks to public statements by its political leaders-partisan, ideological, religious, ethnic, and so forth-to decide what should be done, and is willing, within broad limits, to go along with what the majority of leaders advises. Then, as the consequences of elite initiatives become apparent in the form of policies that succeed or fail, the public judges its leaders accordingly."

Other communications scholars disagree. "People are not so passive. People are not so dumb, and people negotiate with media messages in complicated ways that vary from issue to issue," says William Gamson, who promotes a theory of political consciousness that emphasises the role of "personal strategies" in mitigating media frames. Put simply, on those issues where Americans have access to additional viewpoints and sources of information, such as personal or recounted experience, the effect of media exposure is lessened. The problem for issues that are far removed from opportunities for direct observation, like the Arab-Israeli conflict or nuclear power, is that "media discourse is typically their first resort."

Ironically, news media may be even more influential on policy elites than on the public. The lack of contact between policy elites and the general public may make the former all the more reliant upon the media as a proxy for public opinion. In a study of the actual impact of what he termed "icons of outrage," or those famous photos widely credited with having had an impact on foreign policy attitudes among the public,

David Perlmutter found instead a "first person effect where discourse elites feel that a picture has an effect on them (or should have one) and then, often falsely, project this effect on the general viewing public."

In other words, highly news attentive people, such as public officials, assumed that the images being broadly distributed by the media affected others in precisely the same way and to the same degree that the images affected them. This was not always the case. But, regardless of actual public opinion, Perlmutter found that widely disseminated news pictures, such as those associated with events like the revolt of Chinese dissidents in Tiananmen Square, have a powerful effect on policymakers: "Policy is explained by pointing at specific images in the press."

Framing

The attention to volume and placement of media coverage that is the focus of agenda-setting does not tell the whole story about the influence of communications on public opinion. The type of story that is told by the news media also powerfully affects the public's understanding of social issues. The media's influence on how we think about social problems lasts far beyond our memory of a particular newscast or news topic.

The way the news is "framed" on many issues sets up habits of thought and expectation that, over time, are so powerful that they serve to configure new information to conform to this frame. Framing refers to the way a story is told-its selective use of particular symbols, metaphors, and messengers, for example-and to the way these cues, in turn, trigger the shared and durable cultural models that people use to make sense of their world. The frame is the organising principle, what a story is "about," supported by the frame elements of messenger, metaphor, etc., which combine to support the overall idea.

Understanding which frames serve to advance which policy options with which groups is central to communications strategy. For example, the documented tendency in U.S. media to focus on U.S. contributions to foreign aid to the virtual exclusion of those of other countries is undoubtedly responsible for the equally documented assessment that Americans resist increasing foreign assistance because they believe the U.S. is "doing it all."

Frames are important because research suggests people use mental shortcuts to make sense of new information and these mental shortcuts rely on small sets of internalised concepts and values that allow us to accord meaning to unfolding events. Put simply, the central organising principle in any communication-the frame-triggers what Lippmann called "the pictures in our heads," the models we have developed over time to make sense of our world. Once evoked, frames provide the reasoning to process information quickly and to solve problems, drawing upon our internal reservoirs of expectations about how the world works.

As linguist Deborah Tannen has observed, "People approach the world not as naïve, blank-slate receptacles who take in stimuli... in some independent and objective way, but rather as experienced and sophisticated veterans of perception who have stored their prior experiences as an organised mass. This prior experience then takes the form of expectations about the world, and in the vast majority of cases, the world, being a systematic place, confirms these expectations, saving the individual the trouble of figuring things out anew all the time."

Stephen Reese offers a particularly inclusive working definition of frames: "Frames are organising principles that are socially shared and persistent over time that work symbolically to meaningfully structure the world." Further, frames have consequences. As Charlotte Ryan observes: "Every frame defines the issue, explains who is responsible, and suggests potential solutions. All of these are conveyed by images, stereotypes, or anecdotes."

The relative use of episodic and thematic news frames by the news media is a key factor in how public opinion is shaped.

As Iyengar describes these two types, episodic news frames, which predominate on U.S. television newscasts, depict public issues in terms of concrete instances. That is, they focus on discrete events that involve individuals located at specific places and at specific times, as in nightly crime reports. By contrast, thematic frames place public issues in a broader context by focusing on general conditions or outcomes, such as reports on poverty trends.

The type of news frame used has a profound effect on the way in which individuals attribute responsibility. Because television news is heavily episodic, its effect is generally "to induce attributions of responsibility to individual victims or perpetrators rather than to broad societal forces." And, while it is true that print media tend to be more thematic than broadcast media, the dominant frames used in many print news stories nevertheless reinforce a consumer stance to public issues such as health care, framing the issue as an individual product instead of as a societal problem.

Persuasion

Persuasion is the ability to recognise and manipulate attitudes, defined by Carl Rogers as "a positive or negative feeling toward some individual or object that serves as a predisposition to action." The original persuasion research is credited to Carl Hovland, who studied the effectiveness of the "Why We Fight" recruitment films created for the U.S. military in World War II. Hovland's work set the model for subsequent research and suggested that appeals to individuals that aggregate to mass action remain the goal of most persuasion campaigns. Such persuasion campaigns rely strongly on behavioural theories and research to choose among informational approaches that motivate and guide the action of individuals.

It is important to distinguish between the individual outcome and the collective action associated with social movements, in which people mobilise to change the opportunity and reward structure of a society which is seen to constrain behaviour change in the first place. Persuasion campaigns focus on the impact of a small number of factors on the target individual's desired behaviour, including such inputs as source credibility, rewards within the message, repetition, and intelligence of the receiver. These factors add up to the "input" in the model.

On the output side, McGuire has analysed a "hierarchy of effects" of the persuasion process: "[T]he public must be exposed to the message and, having been exposed to it, must attend to it, like it, learn what and how, agree, store and retrieve, and decide on the basis of it, down to behaving on the basis of that decision, getting reinforced for so behaving, and engaging in post compliance activity (such as proselytising others or reorganising one's related beliefs) that consolidates the new position induced by the communication."

Persuasion theorists focus on the responses of the target audience to messages which are largely seen as "pushed out" through media, but not interactive to the degree that cognitive theorists would suggest is the case. From the cognitive theory literature comes the popular concept of "inoculation"-overcoming the target's resistance to a message by anticipating and including the rebuttal in the original message. For example, a persuasion campaign oriented to improving children's health might adopt a message like, "Oral health: it's not just about your teeth," building off the documented impression that one of the major personal obstacles to brushing is the erroneous belief that the health of the mouth does not influence overall health.

Evaluated from a framing perspective, critics of this approach would say that reminding people of what they believe simply allows them to make the fast and frugal cognitive connection to their enduring belief system and to be done with the message. Moreover, the call to action ignores the biggest obstacle to better oral health-lack of access to dentists-and is therefore, misplaced energy as it further reinforces personal responsibility in place of public solutions. The application of persuasion versus agenda-setting communications strategies can be illustrated by considering whether the desired outcome is in the realm of personal or public behaviour.

Garbage recycling, for example, would be a prime candidate for a persuasion campaign if the goal were to use media strategically to change the garbage handling behaviour of individual householders. Such a hypothetical campaign might use one's standing in the community to induce the target to make sure their recycling bins show they are a good neighbour. By contrast, an agenda-setting campaign would try to get voters to support environmental legislation, such as taxcredits for businesses that recycle. This type of campaign might calculate the potential savings to the community if its three major employers were to institute recycling campaigns and would call on voters to make recycling everybody's business by supporting tax incentives.

The difference between these two approaches would be largely determined by the type of media frames used, with the persuasion frame defining the problem as personal and the agenda-setting frame defining it as public in nature. There is another important distinction between agenda-setting and persuasion. Persuasion tends to focus on the people who have the problem, while agenda-setting focuses on the people who have the power to change the problem through political power.

Thus, persuasion campaigns are oriented almost exclusively to at-risk populations, even though "our knowledge of who is at risk for a problem is imperfect, and persons at risk usually constitute only a small proportion of the total audience in the coverage area of most media campaigns." In this view, the agenda-setting approach to communication strategy speaks to the empowerment of individuals over their situations whereas the persuasion approach suggests blaming the victim and ignoring the power structure of social rewards.

Communications Practice

Communications campaigns have traditionally been classified according to their end target or locus of change: the individual consumer or the mass public. Those aimed at the individual tend to draw their strategies and tools from a commercial perspective, using public relations, marketing, and advertising as the foundation for their campaigns. By contrast, publicly oriented campaigns tend to rely upon the theory and practice of politics as their foundation.

Communications practices that address social issues from the personal perspective are founded on the central tenets of product marketing. People are considered rational economic actors for whom a product campaign can be devised with the goal of influencing individual behaviour. Communicating social issues, thus, is about applying marketing techniques to advance social causes. From this perspective, issue publics are essentially consumer target audiences, and practices like voting or developing a political or partisan identity are equated with becoming brand users. Typically, a particular behaviour is the desired end-product; the goal is to get certain people to choose to do certain things.

Public Relations Practice

In public relations practice, the central assumption is that effective relationships with consumer audiences are a function of the extent to which the organisation and its issues are in good standing with the appropriate publics. Based on the early formulations of people like Edward Bernays, public relations was primarily used by the private sector to draw attention to the organisation itself for the purposes of enhancing the organisation's image and raising resources to support the organisation's goals. In the modern period, public and private organisations utilise public relations to disseminate information, heighten issue awareness, lobby public officials, and generally attempt to create an environment that is receptive to the organisation's message.

As a practice, public relations embraces "publicity, press-agentry, propaganda, and advertising." The Communications Consortium Media Center has recently adapted public relations to the nonprofit sector by creating the concept of "strategic communications," which it defines as the ability of organisations to treat "media relations and communications as important, fully integrated, consistent, and ongoing functions," complete with sufficient investments. While strategic communications can be adapted to either individual or public goals, we have placed this approach within the public relations school of practice because it essentially promotes "best practices" among the nonprofit sector in classic public relations terms; for example, by adapting such traditional tools and techniques as effective spokesperson training and crisis management to social issues.

When foundations engage in public relations, they often do so to promote attention to a grantee or recognition of a signature programme. While public relations may be important to organisational goals, as a practice it is often insufficient to meet the larger public goals associated with communications campaigns. One criticism of public relations is based on its emphasis on the organisation over the issue: Public relations tends to ignore agenda-setting in favour of organisational identity.

Public Service Advertising

Public service as an advertising category was pioneered by the Advertising Council in the early 1940s. The goal of this hybrid invention was to bring the experience of traditional product advertising techniques to serve people and social causes. The underlying assumption is that memorable communications creating a favourable image will lead to the actions suggested, for social issues just as for products. This variation assumes that information, often presented as an emotional appeal, can persuade and motivate people to alter their thinking or behaviour in relation to social and health issues as well as conventional consumer choices.

The advertising industry first began to deal with social issues during the Second World War when product rationing and wartime manufacturing conversion caused the advertising industry to be concerned about declining advertising revenue. To address the feared decline, ad industry executives formed The War Ad Council in 1942 to use advertising to encourage support for the war and to maintain corporate image by associating corporations with patriotic themes as a replacement for product-specific advertising. After the war, the Ad Council continued, turning its attention to a broader array of social issues.

Sixty years after its creation, public service advertising is now commonplace. As an approach, Ad Council campaigns represent the characteristics of traditional public service advertising. However, public service ads have also evolved into a tool used by other schools of communications, and may be influenced by their perspective; so it is important to distinguish between public service campaigns as a school of practice and the specific tool of public service announcements (PSAs), which can be used in service to numerous types of campaigns. The typical public service campaign relies on television, print, and/or outdoor ads.

Most public service advertising relies on donated media, although there is recent movement toward paid media schedules. Traditional public service advertising frames the issue in terms of personal responsibility and benefits and, while it attempts to place an issue on the nation's agenda, it does so for personal, not public, action. Critics of this approachcharge that this perspective is inherently a "blame the victim" orientation, reducing political issues to personal problems. Because people may not distinguish between public service campaigns and other sources of information about a particular social issue, PSAs can have the effect of reinforcing negative stereotypes about who is responsible for social problems.

With regard to specific practices, public service advertising has at least two weaknesses. First, its reliance on donated time means that ads typically do not receive favourable exposure. Second, because the commercial outlets where PSAs routinely air have no intention of alienating their advertisers and audience, "non-controversial" issues are the norm for PSA campaigns. This, of course, makes this strategy less appealing for communications of value to the most distressed communities and dispossessed citizens.

Social Marketing

In the early 1970s, Philip Kotler and Gerald Zaltman began to explore whether "marketing concepts and techniques could be effectively applied to the promotion of social objectives." Their mission was to develop a theory for applying commercial marketing techniques to advance social causes. This approach is called social marketing. Compared to public service campaigning, social marketing is more sophisticated in its integrated use of formative research and in the wide array of communications techniques it employs: from focus groups to survey research and individual interviews. However, these methods are used in ways consistent with the individual approach to campaigning, i.e., to determine whether the enduser of the communication was receptive to the message.

As Lawrence Wallack observes: "Social marketing provides a framework in which marketing principles are integrated with social-psychological theories to develop programmes better able to accomplish behaviour change goals." In other words, critical to the definition of social marketing is the notion of influencing individual behaviour for the good of that person or general society. Social marketing focuses explicitly on mass consumer needs and behaviours. The approach is based on the process of conceiving, pricing, promoting, and distributing ideas and services that satisfy individual and organisational preferences, which is accomplished by focusing on the "Four P's": product, price, place, and promotion.

Political Perspective

The political or civic perspective is attentive to the power structure in a society and to the influence of citizens on elites. Schools of communications practice with this perspective aim to convince large masses of people to give priority to certain issues and to convince policymakers to act on the public will or in the public's interest. Typically, a particular attitude or volition is the desired end-product; the goal is to get people to understand an issue in a certain way and express themselves to policymakers.

Media advocacy practice

Media advocacy stands the tenets of social marketing on their heads by conceiving of media as a product that requires highly critical consumption. The audience is not considered simply a passive receiver of media messages; rather, media are considered an arena for contesting power in society. In its broadest sense, this communications approach argues for the utilisation of the media as a tool to advocate for people without the power to control the conditions that affect their lives.

Media advocacy practice attempts to influence media portrayals of a group and its issuesin order to promote the preferred policy agendas and solutions of the group-or of organisation(s) advocating for the group. Media advocacy has been most closely associated with public health issues, from tobacco control to gun violence, and begins with the assumption that "the root of most health problems lies not in people simply lacking proper health information-an information gap-but primarily in groups not having the power to change social and economic conditions-a power gap."

Media advocacy poses three core questions to its practitioners: "What do we want? Who has the power to make it happen? What do they need to hear?" The answers to the first two questions engage advocates in identifying desired policy changes and the public actors who control them. To answer the third question, polling and focus groups are sometimes used to get the message right so that advocates can seize upon the images and organising themes that effectively transform a private issue like teen smoking into a public concern. Community groups are involved in crafting the media messages so that they reflect "the broad values and goals of the group." The practice of media advocacy is explicitly focused on agenda-setting, considering news and editorial media as keys to achieving policy change.

Media advocacy practitioners have developed instructional materials to help community groups understand the principles of framing and to conduct their own content analysis of frames in the news. Likewise, advocates have conducted newsroom seminars to encourage journalists to widen their perceptual lens. In this emphasis, the practices of the media advocacy school of communications are in direct opposition to the techniques of persuasion, which target individual behaviour. Media advocates try to persuade elected officials to change policies that constrain individual behaviour and choice.

A great irony of media advocacy work is that while it has served as a democratising corrective to social marketing approaches, it has produced an antidemocratic bias of its own. Because much of the work of media advocates focuses on a small core of activists concerned with changing the culture and behaviour of media and policy elites, it underestimates the value of mass opinion in convincing elites and sustaining the frame of public responsibility. Among media advocacy promoters, the balance between attention to expert and elite policy agendas, and mass publics, is skewed toward the former.

Grassroots social mobilisation

For many years the Boston Media Research and Action Project (MRAP) has trained grassroots organisations to influence media content. In particular, sociologists William Gamson and

Charlotte Ryan have drawn on the study of social movements to call attention to the power differentials between community-based organisations (and their constituencies) and media institutions. According to their line of reasoning, advocates must develop strategies that allow marginalised groups to properly interpret and effectively access media channels.

Grassroots social mobilisation seeks to use the media to influence the allocation of public resources in a more equitable manner. Using the techniques of this school of communications practice, community groups can have a democratising influence on the construction of solutions to social problems. Much of the work of grassroots advocacy centers on building the communications capacity of community-based organisations. The implicit theory of change is that people are empowered when they have a better grasp of how and why media influence those issues important to their organisations and communities.

For instance, practitioners use trainings, workshops, and Web-based materials to support the communications activities of organisations that are generally unable to mount full-scale communications programmes and activities within their organisations. One relatively low-cost investment in understanding media had a profound impact on the public portrayal of a low-income neighbourhood.

Public policy campaigns

Public interest or public policy campaigns apply the tools and strategies of electoral campaigning to non-election campaigns, often with the goal of passing a particular piece of legislation. This approach utilises the narrow strategy of controlled policy messages primarily aimed at policymakers. These campaigns are designed to directly influence decisionmakers-as opposed to influencing either the media or public opinion as an indirect method of influencing decisionmakers. Policy campaigns typically involve writing reports, mass mailings, and lobbying public officials.

They may also incorporate elements of social marketing, such as paid advertisements, although they often do so with carefully calculated media buys aimed at reaching members of Congress or other policy elites-the quarter page ad on the opinion page of the Washington Post. Trade associations, labour unions, and public interest groups all participate in this kind of campaigning: drafting policy reports in support of specific policy objectives, developing relationships with powerful actors in the policy process, and providing information to the general public.

Change in public opinion, however, is seen only as a means to influence policymakers. For instance, campaigns of this sort use "publicity polls" to demonstrate high levels of support for the policy of interest, as opposed to the kind of formative research used in social marketing. Critics of this school point to its heavy dependence on rational choice and a traditional information-processing model, and its tendency to rely on facts and information gain to predict support.

Strategic Frame Analysis (SFA)

Designed consciously to address perceived shortcomings inherent in both the personal and political models of communications, strategic frame analysis (SFA) is a multidisciplinary, multi-method approach that pays attention to the public's deeply held worldviews and widely held assumptions. SFA acknowledges the power of the media and the role of both elite opinion and grassroots activism; on the other hand, it also incorporates thinking and practice on the nature of mass publics. Developed by the FrameWorks Institute and UCLA's Center for Communications and Community, it has been applied to such varied issues as community development, the environment, gender equity, and child and youth development.

Strategic frame analysis is different from other communications approaches in several important respects. At a broad level, this practice is a marriage of both basic and applied research. The foundation is a perception among issue advocates that current policy solutions are being driven by skewed public perceptions of reality which result in proposals that differ markedly from those proposed by experts. The SFA approach incorporates research to test the assumption that public perception is indeed at variance with expert remedies, as defined by scholars and policy advocates. The SFA approach explores the contribution of media to this distortion, documenting the specific impact on public attitudes of the dominant frames of news coverage.

For example, content analysis of the portrayal of adolescents on local news conducted by the Center for Media and Public Affairs for the Frame- Works Institute revealed that the three most frequently reported topics of youth news on six local stations in 1999 were crime victimisation, accidents involving young people, and violent juvenile crime, accounting for nearly half (46 percent) of all coverage of youth. This news portrayal flies in the face of expert assessment; James Youniss and Allison Ruth have shown that, for example, on virtually every social indicator, "youth today are at least as healthy or healthier than their parents' generation."

Using survey research methods adapted to SFA, FrameWorks researchers were able to demonstrate empirically that this "at risk" view of the world has serious consequences for those who seek to engage the public in supporting such programmes as mental health counselling for teens, after-school programmes, opportunities for volunteer work, team sports, etc. The dominant news frame of teens in trouble does nothing to build public will to advance policies for youth. Survey respondents were exposed to a series of questions designed to prime a particular way of thinking about youth before responding to a series of key indicator questions.

The only policy receiving a statistically significant increase in priority under the teens in trouble prime was to require parental involvement in the schools. Furthermore, descriptive statistics, whether positive or negative, did nothing to shift perceptions of youth or encourage support for policies to benefit youth. By contrast, when respondents were presented with positive images of youth, virtually every policy moved closer to solutions espoused by adolescent experts. This use of research methods to document and experiment with frame effects is one unique contribution of SFA.

Drawing from an identification of different models people hold of a particular issue, tests are developed to determine their impact on policy positions. A range of methods are used-from survey research to media effects experiments. The results of this work are then shared with issue advocates through trainings, toolkits, and interactive online courses designed to help advocates frame their communications in ways that have the greatest potential for encouraging public reconsideration of an issue (e.g., alternative policy solutions). For example, in the case of the SFA research on adolescent issues, policy advocates were shown how to prime for better policy support by using different images of youth associated with volunteer service, team sports, and performance arts.

In addition to examples of each approach, advocates were shown the impact of these communications choices on policy support, with reference to the research. This approach is strategic in the sense that it empirically tests for the impact of dominant frames on public reasoning and volition and then develops and tests alternative reframes. Reframing is intended to change "the context of the message exchange" so that different interpretations and probable outcomes become visible to the public. The objective is to enable issue advocates to assess the extent to which rival frames produce different decision outcomes.

Working with policy advocates in preparing for the release of a major report, for example, SFA research is used to outline the message strategy, to provide specific examples of the reframe, and subsequently, to monitor the degree to which resulting news coverage was "on frame." On issues from environmental policy to children's issues, SFA has been able to drive the public discourse in a different direction from the episodic, crisis-oriented frame often adopted by advocates and journalists alike in describing social problems.

Because it tests competing theoretical arguments, strategic frame analysis offers policy advocates a way to work systematically through the challenges that are likely to confront the introduction of new legislation or social policies. It informs their work by helping them anticipate attitudinal barriers to support and developing research-based strategies to overcome public misunderstanding. By understanding that most depictions of at-risk teens are likely to result in public attribution of responsibility to parents, advocates can dispense with this ineffective communications strategy in favour of one that demonstrates the values youth acquire from such programmes as arts, sports, and volunteering and to use these frames to open up a discussion that is far closer to the asset-based approach championed by many youth development experts.

Strategic frame analysis pays attention to agenda-setting by acknowledging the influence of media on opinion and on the public's frame repertoire. Using qualitative and quantitative tools heretofore applied primarily to persuasion campaigns, it analyses the impact of various frames on people's attitudes to public policies. Like other schools of practice, strategic frame analysis has limitations. For example, the breadth of inquiry requires a substantial commitment of resources. SFA is costly also because it is an approach that is most effective in long-term engagements-compared, for example, to the more immediate "pitch and place" tactics of social marketing and public policy campaigns designed to produce quick legislative results. Additionally, SFA relies on a high-level of expertise in the analysis of frames and the manufacture of new frames.

Typically, experts in such fields as political psychology, cultural anthropology, and cognitive linguistics are engaged in the analytical process. While SFA practitioners disseminate and explain the results, the approach is less democratic than media advocacy in the production of messages; while SFA gleans potential frame solutions from community advocates, it insists on validating these hypotheses through research. And while community voices are engaged in these campaigns, considerable research is devoted to understanding which messengers are most likely to result in greater public support for an issue.

Finally, SFA's orientation to public as opposed to private action directs its attention to the most commonly held cultural frames, leaving it vulnerable to charges that it overlooks minority views in favour of the most widely shared framing solutions, and that it does not pay adequate attention to the views of policy elites that control the power structure without regard to public opinion.

Tools and Techniques for Communication Practice

Each of the above schools of practice represents a particular perspective on the task of integrating what we know about how communications media affect individual consumers and mass publics with the principal techniques of communications practice. Another way to approach the arena of communications is to consider the specific range of tools and techniques that can be enlisted to support different organisational objectives. This is organised around Harold Lasswell's enduring five-questions model of communications: "Who says what to whom via what channels with what effects?" Later researchers added a sixth important question: Why? These are described below.

Why Communicate?

Organisations must first be able to answer the question: What is the problem?

The initial step toward a solid communications plan is the accumulation of descriptive data and expert opinion to explain the overall problem the organisation wishes to address. In so doing, it is important to determine whether communications planners perceive it to be a public or a private problem, and the extent to which public attitudes and perceptions are also part of the problem. For example, documented stereotypes about race and teenage pregnancy might have been a mitigating factor in generating support for a teen after-school programme. By establishing the social context, an organisation can begin to understand the role that communications plays in the definition of the problem, as well as in the solution.

The second step is to identify the organisation's policy agenda or other solutions to ameliorate the problem. Too often, groups have failed to identify precisely what short-term and long-term outcomes they hope to achieve as a result of their overall effort. In order to measure effectiveness of communications over time, the group must advance a position, a policy, or some prescriptive solution to the problem which can serve as a benchmark against which to measure public understanding and support.

The third step is to identify the organisation's theory of change. A theory of change defines how the world works. "[A] theory of change can sharpen the planning and implementation of an initiative," facilitate the evaluation process, and make clear why one is communicating, as opposed to adopting other strategies, from lobbying to service delivery. The articulated theory should also make clear the organisation's approach to the core concepts of agenda-setting, framing, and persuasion, and point to some schools of practice as more relevant than others.

Finally, it is important to determine the precise role that communications can play as part of an overall strategy for solving the problem identified. For example, the overall strategy for sustaining and expanding a proven approach to youth involvement in after-school programmes might seek to secure more state and local funds for programmes that reduce high school drop-out rates. A number of strategies would be planned, only some of which are communications-oriented.

The problem that communications must solve might be making voters aware that cost-effective solutions to teen drop-out rates exist and are not fully funded. Another problem communications might solve is to make policymakers aware that voters strongly support investing in programmes to reduce high school dropout rates. In either case, the point is that the communications focus is not synonymous with the social problem itself.

At the problem identification stage of planning a communications strategy, the questions that organisations need to address include:

— What is the social problem we are addressing?
— What are its characteristics?
— What do people already know about it, and how do they think about it?
— What have been the dominant frames of media coverage of the issue?
— What do we think should be done to improve/solve it?
— What do experts believe should be done to improve/solve it?
— What is our policy agenda or what are our objectives in tackling this problem?
— What is our theory of change, e.g., how do we think our efforts can prove helpful?
— What objective indicators would suggest to us that opinion/policy/behaviour is moving in the right direction?
— What is the appropriate role for communications in the broader strategy?
— What schools of communications practice seem best oriented to this problem?

Communicate to Whom?

The appropriate target publics for a communications campaign should become obvious as an organisation assesses the problem and its theory of social change. However, communications planners sometimes confuse the locus of the behaviour or attitude change desired-individuals, mass publics, specific subgroups, or elites-which can undermine an entire communications strategy. The question of who has the power to make change needs to be distinguished from the easier issue of who wants to listen to your message.

"Audience segmentation" is the term used to disaggregate mass publics by specific demographics such as race and gender, partisanship, socio-economic status, or such "psychographics" as Soccer Moms or Yuppies. The more definitive you can be about the specific audience you seek, the more likely you are to be able to plan a very targeted and efficient campaign. Given limited resources, for example, a campaign that sought to enlist people in protecting the health of oceans might look first to those who live along the coastal waterways, targeting media resources to California and Florida in an effort to take that visibility nationwide at a future date.

At the same time, for a campaign focused primarily on agenda-setting, an organisation may need to sequence its communications in order to take advantage of the impact of one audience on another and avoid the cost of a mass campaign e.g., beginning with "influentials," moving to op/eds and editorial pages, and using these to reach policymakers. For example, the policy campaigns reviewed earlier focused their media purchases narrowly on those outlets most visible to lawmakers and policy influentials and did not waste time or money reaching those lawmakers' direct constituents with mass advertising. In sum, the questions to be addressed about audiences are:

— Which people are critical to achieving our goals?

— Are there subsets of this group that make more sense to our campaign goals than others?
— Are there sequences of groups that can build from one another?
— Are there important intermediaries that already reach these audiences?
— What other organisations, groups, and individuals are vested in this issue?

Communicate What?

In a review of communications campaigns over two decades, scholars conclude that "most are underdeveloped at the preparation, production, and dissemination phases of implementation due to poor conceptualisation and inadequate formative evaluation research inputs.... This situation is in distinct contrast to commercial advertising campaigns, where strategies for influencing the audience are based on extensive pre-campaign research activities, such as market segmentation analysis, consumer opinion surveys, focus group interviews, and message pretesting." Nowhere is this lack of planning and investment more evident than in the area of message development.

Indeed, crafting a message is often the first task groups set out to tackle in creating a campaign, when it should be the logical endproduct of an organic strategy development process. Those campaigns in which the group has predetermined a message are usually doomed to failure. Message development has to move the target audience from the position, attitude, or behaviour it currently holds to a new position, more closely aligned with the campaign goals. This requires translation of an organisation's policy agenda into language, values, and frames that the target audience can consider, which must be done with ample consideration of what the audience currently knows and believes about the issue.

Indeed, an effective message results from taking the audience's pulse on an issue and gauging its predispositions, and then determining how to effectively redirect its attention. Message testing is needed to confirm that the message will actually have the desired effect. The key questions about messages for a communications campaign are:

— What are we asking people to do, think, or feel as a result of this communication?

— How do we know this message will yield this result?

— Does our message strategy take into consideration the dominant frames of media coverage of this issue?

— Does our message strategy reflect what we know about public opinion in general and the particular opinions of our target audience?

— Have we adequately translated the message from the language and complexity of expert understanding to suit the educational level, perspectives, and values of our target audience?

— How will our messages stand up to confrontation and criticism?

Who Is Communicating?

From the beginning of communications research, the importance of the messenger to the public's acceptance of the message has been understood. Trustworthiness, however, presents more of a challenge. Trustworthiness can be satisfied by an assessment of the speaker's character. But, in the absence of such personal information, listeners often evaluate trustworthiness on the basis of a speaker's "costly effort." That is, they ask whether the speaker has "put their money where their mouth is" through an action or whether the speaker would have anything to gain by lying.

Listeners are looking for sincerity, but also for vested interest-hence, the psychological basis for the concept of "unlikely allies": a police officer is a more persuasive spokesperson for the importance of early childhood education than a child advocate because s/he has no apparent reason to lie on this issue. And, contrary to popular wisdom, "You do not necessarily learn more from people who are like you, nor do you learn more from people you like. This is why most people turn to financial advisors, instead of their mothers, when dealing with mutual funds, and back to Mom when seeking advice about child rearing." In choosing who should represent the communications sender (the messenger), as opposed to the receiver (the audience), organisations must answer the following questions:

— Who is both knowledgeable and trustworthy on our issues?

— Who is likely to be perceived as an honest messenger by the target audience?

— Who is likely to be able to satisfy these criteria AND generate media attention?

How To Communicate?

Whether an organisation chooses to broadcast over the Internet or television, pass out pamphlets at malls, or orchestrate a cell-phone crusade, take advantage of "silent radio" that runs advertisements on the kiosk as you wait to pump your gas, put up posters in libraries, or send handwritten letters to members of Congress depends upon the predetermined campaign goals and theory of change under which the campaign is operating. The choice of media should be made on the basis of matching the medium to the communications goals and targets.

This suggests that if you don't need television to reach your intended audience, you shouldn't pay for it simply because it seems like a missing component in a communications campaign. Indeed, there is no "pre-packaged" formula of media channels that comprise communications campaigns. The channels must be selected because they effectively reach the targeted audience. The one hallmark of most campaigns, however, is that repetition is a prerequisite to change. Constructing a campaign that puts an effective message in front of the most people in the target audience the most often over the longest period of time is the goal of this aspect of communications planning.

Certain theories of change and schools of communications practice drive toward the choice of particular media. For example, media advocacy is oriented toward news, op/ed, and editorial placements as the key vehicles to influence policymakers and policy elites. Those who seek to change social norms often attempt to demonstrate behaviours in entertainment media, so that people will see their favourite stars buckling up, designating drivers, or using condoms and, presumably, emulate the action.

Policy campaigns might buy one full-page ad in the state capital edition of a daily newspaper, hoping to convince state lawmakers that the public is on notice with respect to a particular issue or piece of legislation. In each case, the theory of change drives the selection of the strategic media placement. The questions an organisation needs to address in selecting effective media are:

— Is our placement strategy consistent with our theory of change?
— Have we chosen media that make sense for our message and our audience?
— Is the mix of media driven by our campaign goals?
— Have we ensured adequate frequency or exposure to accomplish our goals?

What Are the Communications Outcomes?

Taking too much responsibility for broad-scale social change is a common problem in communications evaluation. This evaluation practice ignores the interactive nature of communications with uncontrollable variables, from acts of God and governments to access to communications channels. Another problem in communications evaluation is failing to isolate the contribution of the communications activities from other variables-either those that may prevent attainment of communication goals or those that are more likely than communications to induce change.

In the world of philanthropy, most communications grantees will look like failures when the effects of their work are improperly specified, but many will look like huge successes for the same inaccurate reasons. The only systematic way to judge the contribution of communications activities to long-term social change is to monitor media content and public opinion over time. While this is far too costly for most individual grantees, it is the kind of activity that major foundations can and should support as they enter signature programmes.

When one or more foundations orient grantmaking toward an issue-whether it's child care, foreign aid, or community development-those foundations should invest in annual reviews of media content and public opinion, and should take a longer view toward influencing these arenas. When foundations target certain geographic areas or populations, they should invest in baseline and annual reviews of media and opinion.

McGuire suggests that each campaign should set out a series of probable effects that are likely to result from the communications interventions and which allow the initiating organisation to gauge the effectiveness of its strategy at each important stage. Rather than the typical approach described by Dungan-Seaver, campaigns need to evaluate the degree to which the communications results in a better understanding of, and support for, the policies which are being advanced. Name recognition or even sympathy for a cause is not necessarily synonymous with policy preference.

Many communications campaigns operate on shoestrings, it is important to distinguish between the success that the campaign could have achieved, had it been adequately funded, and the marginal success it was able to achieve with limited investment. The latter achievement should not be misconstrued as an indictment of communications campaigns in general or the campaign strategy in particular. Not until foundations are willing to invest adequately in communications campaigns can they be judged according to the higher standards to which advertising campaigns are held accountable. The questions to be addressed with respect to communications effects are:

— How will we know we are having an impact?

— Are there different indicators for short-term and long-term impact?

— Are our outcome goals in line with our theory of change?

— What specific actions/beliefs/outcomes will we monitor as indices of improvement?

— Have we set our goals too high for the budget associated with our campaign?

5

Agenda-setting Role of Mass Media

Newspapers set a nation's agenda, to focus public attention on a few key public issues, is an immense and well-documented influence. Not only do people acquire factual information about public affairs from the news media, readers and viewers also learn how much importance to attach to a topic on the basis of the emphasis placed on it in the news. Newspapers provide a host of cues about the salience of the topics in the daily news—lead story on page one, other front page display, large headlines, etc. Television news also offers numerous cues about salience—the opening story on the newscast, length of time devoted to the story, etc. These cues repeated day after day effectively communicate the importance of each topic.

In other words, the news media can set the agenda for the public's attention to that small group of issues around which public opinion forms. This mediated view of the world is that the priorities of the media strongly influence the priorities of the public. Elements prominent on the media agenda become prominent in the public mind. Social scientists examining this agenda-setting influence of the news media on the public usually have focused on public issues. The agenda of a news organisation is found in its pattern of coverage on public issues over some period of time, a week, a month, an entire year. Over this period of time, whatever it might be, a few issues are emphasised, some receive light coverage, and many are seldom or never mentioned. It should be noted that the use of term "agenda" here is purely descriptive. There is no pejorative implication that a news organisation "has an agenda" that it relentlessly pursues as a premeditated goal.

The media agenda presented to the public results from countless day-to-day decisions by many different journalists and their supervisors about the news of the moment. The public agenda—the focus of public attention—is commonly assessed by public opinion polls that ask some variation of the long-standing Gallup Poll question, "What is the most important problem facing this country today?". Comparisons of the media agenda in the weeks preceding these opinion polls measuring the public agenda yield significant evidence of the agenda-setting role of the news media.

Since that initial study during the 1968 U.S. presidential election, more than 300 hundred published studies worldwide have documented this influence of the news media. It should be noted that this evidence encompasses a wide variety of research designs, including numerous panel studies, time-series analyses, and controlled laboratory experiments. To summarise the extent of this influence—and to facilitate comparisons from one research setting to another—social scientists frequently calculate the correlation between the ranking of issues on the media agenda and the ranking accorded those same issues on the subsequent public agenda.

This quantitative measure provides a substantial degree of precision for our comparisons, much as a thermometer's precise numbers are better than simply saying it seems cooler today than it was yesterday. The vast majority of comparisons between how issues are ranked on the media agenda and how the public ranks the importance of these same issues yield correlations of +.50 or better. That reflects a substantial degree of influence.

Agenda-setting effects also have been found at the local level, and the evidence for both national and local effects is found in a wide variety of settings around the world. In Spain, unemployment and urban congestion were the major concerns of Pamplona, Spain, residents in the spring of 1995. Comparisons of all six major concerns on the public agenda with local news coverage in the preceding two weeks found a high degree of correspondence. The match with the dominant local daily newspaper was +.90; with the second Pamplona daily, +.72; and with television news, +.66.

Agenda-setting at the community level also occurred in a 1986 Japanese mayoral election. Voters in Machida City, a municipality of 320,000 residents in the Tokyo metropolitan area, regarded welfare policies, urban facilities, and local taxes as the three most important issues in the election. Comparison of the public agenda, which had seven issues in all, with the coverage across a three-week period of the four major newspapers serving Machida City yielded a modest, but positive, correlation of +.39.

In Argentina, agenda-setting effects were found in the 1997 legislative elections in the Buenos Aires metropolitan area. Corruption was prominent on both the public and media agendas throughout the fall, always ranking first or second. But in September there was only modest overall agreement (+.43) between the public agenda and the combined issue agenda of five major Buenos Aires newspapers. However, as election day approached in October, the correspondence between the agendas soared to +.80, an increase that suggests considerable learning from the news media in the closing weeks of the election campaign.

Returning to the national level, in the U.K. during the final decade of the 20th century (1990-2000) there was significant correspondence (+.54) between public concern about international issues and the pattern of international coverage in The Times. In sum, the news media have a substantial influence on the content of the public agenda, and the phrase "setting the agenda" has become commonplace in discussions of journalism and public opinion.

Media Influence on the Pictures

The agenda-setting influence of the news media is not limited to this initial step of focusing public attention on a particular topic. The media also influence the next step in the communication process, our understanding and perspective on the topics in the news. If you think about the agenda in abstract terms, the potential for a broader view of media influence on public opinion becomes very clear. In the abstract, the items that define the agenda are objects. For all the agendas, the objects are public issues, but they could be other items or topics, such as the agenda of political candidates during an election. The objects are the things on which the attention of the media and the public are focused.

In turn, each of these objects has numerous attributes, those characteristics and traits that describe the object. For each object there also is an agenda of attributes because when the media and the public think and talk about an object, some attributes are emphasised, others are given less attention, and many receive no attention at all. This agenda of attributes is another aspect of the agenda-setting role of the news media.

Walter Lippmann's phrase, "the pictures in our heads," the agenda of issues or other objects presented by the news media influence what the pictures in our heads are about. The agenda of attributes presented for each of these issues, public figures, or other objects literally influences the pictures themselves. Images held by the public of political candidates and other public figures are the most obvious examples of attribute agenda-setting by the news media. During the 1996 general election in Spain, the descriptions by voters in Navarra of the three major party leaders showed considerable correspondence with the media's presentation of these men.

For the local newspapers, the median match with the local voters' descriptions was +.70; for the national newspapers, +.81; for national television, +.54. Similar matches between the imagery of the news media and the images in the public mind have been found in U.S. national elections. Comparison of New York Democrats' descriptions of the contenders for their party's presidential nomination in 1976 with the agenda of attributes presented in Newsweek's early January sketches of these men found significant evidence of media influence. Especially compelling in this evidence is that the correspondence between the news agenda of attributes and the voter agenda of attributes increased from +.64 in mid-February to +.83 in late March. Voters not only learned the media's agenda, but with some additional exposure over the weeks of the primaries they learned it even better.

Turning to a very different political and cultural setting, the voters' images of the three candidates for mayor of Taipei were compared with the descriptions of these men by the local newspapers and TV stations. The agenda of attributes included 12 categories representing a wide variety of personal and political attributes. Comparisons of the voters' images with the agenda of attributes in the China Times and United Daily News ranged from +.59 to +.75. The median value of these six comparisons was +.68. None of the comparisons with TV news were significant, no doubt because the voters were well aware that all three television stations at that time were under the direct domination of the government and long-ruling KMT political party. This is a specific evidence in support of the general observation that the appearance of agenda-setting effects requires the existence of reasonably free and open media and political systems.

There also are examples of attribute agenda-setting for public issues. The aspects of issues selected for attention by the media influence the public's perception of these issues. Nationally, during the 2000 presidential election in the U.S., the correspondence between the news media's presentation of social welfare and the way in which U.S. voters talked about this issue was +.60. For a very different set of issues, the environment, the results are very similar. For global environmental problems, there was a strong level of correspondence (+.78) between the presentation of this issue in Japanese newspapers and the way that Tokyo residents thought about eight aspects of this issue.

For an environmental situation in the U.S., there was a similarly strong level of correspondence (+.71) between the pictures in people's minds and local newspaper coverage on six aspects of a project to develop a large man-made lake in central Indiana. Which aspects of an issue are covered in the news—and the relative emphasis on these various aspects of an issue-makes a considerable difference in how people view that issue. From the pattern of the total news coverage, the public learns what journalists consider the important issues are and who the prominent public figures of the day are.

From the details of this coverage—the agenda of attributes presented by the news media—the public forms its images and perspective about these issues and public figures. Influencing the focus of public attention is a powerful role, but, arguably, influencing the agenda of attributes for an issue or political figure is the epitome of political power. Determining the way that an issue is framed—setting the ground rules for deliberation, if you will—can significantly influence the ultimate outcome.

Public Agenda of Media

Although the influence of the media agenda can be substantial, it alone does not determine the public agenda. Information and cues about object and attribute salience provided by the news media are far from the only determinants of the public agenda. This substantial influence of the news media has no way overturned or nullified the basic assumption of democracy that the people at large have sufficient wisdom to determine the course of their nation, their state, and their local communities. In particular, the people are quite able to determine the basic relevance—to themselves and to the larger public arena—of the topics and attributes advanced by the news media. The media set the agenda only when citizens perceive their news stories as relevant.

The spectacular failure in the U.S. of the intensive news coverage on the Clinton-Lewinsky scandal to set the public agenda and sway public opinion, an effort that failed despite gargantuan and persistent coverage frequently described as "All Monica, all the time," speaks in a loud voice about the limits of media influence. Overwhelmingly, the U.S. public rejected the relevance of that scandal as the basis of their opinion about the president's success or failure in governance. The presence—or absence—of agenda-setting effects by the news media can be explained by a basic psychological trait, our need for orientation.

Whenever we find ourselves in a new situation, there is an uncomfortable psychological feeling until we explore and mentally grasp at least the outlines of that setting. Recall, for example, your initial feeling upon visiting a foreign city. This innate need for orientation also exists in the civic arena, especially in those elections where citizens are faced with unfamiliar candidates or referendum questions on which they are less than fully knowledgeable. In all these situations, and many more, people experience a need for orientation. Because it is a psychological trait, the degree of need for orientation varies greatly from one individual to another.

For some individuals in any situation, there is a high need for orientation. For other individuals, there is little or no need for orientation at all. They just aren't interested. Need for orientation is defined by two components: relevance and uncertainty. Relevance is the initial defining condition that determines the level of need for orientation for each individual. If a topic is perceived as irrelevant—or very low in relevance—then the need for orientation is low. Individuals in this situation pay little or no attention to news media reports and, at most, demonstrate weak agenda-setting effects.

For individuals among whom the relevance of a topic is high, their degree of uncertainty about the topic determines the level of need for orientation. If this uncertainty is low, that is, they feel that they basically understand the topic, then the need for orientation is moderate. These individuals—for whom a situation has high relevance and low uncertainty—will monitor the media for new developments and perhaps occasionally dip into a bit of additional background information. But they are not likely to be avid consumers of news reports about the topic. Agenda-setting effects among this group are moderate.

Finally, among individuals for whom both the relevance and their uncertainty about a situation are high, need for orientation is high. These individuals typically are avid consumers of the news, and strong agenda-setting effects typically are found among these individuals. Table one illustrates two patterns that vary according to individuals' levels of need for orientation: attention to the news and agenda-setting effects. Both frequent use of the news media to follow an election and the agenda-setting effects of the news media on the perceived importance of the issues steadily increase with the level of need for orientation among members of the public.

Table 1. Need for Orientation Effects

	Level of Need for Orientation		
	Low	Moderate	High
Frequent users of newspapers, TV and news magazines for political information	54%	63%	74%
Agenda-setting effect of TV (Issue agenda)	+.05	+.41	+.55
Agenda-setting effect of newspapers (Issue agenda)	+.29	+.59	+.68

When the news media do provide information that citizens find relevant and useful in coming to a decision about how to cast their ballots, there is a substantial audience—and there is substantial media influence on the priorities that citizens assign to the issues of the day.

Effects of Agenda-Setting

Attitudes and behaviour are usually governed by cognitions —what a person knows, thinks, believes. Hence, the agenda-setting function of the mass media implies a potentially massive influence whose full dimensions and consequences have yet to be investigated and appreciated. To begin at the beginning, the salience of objects in the mass media is linked to the formation of opinions by the audience. With the increasing salience of public figures in the news, for example, more people move away from a neutral position and form an opinion about these persons.

An examination of US presidential candidates in all five elections between 1980 and 1996 found exceedingly strong correlations between the pattern of media emphasis, which varied widely across these elections, and the number of citizens who expressed ambivalent opinions about the candidates by checking the midpoint of various rating scales. Twenty of the comparisons between media salience and opinions about a candidate as measured in the National Election Study were significant with a median value of -.90. Note that these correlations are negative because high salience for a candidate in the media was associated with a low number of people selecting the neutral mid-point on the rating scales.

Analogous links have been found between issue salience and people's attitudes. In the German state of Baden-Wurttemberg, the personal salience of two major issues, the re-unification of East and West Germany and East German migrants, was strongly linked to both the strength and direction of personal opinions. For the strength of opinion on both issues, personal salience was a far stronger predictor than media exposure or demographic characteristics. For the direction of opinion, personal salience was a slightly stronger predictor than age for German re-unification and only slightly weaker predictor than education (and equal to the use of television) for East German migrants.

Priming Public Opinion

By far the best documented consequence of object and issue salience is the priming of perspectives that subsequently guide the public's opinions about public figures. By calling attention to some matters while ignoring others, television news [as well as the other news media] influences the standards by which governments, presidents, policies, and candidates for public office are judged. The psychological basis of priming is the selective attention of the public. People do not, indeed, can not, pay attention to everything.

Moreover, in making judgments—whether in casting a ballot on election day or simply in responding to a pollster's question—people use simple rules of thumb and intuitive short-cuts. Rather than engaging in a comprehensive analysis based on their total store of information, citizens routinely draw upon those bits of information that are particularly salient at the time judgment must be rendered. In other words, citizens rely upon the agenda of salient objects and attributes in their minds, the agenda that is shaped to a considerable degree by the mass media.

An extensive series of agenda-setting experiments conducted by Shanto Iyengar and Donald Kinder produced significant evidence of a priming effect by television news on people's opinions about the president's overall performance in office. Among subjects exposed to extensive news coverage on one or more of five different issues—defence, inflation, arms control, civil rights, and unemployment-their ratings of presidential performance on the issue or issues receiving heavy news coverage influenced their overall opinion about the president's performance more than among persons not exposed to this news coverage. This influence existed whether or not the news story implied a substantial degree of presidential responsibility for the issue.

In subsequent experiments where the degree of presidential responsibility for an issue was explicitly manipulated, the impact of problem performance ratings on opinions about the president's overall performance was greater when the news stories emphasised presidential responsibility. Turning to a very different setting, public opinion about Hong Kong's last British governor was strongly influenced by news coverage on his proposals to broaden public participation in the election of the Legislative Council. Tracked in consecutive weekly polls from the fall of 1992 when the governor made his initial policy speech, public opinion about his overall performance was significantly primed by the pattern of news coverage on his reform proposals in Hong Kong's three leading newspapers.

Both the distinction and link between traditional agenda-setting effects and priming as a consequence of these effects is illustrated by American public opinion regarding the Persian Gulf War. Extensive television coverage resulted in the high salience of the war on the public agenda as the most important problem facing the country, a traditional first-level agenda-setting effect. Analyses of public opinion about President Bush from 1988 to 1991 further indicated a shift in the basis of his popularity from economics to foreign policy, a priming effect. And demonstrating the effects of attribute agenda-setting on opinions, members of the public who reported higher levels of exposure to television news, which emphasised military options in its framing of the war, favoured a military rather than a diplomatic solution in the Persian Gulf.

This priming effect also occurs for political parties. Among German voters, political party preference during 1986 was influenced by the television news agenda. Preference for the Christian Democrats was substantially influenced by news coverage of two issues, the energy supply and East German situation. Preference for the SPD was influenced by three issues, East-West relations, environmental protection, and pensions. Similar patterns were observed in the weekly opinion polls for other political parties. Although the overall pattern is one in which issues on the television news agenda resonated in unique ways with political partisanship, the general finding is that salient issues on the media agenda were strongly linked with shifts in political partisanship during the year.

Effects of Tone

Mass communication effects can result from the sheer volume of exposure. First level agenda-setting effects demonstrate that phenomenon. But as both attribute agenda-setting and priming demonstrate, closer attention to the specific content of mass media messages—including the tone of those messages—provides a more detailed understanding of the pictures in our heads and of subsequent attitudes and opinions grounded in those pictures. In Germany, the tone of the news about Helmut Kohl in news magazines and major newspapers influenced public opinion between 1975 and 1984 about his political performance, first, as leader of the opposition and, later, as chancellor.

Shifting patterns of positive and negative tone in the media, summed across six attributes of Kohl, prompted significant shifts in his level of approval among the German public. The median correlation between the affective tone of six news media's attribute agendas and subsequent public opinion with a lag time of six months was +.48. In the US, a day-by-day observation of the final three months in the 1992 and 1996 presidential elections found that the tone of television news coverage about key campaign events influenced voters' preference for the candidates. Favourable coverage of Republican campaign events on four national television networks increased support for the Republican candidate. Conversely, favourable coverage of Democrat campaign events decreased support for the Republican candidate. The strength of these media effects on voters' opinions was similar in the two years.

Effects of tone are not limited to attitudes and opinions about political leaders. Negative newspaper headlines about the economy influence the public's perceptions about the health of the economy. In turn, these opinions become self-fulfilling prophecies as people adjust their behaviour to fit their beliefs. Comparisons of economic headlines in the New York Times, monthly measures of consumer sentiment about the health of the economy, and major monthly statistical indicators of the actual economy from 1980 through 1993 found a series of significant effects.

Influence on Observable Behaviour

The salience of issues and other topics on the media agenda also influences observable behaviour. Extensive news coverage of crime and violence, including a murder and rapes, on the University of Pennsylvania campus a few years ago contributed to a significant drop in applications by potential first-year students, according to the university's dean of admissions. This decline occurred predominantly among women. Moreover, other comparable universities experienced an increase in applications during the same period. Another example of media influence on the behaviour of young adults is Harvard University's successful use of entertainment television programming to spread the idea of "the designated driver," that member of a party group who abstains from drinking in order to safely drive his or her friends home afterward.

A 1988 Indiana Poll brought together all these aspects of agenda-setting and its consequences. Replicating a familiar pattern, the salience among the public of a major issue of that time, the US federal budget deficit, was significantly correlated with the frequency of exposure to both newspapers and television news. In turn, issue salience in conjunction with use of both newspapers and television news predicted public opinion about a possible solution to the problem as well as what people knew about the issue. Further, issue salience in conjunction with use of a single medium, television news, predicted the strength of people's opinions while issue salience in combination with newspaper reading predicted actual behaviour, such as writing a letter or attending a meeting. Here in a single setting is evidence of significant relationships between media exposure and issue salience and of subsequent effects by both on knowledge, opinions and observable behaviour.

6

Role of Mass Media in Modern Democracy

Mass media play an outstanding role in democracy. The media are supplying the political information that voters base their decisions on. They identify problems in our society and serve as a medium for deliberation. They are also the watchdogs that we rely on for uncovering errors and wrongdoings by those who have power. It is therefore reasonable to require that the media perform to certain standards with respect to these functions, and our democratic society rests on the assumption that they do. The most important democratic functions include surveillance of sociopolitical developments, identifying the most relevant issues, providing a platform for debate across a diverse range of views, holding officials to account for the way they exercise power, provide incentives for citizens to learn, choose, and become involved in the political process, and resist efforts of forces outside the media to subvert their independence.

However, there is a growing concern that the mass media are not fulfilling these functions properly. Media critics claim that commercial mass media controlled by a few multinational conglomerates have become an antidemocratic force supporting the status quo. The news are more entertaining than informing, supplying mostly gossip, scandals, sex, and violence. Political news are more about personalities than about their ideologies. In the absence of serious debate, voters are left with paid political propaganda containing only meaningless slogans making them disinterested and cynical about politics. It is also claimed that the watchdogs are barking of the wrong things.

The media hunt for scandals in the private lives of politicians and their families, but ignore much more serious consequences of their policies. They go after wounded politicians like sharks in a feeding frenzy. All too often, the media make us afraid of the wrong things. Minor dangers are hysterically blown out of proportions, while much more serious dangers in our society go largely unnoticed. The exaggerated fears often lead to unnecessary measures and legislation and "gonzo justice". Critics also complain that the media fail to report wrongdoings in the industry.

For example, many media have suppressed information about the health hazards of smoking due to pressure from advertisers. Even more alarming is the claim that certain mass media (especially women's magazines) are promoting worthless alternative health products, thereby effectively conspiring with the industry to defraud consumers of billions of dollars every year. Dehsen's *The Concise Encyclopedia of Democracy* makes only brief mentioning of the possibility of political, commercial or other influences on the mass media. Most other treatises on the theory of democracy make no mentioning at all of any such problems.

The political and cultural consequences of this alleged misinformation of the public are not fully explored. What are the effects of the commercialisation of news on the democratic process? Which way does this influence push the development of our society? The study of these questions is difficult because it must integrate findings from many different 3 scientific disciplines. This paradigm provides an excellent integrating framework for three reasons:

1. its emphasis on non-equilibrium phenomena as an important factor in socioeconomic change,
2. its population-based focus on selection events as an explanation of emergent phenomena, and
3. its ability to describe the coevolution of institutions and their social environment.

Media Economics

Most newspapers, radio- and TV stations get most or all of their income from advertisements and sponsoring. The media will therefore seek to optimally satisfy the interests of their advertisers, which are not necessarily coincident with the interests of the readers, listeners and viewers. The predominant view among economists is that free competition generally benefits society because it provides the most differentiated supply of commodities to the optimal price. This line of reasoning dominates European as well as American media policy. It is well known, however, that free competition does not always consider all interests.

The term market failure describes the situation where the free market forces do not automatically lead to maximal welfare (often defined as the sum of benefits to all parties). Market failure may occur, for example, when consumers are unable to evaluate the quality of a commodity, when third party interests are affected (externalities), or when production has large fixed costs. In the case of media financed by advertisements exclusively, the interests served are those of the advertisers.

The interests of the media consumers are satisfied only insofar as these are coincident with the interests of the advertisers. There is no guarantee that public interests are served well. This is the reason why many countries have public radio-and TV stations with public service obligations.

Liberalising the media market and relying on the free market forces are policies that are often used for the express purpose of making sure that all interests are served. Many theorists ignore, however, that the media not only satisfy consumer preferences, but also form them.

Many economists assume that competition increases diversity. Numerous policy discussions have recommended increased competition as the best way to assure diversity which, it is assumed, will make sure that all interests are served well. However, this strategy has failed time and again because the underlying assumptions are wrong. It has been known for many years that there is a strong tendency towards wasteful duplication of the most popular program forms under free competition.

There is considerable uncertainty over whether competition increases or decreases the diversity and quality of media products. While moderate competition may increase diversity, it has been found theoretically as well as empirically that excessive competition may lead to decreased diversity. Assume, for example, that a country has two competing commercial TV-stations with each one channel. In this case they will most likely both try to maximise their market share by sending the same kind of programs that appeal to the broadest possible audience. But if, on the other hand, both channels are owned by the same TV-station, then the owner will seek to minimise competition between the two channels by sending different types of programs on the two channels.

Most studies of the effect of market structure on the quality of mass media products use diversity as the only measure of satisfaction of consumer needs. Diversity is the most objective criterion and the one that is most easily measured. Some authors explicitly state their unwillingness to use more subjective quality measures, but a few scientists have demonstrated that it can be done.

McQuail provides a detailed discussion of quality criteria, Napoli finds that market incentives are not sufficient for promoting public affairs programming, and Zaller (forthcoming) concludes, "for every set of cases in which I am able to make plausible comparisons, higher levels of market competition are associated with lower levels of news quality". Diversity may indeed be a poor measure of quality. If we assume that there is a positive relationship between production costs and the quality of a media product, and if we further assume that the total revenue from a particular niche of the media market is limited, then we can conclude that the more competitors there are to share the niche, the less income will each competitor have to spend on improving quality. This simple model suggests that there may in fact be a negative relationship between diversity and quality.

It has been criticised that the diversity that is measured is a diversity of form, not of contents, and even less does it represent a diversity of opinions or ideologies, nor a satisfaction of consumer interests. A diversity of program formats is hardly related to fairness, relevance, thorough investigation, or other requirements that we expect a democratic press to meet. The available studies of diversity therefore fail to capture the central problems related to the democratic role of the media. It is necessary that media economists introduce other quality measures in studies of the relationship between market structure and the quality of mass media products. Lacking better criteria, we may use production costs as a reasonable measure of quality.

Many mathematical models are based on the assumption that a TV program or other media product satisfying a specific demand is produced at fixed costs. The product is either produced or not produced, depending on whether it is profitable. This simplification fails to cover the easily observable fact that a media product satisfying a specific demand may be produced in varying degrees of quality at varying costs. If many competitors share the same product niche then each competitor will have less income to cover production costs and will therefore be forced to make a product of lower quality. For example, if many competitors share the market for political news, then each competitor will have few resources for investigative journalism and will only be able to uncritically relay the messages from politicians and news agencies.

You may expect that at least free competition leads at to an optimal satisfaction of the interests of the advertisers, but this is not the case according to a study of the American radio broadcasting market. Theoretical calculations show that free 6 competition may favor products with high variable costs rather than products with high fixed costs; because as the number of suppliers gets higher, each supplier has less income for covering the fixed costs. When applied to mass media, this theory means that more competition may lead to lower quality if we assume that there is a positive correspondence between production costs and quality.

If we assume that media products of higher quality can attract a larger audience, then we must conclude that excessive competition benefits neither consumers nor advertisers. Denmark is regarded as a good test case because it had a state monopoly TV station until 1988 when one, and later more, commercial TV stations were introduced. The introduction of competing TV stations were motivated by the desire to improve the quality and diversity of the program supply and to make sure that minority interests were satisfied.

A government commission recommended competition as the means to obtain these goals, in spite of the fact that they were aware of experiences from England and Sweden showing that competition might reduce program quality. The commission was not aware of any theory that could explain the latter effect. A recent investigation has shown that the competition has not improved the quality of news production, confirming the prediction by Sepstrup. In Sweden, where the market situation is similar, it has been observed that TV news have become more dramatic, sensationalist, and less informative, as the competition has increased. In Finland, an increase in the number of TV channels has not led to increased diversity of the available programs.

Characteristics of Media Market

The development of the mass media during the last several decades is characterised by the following main tendencies:

— *Convergence*: Different media like newspapers, radio, television, telephone and internet are increasingly being fused together, technologically as well as economically.

— *Concentration*: Media companies are being merged together and controlled by fewer owners. This concentration is horizontal (several media under the same owner) as well as vertical (several links in the "food chain" under the same company group). Different media bring news from the same sources.

— *Globalisation*: The media are owned by multinational companies broadcasting across borders.

— *Commercialisation*: Advertisements are sneaked into entertainment as well as news stories. The distinctions between advertisements, news and entertainment are increasingly blurred. Audience groups with less spending money are not considered.

— *Commercial influence*: Advertisers and owners have influence on editorial decisions.

— *Trivialisation*: More sex and violence. More prying into the private lives of celebrities. The media avoid controversial issues and serious debates. Debates are reduced to an entertaining clash between personalities, resembling a boxing match, where the issue of controversy has only secondary importance.

Several media scholars agree that the main cause of these tendencies is the liberalisation of the media market. Stories are selected for profitability rather than relevance.

Popularisation

The simulation of proximity is an important element in popularisation. A political decision can be difficult to explain in abstract terms. It helps when the medium shows an ordinary person telling what the consequences of the decision is for him or her. The audience feel that a story is more convincing when they see an example they can identify with. But in fact it is less credible because the example may not be representative. A magazine can show a person who felt better after taking a certain brand of alternative medicine, and fail to show the 99% who felt worse after taking the same medicine.

Advertising has a profound influence on the choice of programs. TV advertisers prefer to have their commercials shown in association with soft entertainment. Ideal from the advertisers' point of view are shows such as competitions where one can win sponsored merchandise, or soap operas that portray a privileged lifestyle where luxurious goods give status. This does not provide good conditions for the political debate. It is difficult to find sponsors for serious political debates because these do not make the viewers relax and because some of the viewers will disagree with the points of view presented.

Furthermore, the commercial media are not very inclined to cover controversial issues in a balanced way. People prefer to hear points of view that they agree with. It is therefore adverse to the media's economy to view a controversy from both sides and present alternative points of view. The media are prone to choose side in a controversy; and if later evidence should favor the opposite side, they are likely to keep silent about the matter rather than loosing face. Disclaimers are not profitable. This is a self-amplifying process. The more the media create consensus about a particular issue through biased coverage, the fewer proponents of the opposite view will there be to balance the issue, and the more difficulties will these proponents have in gaining access to the media.

Nowhere is this bias problem worse than in crime reporting. The media often take a stance on the question of guilt before a verdict has been made. The police and the prosecutor are often very willing to express themselves because it gives them a PR gain and an opportunity to ask the public for help in solving crimes, while a suspect has few, if any, possibilities and resources for replying. It is very unlikely that judges can resist being influenced by this when a media frenzy has created a public outcry against a suspect.

The legal possibilities of forcing the media to publish disclaimers or to give a voice to alternative points of view are quite illusory, and the means of sanctions are far from effective. The printed media cannot compete with the ability of the electronic media to keep their audience spellbound by strong sense impressions. The newspapers have their strength in the possibilities for in-dept analysis of social and other topics. However, this possibility is not fully exploited because the journalistic resources are limited by economic competition, and because this parameter of competition only gives access to a limited niche of the reader market.

Many papers and magazines therefore compete on news about celebrities and topics that appeal to the emotions. Everything that is dangerous, deviant or wrong has a prominent place, especially in those papers that are mainly sold from newsstands. They want to have a new scandal on the front page every day in order to tempt people to buy the paper. We may expect to see similar approaches when electronic pay-per-view media become common. Radio- and TV-channels based on advertising use fewer horror effects, because this would conflict with the principle of bringing the viewers into a buying-mood. This does not improve the journalistic and artistic quality, however. Many media workers are frustrated that their creativity is curbed by the economic structures, and the situation is hardly better for advertisement-free commercial media, such as home video and pay-TV.

Selection of News

Traditionally, media scholars have described the selection of news with concepts like gatekeeping and newsworthiness. These concepts are based on a scenario where an editor or journalist sorts incoming news according to news value and political criteria. Social problems involving fear and danger are very attractive to the media and such topics often make up a significant part of the stories. The excessive focus on fear and danger has important political implications. The dissemination of news may occasionally be so selective and biased that you may accuse the media of manipulation and propaganda, for example in connection with war. But in general we do not have to impute dishonest motives on producers in order to explain media distortion.

Most cases of selection in the news media can be explained by structural factors, such as the organisation of news agencies, financing, dependence on sources, and ratings competition. The news coverage is determined by such factors as the journalist's knowledge, predefined news formats, deadlines, the authority of sources, and the possibility of obtaining good pictures. The media may not publish a story if it does not fit into an existing format or if it does not relate to an existing theme. The media are self-referential to such a degree that the newsworthiness of a story may be a self-fulfilling prophecy. A topic is interesting because all the media tell about it.

Violent crimes and sex crimes are areas where the news reporting is highly selective. The media prefer emotional stories, sobbing victims, and stories that fit into the political agenda and confirm the image of the criminal as a monster. The use of expert sources has been found to be extraordinarily selective. The media play a key role in the public debate on risks and dangers, but their coverage is highly selective. At times the media exaggerate minor risks where reassurance would be more sensible. In other cases they ignore serious risks, e.g. when new technologies are uncritically described as progress.

It is an essential problem when informing about risks and dangers that the concept is abstract and invisible until it manifests itself in a specific accident or disaster. The media do not like to report on hypothetical risks. They need a real event that the theoretical discussion can be related to and real people to give the story a human-interest dimension. Risk analysts have been criticised for ignoring these problems and not focusing enough on the mass media. The media may be attracted to risks, but not unconditionally so. They are not good at maintaining attention to a theoretical risk when there are no actual events to make the topic newsworthy.

There is an unusually fierce competition between sources when it comes to informing about risks, dangers and other social problems. Various interest groups, politicians and experts seek to promote each their agenda on which dangers to fear. The media inevitably play a key role in this conflict because their choice of sources influences the definitions of dangers. The politicians have to take a stance to whatever problem the media place high on the agenda. The media's decision on who is allowed to define a problem, or whether the problem is mentioned at all, is not controlled in a democratic way.

Influence of Mass Media on People

There are many different theories about how mass media influence people's attitudes, worldview, and behavior.

While historical as well as contemporary observations are full of examples attesting to the power of the mass media to influence people, early experimental studies have failed to confirm the assumption that mass media have a strong power to change people's attitudes. This discrepancy between experiments and real world observations was solved with the introduction of theories of cognitive processing, such as agenda setting, framing, and priming.

Human Cognitive Processing

The human cognitive capacities are limited. The newsmedia contain huge amounts of information, much more than any person can possibly handle. It is therefore theorised that humans are economising the processing of the information they receive from newsmedia as well as from other sources. The first step in the handling of information is selection. People chose which newsmedia to read, watch, and listen to, according to their needs and preferences. They are screening the media for interesting information, ignoring topics that appear to be irrelevant to them, redundant, boring, or too complicated to comprehend.

People routinely reject stories that appear too remote or too complicated simply to save time and energy. Stories that catch people's attention are those that are relevant to their personal interests, but also general human-interest stories such as reports about crimes and accidents, health, sports, entertainment, and celebrities. The producers of news have learned to snare people's attention by giving most stories a personal touch. Once a story has been selected for attention, the cognitive processing of the story is further economised by schematic thinking. Humans use what has been called knowledge structures or schemata as mental templates that people and events are fitted into.

This process facilitates the integration of new information into existing knowledge. Since news sources usually present the news in isolated snippets without sufficient background, the schemata allow the receivers to embed the news into a meaningful context. This process also facilitates discarding redundant information that already exists in the schema as well as information that conflicts with previous knowledge that still appears to be sound. People often misunderstand stories, either because they do not have an appropriate schema for interpreting the story, or because they apply the schema that comes first to mind rather than the schema that is most appropriate. Well-informed people have a rich collection of schemata that makes it easier to process new information. Thus, the information-rich become still richer.

Effect of Agenda-setting

The effect of agenda-setting is epitomised in the famous quote by Bernard Cohen, saying that the press "may not be successful much of the time in telling people what to think, but it is stunningly successful in telling its readers what to think about". People need to orient themselves in a complex world full of complex issues. In the absence of other cues, people tend to judge the importance of issues from their salience in the media and to focus their attention on those presumably most important issues.

There is plenty of evidence that the media have a strong influence on people's perception of which issues are important and which problems they want their government to do something about. The agenda-setting influence of the news media increases when the need for orientation among the audience is high. The agenda-setting effect is lower for obtrusive issues that people can observe directly, as well as for other issues that the audience is well informed about. The media have little power to set the agenda when people have sufficient political knowledge to counterargue the claims made by the media.

Furthermore, the agenda-setting effect is stronger for concrete issues that are easy to visualise than for abstract issues. While the powerful effect of agenda-setting is generally accepted among media scholars, there is some uncertainty about who sets the agenda. Some studies show that politicians have a strong influence on the agenda of mass media, at least in areas such as economic policy. The media may themselves put attention-catching issues on the agenda for economic reasons, especially sensationalistic issues involving danger, crime, sex, and celebrity scandals.

Effect of Priming

Closely related to agenda-setting is the effect of priming. Priming refers to the fact that one piece of media information can influence how we interpret subsequent pieces of information by making us tune in to certain areas of thought. Thus, the news media can influence the criteria by which political candidates are judged by calling attention to some issues and ignoring others before the speech of the candidate. For example, the support for US president Bush dropped significantly in 1992 because an intense media focus on economic recession made voters shift from evaluating the president in terms of his handling of the Gulf war to evaluating his handling of national economy.

The priming effect is often explained in terms of schematic thinking. When evaluating new information or making a decision, people tend to apply the information and schemata that are most readily accessible or available in memory at that moment, rather than conduct a complete and comprehensive search and examination of information. A schema may be readily accessible to the individual either because it has recently been activated and remains in short-term memory, or because it is linked in memory to other constructs which have been activated.

Framing

Another cognitive effect, which may be explained as a consequence of schematic thinking, is framing. Framing refers to the frame of reference within which an issue is described. For example, a news broadcast about the development of new nuclear weapons can variously be framed as a story about technological progress, about military budgets, about military strategy, about balance of power between nations, about arms race versus disarmament, or about radiation hazards. The way the story is framed can have a strong influence on people's attitudes towards the issue.

It is often assumed that framing is a kind of second-level agenda setting in the sense that it makes certain aspects of an issue more salient in such a way as to promote a particular problem definition. However, it has been argued that framing influences how audiences think about issues, not by making aspects of the issue more salient, but by determining which schemata are activated in the interpretation of the incoming information. Since every story must have a frame, whether the journalist pays attention to framing or not, we cannot assume that the effects of framing are always intentional. Several theorists make a distinction between frames in the media and frames in the minds of the audience.

A media frame is "a central organising idea or story line that provides meaning to an unfolding strip of events..." Audience frames are defined as "mentally stored clusters of ideas that guide individuals' processing of information". These definitions should be preferred because they have a better theoretical foundation and because they make no assumption about whether a particular media frame is intended to promote a particular audience frame.

The commercialisation and trivialisation of news media has a strong influence on how issues are framed in the commercial news media. Framing political news around the strategies of politicians rather than issues makes the audience perceive the motives of politicians as egoistic, whereby a cynical view on politics may be fostered. Stories about social problems are often framed with a focus on people rather than principles, single events rather than themes, and easily understandable proximate causes rather than deeper and more complex causes. This choice of framing influences the attribution of responsibility for the problems, the causal attribution, and the remedies that will be chosen to ameliorate the problems in question.

The media will often find some person to blame for a problem, but without a deeper focus on the social structures that caused the problem, it is unlikely that an effective solution to the problem will be found and accepted. Entertainment abhors ambiguity. Once a particular interpretation has been applied to a conflict, it is unlikely that the media will reframe the issue. Without seeing an issue from more than one side, it is unlikely that the conflict or problem will be solved in a sensible way.

For example, S. Iyengar mentions violent crime, which ranges high on the media agenda. The personalised framing of crime stories is likely to make the audience see the cause of the problem in moral defects of the perpetrator. The lack of focus on deeper causes such as poverty, discrimination, poor education, and blocked opportunities may keep the audience from supporting more effective preventive remedies against crime. The commercial need for personalisation of stories also make the media focus on victims of crime. Grieving victims make good stories with a strong emotional appeal. The strongly emotional content of these stories is likely to evoke the primitive feelings of revenge in the audience and a call for 14 stronger penalties, regardless of whether punitive measures can solve the problem.

Crime reporting is just one example of this effect, and admittedly a controversial one (differing frames may indeed explain why this issue has become controversial). The pervasive media focus on people rather than principles, events rather than themes, and simple rather than deep causes, is adversely affecting the problem-solving capabilities of democratic societies on a broad variety of issues, ranging from poverty to international conflicts.

Cultivation Theory

Not only news and documentaries can influence people's perception of the world, but also fiction and entertainment shows. Cultivation theory is a research tradition, which assumes that there are certain repetitive and pervasive patterns of images and ideologies dominating most genres of television shows and films. If people spend several hours a day, year after year, watching television, and if every show they watch is full of violence, then people may come to believe that the world is full of violence. This is the kind of hypotheses that cultivation studies are trying to prove.

There can be no doubt that the television world is different from the real world. News and drama alike contain more crime and violence than the real world. The proportion of violent crimes to nonviolent crimes is much higher in TV than in the real world. The characters portrayed in TV drama are not representative of the population at large. There are more men than women and an over-representation of people in prestigious professions. Numerous studies have found that heavy TV-viewers tend to over-estimate the amount of violence in society, the risk of falling victim to a violent crime, the fraction of the population engaged in law enforcement, the fraction of the population with prestigious professions, the fraction of the population that have marital discords and extramarital affairs, etc. The observed effects are relatively weak, but consistent and statistically significant.

The effects of receiving the high dose of crime and violence from television have been called the mean world syndrome. Heavy TV viewers may come to perceive the world as a gloomy and dangerous place. People become fearful of falling victim to violent crime and take drastic measures to protect themselves and their children—measures that are out of touch with the objective risk. The fearful people become authoritarian and easy victims of political manipulation.

Many Cultivation theorists assume that the pervasive patterns of TV images are shaped by commercial influence. Most cultivation studies are carried out in the USA where the commercial influence on television is strong. A few studies in countries where non-commercial television has a significant impact, find the "mean world" effect to be smaller than in the USA. The hypothesis of commercial influence is further supported by a few international comparisons that find the cultivation effects to be stronger in countries where commercial television dominates than in countries with predominantly noncommercial television.

The very broad-based focus has made cultivation studies vulnerable to criticism. The lumping together of all genres and all viewing patterns is likely to dilute the observed effect. This may be the reason why the observed correlations are weak. Evidently, some TV genres contain more violence than others, and different genres have different effects on people's worldview.

Critics of cultivation research point out that the correlations may be spurious, while adherents of the paradigm emphasise that no strong mediating variables have been found and that the results are quite stable over different research conditions. Most cultivation studies are based on surveys. A survey can prove correlation, but not causation. It is theoretically impossible to tell on the basis of a correlation between TV viewing habits and attitudes whether viewing habits influence attitudes, or attitudes influence viewing habits, or whether some unidentified extraneous variable influence both. In fact, one study, which observed an association between the viewing of crime drama and authoritarian aggression, found both directions of causality to be equally plausible.

The position of cultivation theorists towards the question of causality is sometimes quite inconsistent. Leading theorists state that causal models are impossible, or even irrelevant. Yet the same theorists discuss causal models all the time. In fact, the whole paradigm rests on the assumption that cultivation is a long-term cumulative effect, and this assumption makes no sense unless a direction of causality is assumed. An irrefutable proof for the direction of causality is only possible with experimental manipulation of TV viewing patterns.

Unfortunately, most cultivation researchers discount such experimental studies because experiments focus on particularistic short-term effects, while the cultivation research project emphasises the long-term combined effect of the viewing of all TV genres. A few experimental studies have found significant effects of relatively short-term exposure on the attitudes of TV viewers, but most experimental studies are concerned with measuring behavior (especially violent behavior) rather than attitudes.

A strong indication of the direction of causality has recently been obtained, however, from an improved understanding of the cognitive mechanisms underlying the cultivation effect. These mechanisms, which have been confirmed experimentally, cannot easily be accounted for if the causality is spurious or reversed. When asked to estimate, for example, the incidence of violence in society, people tend to economise their mental processing effort and give a heuristic answer based on the ease with which instances of violence can be recalled.

A number of testable predictions can be made from this model, and these predictions have been confirmed experimentally. Experimental conditions that induce a more systematic information processing can make test persons discount TV as a reliable source of information and give more accurate answers. Likewise, it is known from cognitive psychology and endocrinology that concrete and emotional accounts make a stronger impression than abstract descriptions.

In accordance with this theory, it has been found by experiments that people judge the incidence of particular phenomena by the number of examples in the media rather than by statistical accounts when both examples and statistics are presented in the media. Likewise, examples that evoke emotions or are presented in an emotional fashion make a stronger and more lasting impression than non-emotional presentations.

Effects for New Issues

Many studies have found that the media have little power to change people's opinions, but more power to reinforce existing views. In fact, several studies have found that media effects are stronger for issues that people are unfamiliar with. Communication studies have traditionally been divided between the study of mass media and the study of interpersonal communication. Recently, it has been argued that this is a false dichotomy because the mass media may inspire interpersonal communication. Rogers attributes the findings of many studies that mass media effects are small to the fact that they do not include the secondary effect of interpersonal communication.

In fact, the two-step flow model of communication has been known for many years: The mass media influence some people who, in turn, influence other people. The influence of the media is not unidirectional. Among the people influenced by the media are the elites and opinion leaders whose opinions appear in the mass media. This circular flow of communication may obviously amplify certain opinions. Another self-amplifying process is the "spiral of silence".

Noelle-Neumann discovered that people might be reluctant to voice unpopular opinions for fear of social isolation. This effect may cause the amplification of mainstream opinions or opinions that are perceived as growing in popularity, while minority opinions are suppressed. Such a mechanism may explain fashions and fads. Several studies have measured the "spiral of silence" effect by asking people whether they would voice their opinion in a hypothetical situation. These studies have found a quite weak, though significant, effect.

One field study, which placed unsuspecting people in a situation where they were actually asked to present their opinion, found a stronger effect. Members of a minority were less willing to express their opinion towards members of a majority than vice versa. These secondary effects, some stronger than others, all point in the same direction: The effect of the mass media is stronger when secondary effects are taken into account than when the direct effect of media messages on each individual are measured.

Sociological Theory

In the sociological theory of Jürgen Habermas, the mass media are seen as controlled by political and economic forces, which have an interest in manipulating the audience. This compromises the legitimacy of the communicative power exercised by the mass media. The political manipulation is a kind of opinion making and PR, where the media not only transmit debates, but also create and shape them. The commercial manipulation uses the carefully designed and tested psychological methods of advertising. The media explore themes and identification possibilities that appeal to the unconscious dispositions of the audience in order to attract attention.

Habermas mentions the following themes as attracting common interest: romance, religion, money, children, health, and animals. The German political scientist Peter Klier criticises Habermas' manipulation hypothesis because absolute objectivity does not exist. Klier thinks that the amount of information in modern society is so huge that media as well as citizens and politicians have to make a very strict selection. Klier thinks that this selection is such a big problem that no manipulation hypothesis is needed for concluding that democracy has a legitimacy problem. He stresses that people's reality image is more determined by the mediareality the more they are dependent on selective media and the less their chances are of getting corrective information from primary sources.

Klier advocates this obvious observation as a counter thesis to the manipulation hypothesis. But this so-called counter thesis confirms the very fact that the media produce a skewed image of reality. We are only left with the question of whether this distortion deserves to be called manipulation. Niklas Luhmann, in his social systems theory, sees communication as a fundamental process in any social system. The communication forms a triple selection process:

1. selection of information at the sender,
2. selective attention at the receiver,
3. the selecting effect of the received information.

The communication is very much controlled by the media in modern society. Luhmann describes the mass media as a self-referential and self-maintaining (autopoietic), almost autonomous system. Unfortunately, Luhmann does not go very far in his analysis of how this media system is integrated into the bigger social system. Luhmann finds that the most important selection criteria of the media are the following: surprising news, topicality, conflicts, quantitative data, local relevance, as well as scandals and norm violations in relation to individual actors and moral judgments.

Luhmann is not clear in the question of whether the media distort reality, because he emphasises that there is no objective measure to evaluate the media reports against. He tries to evade the problem by saying that the media are accused of manipulating, rather than just saying that they manipulate. We also have to accept that the media fit reality into certain frames of reference, because there is no other option. However, this relativist line of thought does not deter Luhmann from giving specific examples of how the media influence society by their selectivity. He mentions the Gulf war, AIDS, and immigrant crimes as examples. He even recognises that the media may provide falsehoods if the need for news and sensations overweigh the risk that the deception be revealed.

Risk in Solciological Theory

Risk is a subset of danger, and a topic that has given rise to at least three different research traditions: risk sociology, risk analysis, and risk communication. Because of the 19 prominence of the topics of risk and danger in the mass media, and because of the important political implications of the intense focus and possible exaggeration of certain dangers, we may find it worthwhile to look more into these areas of study. Risk sociology that is based on Ulrich Beck's book *Risk Society* and Mary Douglas' Purity and Danger. Unfortunately, Beck does not pay much attention to exaggerations of risks. His project is, on the contrary, to investigate understatements of risks. Admittedly, this can be quite relevant in the context he is working in, since certain environmental risks have been underrated and hushed up for many years.

Beck deprecates the importance of statistical calculations of risks because risks are always evaluated in relation to political and moral norms. Beck does, nevertheless, give an example where he considers a risk-claim to be exaggerated, namely the Brent Spar-conflict. But here he blames Greenpeace, not the media, for the exaggeration. As a parallel to framing theory, there is much importance attached to the influence of semantics and symbols in risk sociology. People are not good at evaluating risks and making rational choices based on small probabilities. The choice of which risks to accept and which to combat is a social process depending on the social organisation. The perception of a risk is malleable, as a result of negotiations and struggles between different experts, authorities and action groups who are providing competing views and definitions of technological risks.

In these struggles, the concepts of risks are often used to legitimise or challenge hierarchies of power. However, risk sociologists pay surprisingly little attention to the role of the media in selecting who is given the opportunity to speak and thus to gain power and influence by promoting a particular definition of a particular risk. Mary Douglas tells that what we fear most are the things that disturb our sense of the order of nature. Her studies are based on tribal societies where modern mass media are nonexistent. Subsequently, she has tried to apply the same theories to modern societies, together with Aaron Wildavsky. The analysis of the environment protection movement performed by these two anthropologists has been interpreted as a claim that these organisations create fictive risks in order to consolidate their internal organisation.

Based on risk sociology, Maarten Hajer has submitted the environmental debate to a discourse analysis à la Foucault. According to this theory, the discursive order is defined by story lines (paradigms) which provide the frame of reference and define the moral order of the debate. The story lines determine which objects are communicable in a given culture. Hence, social actors can exercise power if they succeed in defining the story lines. The mass media are only mentioned cursorily, even in Hajer's discourse analyses. Apparently, he only sees the media as a passive service organ for the communication of social actors, while the role of journalists as social actors is only mentioned in a parenthesis.

Sociology of Social Issues

Risk sociologists may have ignored the significance of the mass media, but this is not the case for the sociology of deviance and the closely related sociology of social issues. The objects of study of these disciplines overlap quite a lot with the aforementioned risk sociology. It is therefore very odd that these branches of sociology apparently have developed largely independently of each other with very little mutual inspiration. The sociology of deviance is a study of how society defines certain persons, phenomena or behaviors as deviant and dangerous. The dangerous is thus a social construct. Society can control unwanted behaviors by defining them as sinful or sick. Whoever has success in setting the norms for what is considered deviant and dangerous and promoting their particular interpretation of the deviance has thus gained a key position in the social power apparatus.

Sometimes, a social deviance is considered so dangerous that it must be combated with the most draconian means. Such a manifestation of exaggerated fear is called a witchhunt or moral panic. These persecutions have been compared with magic rituals in accordance with Mary Douglas' theory. In modern society, there is a fierce competition for defining what is dangerous to society. Numerous organisations and lobbying groups compete for setting the agenda for the discussion of social problems in order to gain influence and get more resources for their particular cause. This has very aptly been called the social problems marketplace.

Throughout the times, various professions like priests, lawyers, psychologists, psychiatrists, neurologists, etc. have had monopoly on making statements about certain dangerous deviancies. Thereby they gain power and influence through what has been called issue ownership. Many sociologists have described how certain social problems get inflated to hysterical proportions because of the way they are exposed in the media. Media-created fears have made people change their lifestyles, have changed the nature of social policies and undermined the process of justice.

Risk analysis

Risk analysis is a research tradition based on statistics, psychology and sociology. Risk analysts have found that experts evaluate risks on the basis of statistical criteria, while lay people tend to base their evaluation on political and moral criteria and on how individual risks affect people. The characteristics of different risks have been divided into two main factors according to the so-called psychometric model:

— Factor 1 comprises risks that are unknown to the persons affected, unknown to science, new, involuntary, and with slow effect.

— Factor 2 characterises risks that have fatal, dreaded and catastrophic consequences as well as consequences for future generations.

It has been found that people's fear and their demand for risk-reducing intervention is influenced much more by factor 2 than by factor 1 finds that people's emotional response is primary to their attitude towards risks, and that their evaluation of advantages and disadvantages of risky activities is secondary and at least partially determined thereby. It is also important to what degree people have trust in the organisations or authorities that are supposed to control risks. It is noteworthy, that trust is easier to break down than to build up. Sources of bad news are regarded as more trustworthy than sources of reassurance. A single investigation finding that a certain activity is risky has more impact than a large number of investigations finding no risk.

Risk analysts have set up a model of how the social effects of a risk are amplified or attenuated when channeled through the different units of society. The direct effect of the risk factor in terms of damage or exposure to danger has influence on people's risk perception directly as well as through the mass media. The risk perception so formed gives rise to individual as well as collective reactions, which may have a range of cultural and socioeconomic consequences. These consequences often feed back on the risk factor with the effect that it is either decreased or increased.

Risk Communication

People tend to evaluate the probability associated with a risk on the basis of the amount of information they receive about the risk factor. The perception of a risk is thus shaped by the amount of media coverage and the vividness of this information. The media coverage is determined by factors such as causality, responsibility and blame, according to agenda setting research. Framing also has a strong effect. For example, people's attitude towards a risk or danger depends on whether it has been described in strictly scientific and statistical terms, or the media have focused on uncertainty, economy, health, environment, who is affected, justice, equality, etc.

Scholars of risk communication tell that it is important how the responsible authorities inform the population about risks. The population should be kept informed about the newest knowledge about technological risks and the efforts to reduce these risks in order to build up trust. It is necessary to bridge the gap between technical descriptions and people's personal perception of security. An information vacuum is created if the responsible organisations ignore or deny a risk.

The population, the media, and grassroots organisations will seek to fill this vacuum with information from other sources. The lack of trust that arises leads to an amplification of the conflict with increased media coverage and excessive fear as a result. This may often force the authorities to implement quite drastic measures against the risk that they originally tried to downplay.

Evolutionary Theories

Cultural Selection Theory

Cultural selection theory is a theory that explains social change based on selection events. Humans may make conscious decisions based on intelligent planning as well as unconscious or irrational decisions. All decisions count as selection events. Selection events can also be caused by external influences, the environment, or be necessitated by the logic of the social structure. The systematic study of selection mechanisms shows that the combined effect of many small selection events can bring about macroscopic changes in the social structure. These social changes are sometimes planned and beneficial, but they may as well be unplanned, unexpected and undesired. An important advantage of cultural selection theory over other models of social change is that it better explains undesired developments.

When applying this theory to the mass media, we already know that news and stories are selected by the media, and the selection criteria have already been discussed. But there is also a selection going on at a higher level, namely the economic competition between mass media. The relentless economic competition forces the media to concentrate on those topics that immediately catch our attention and make us buy today's newspaper or stay tuned on the TV channel through the commercial breaks. Serious quality media that do not mesmerise their audience with psychological means get fewer customers and thus less revenue from advertisements.

The reduced income forces them to cut down on journalistic staff whereby the quality is reduced and more readers or viewers fall away. This vicious circle continues until the medium goes bankrupt or changes its policy. The discipline of evolutionary economics applies selection theory to socioeconomic systems. The economic selection that results from competition between news media is taking place at a higher level than the selection decisions of journalists and other gatekeepers.

The economic selection may therefore be able to override the selection at the lower level by forcing those media organisations out of business that do not let economic considerations determine their selection and shaping of stories. This means that the media can, and do, develop in directions that no journalist or editor wishes. Many journalists are frustrated by the increasing tabloidisation of their media and try to improve the standards, but to no avail.

Cultural r/k Theory

Some studies have indicated that the viewing of fear-provoking television programs cultivates authoritarianism. The concept of authoritarianism has been widely used and studied in social psychology for half a century. Unfortunately, this concept is strongly criticised for being vaguely defined and politically biased. Therefore, the cultural r/k theory is preferred here as an alternative to the theory of authoritarianism. With a theoretical basis in cultural selection theory, the r/k theory avoids the political bias and accusations of psychopathology that lies implicitly in the diagnosis of authoritarianism.

The cultural r/k scale, which may be seen as a replacement for the authoritarianism scale, is applicable not only to individuals, but also to entire cultures and cultural products. A culture and its population will, according to this theory, adapt to the environment in which the society finds itself and, more specifically, to the need for defense against factors that threaten the nation or social group. The perception of a bellicose neighbor state as a security threat will give rise to a kind of psychological armament in the citisens who see their nation or tribe as threatened. The solidarity and feeling of group identity will be strengthened. It has been discovered that these social psychological reactions give rise to a whole series of emergent cultural phenomena.

The political structure will be more hierarchical because people feel the need for a strong leader. The ideology will go in the direction of saying that individuals exist for the sake of the society, rather than vice versa. Religious life will be stricter. Discipline will be harsh and the tolerance for deviants will go down. Sexual morals will also be stricter, and the birthrate will go up. Interestingly, it has been found that these cultural changes are also reflected in the artistic production. Architecture, pictorial art, fiction, and even music becomes more formalistic, embellished and perfectionist so as to achieve a cognitive congruence between the art and the social system where political and religious leaders have a grandiose and majestic status.

A culture that exhibits these characteristics is called regal. The opposite tendencies are called kalyptic. A kalyptic culture is typified by peacefulness, tolerance and individualism. You may imagine a continuous r/k scale going from the extremely regal to the extremely kalyptic, where most cultures and their individual members fluctuate somewhere around the middle of this scale. Any danger that is perceived as threatening to the social order and to the nation as a whole can have a regal influence. This effect has been exploited by despots throughout history who have created witch-hunts and fictitious enemies in order to boost social solidarity and thereby consolidate their dwindling power.

The regal development not only makes a social group better armed to resist violent attacks, but also more likely to initiate a violent conflict. A culture will drift in the kalyptic direction in the absence of any serious threats to the nation and to the social order. People will not accept a tyrannical rule when nothing legitimises the call for a strong leadership and nothing justifies the requirement that people make great sacrifices for the sake of their nation. Applying the cultural r/k theory to analysis of the mass media, we can find that excessive fear mongering can have far-reaching consequences if it makes people see their society as constantly endangered. The consequence is that ever more resources are spent on ineffective punitive measures and less on the more effective preventive measures.

These political consequences of the intense media focus on crime and danger are in agreement with the predictions of the cultural r/k theory, though they may be explained without the use of this theory. However, the predictions of the r/k theory are more farreaching than the predictions of framing theories. The more the media cultivate the fear of crimes and other dangers that threaten the social order, the more the culture develops in the regal direction. This is likely to influence not only the crime policy, but to lead to lower tolerance towards all kinds of minorities, more xenophobia, and a tougher foreign policy.

Interdisciplinary Synthesis

Economic theory can clarify the effect of unrestrained competition on the media market. While the immediate expectation of economists is that free competition leads to optimisation, a more thorough analysis shows that this belief does not hold for the media market. A mild degree of competition may in some cases lead to improved quality and diversity, but excessive competition between commercial media has been found theoretically as well as empirically to lead to wasteful duplication of the most popular entertainment genres rather than to a diversity of genres.

Economists are reluctant to use any other measure of quality than diversity of genres, but this is indeed a poor measure of quality. One model even suggests a negative relationship between diversity and quality; and as the cultivation studies show, a diversity of genres does not guarantee a diversity of messages. The commercial media tend to avoid controversial issues. The distinctions between advertisements, news and entertainment are becoming more and more blurred. Audience groups with less spending money are not considered. The result of excessive competition, one may conclude, is a choice of very similar sensationalist and entertaining programs with low production costs and low informational value. This benefits neither consumers nor advertisers.

Journalists and editors often deplore this development and try to improve the quality of their media by advocating principles of journalistic standards and media ethics. These efforts have little effect, however, because the effects of the economic market forces are able to override the lower level effects of journalistic selection. Media studies clearly show the consequences of strong competition between the mass media. The media are trying to generate a sense of personal proximity. Political disagreements are presented as a clash between personalities rather than between ideological principles. The stories often appeal to the emotions rather than to the intellect. Advertisers prefer soft entertainment and shun controversy.

Relaxing entertainment may not suffice for attracting the attention of viewers or readers, however. In order to survive in the competition for attention, the media often turn to emotional and attention-catching subjects involving crime, fear, danger, and of course sex and gossip. There is a remarkable consistency among different scientific disciplines in the finding that certain topics like these are used repeatedly in the media for catching attention. The discipline of risk analysis tells that people's evaluation of risks and dangers is determined by emotional factors rather than by statistical probabilities.

Certain risks have a greater emotional impact than others, and studies of risk communication adds the finding that it makes a big difference whether information about a certain risk is communicated in a way that makes people feel that the authorities are in control of the situation or not. These findings all add up to an understanding of the sociological discovery that people often fear the wrong things and take drastic precautions against the most unlikely dangers while ignoring other much more serious risks. These effects are of course mirrored and amplified by the media.

The sociology of deviance has discovered that certain professionals and organisations can gain power by defining a danger, making people afraid of it, and at the same time claiming their expertise in fighting this danger. This position is so attractive that numerous interest groups are competing fiercely for gaining recognition for their particular social problem, including their particular definition of it, and having this issue placed high on the media agenda. The media may find it quite profitable to cooperate with such an interest group and run a highly emotional and attention-catching campaign about a particular social problem.

Exaggerations are the norm rather than the exception here, and the situation may soon develop into a moral panic or witch-hunt. Some of the most important factors that influence the form and contents of the mass media, it is time to analyse how these media affect the viewers, listeners, and readers. A politician wanting re-election cannot ignore a sensationalist media campaign or moral panic. Even in the rare case where a politician can resist the emotional appeal of the media and see the hard facts behind the stories, he or she still has to "do something" to satisfy the public opinion. The consequence is that laws about problems with a high media-appeal may be changed frequently without a rational analysis.

Another topic, which is often used for catching attention, is, obviously, sex. Stories about sex may be either positive ("sex is good") or negative ("sex is bad and dangerous"). Both types of stories are equally good for catching attention. The high prominence of sex on the agenda may thus influence the sexual morals of the society in either the liberal or the restrictive direction, depending on which kind of stories fit best into the agenda of the time.

Economic considerations influence not only the subject matter of media stories, but also the form. Commercial media prefer to present issues in a personalised way. Ideological disagreements are presented as conflicts between persons. Likewise, social problems are explained by presenting examples of persons who are afflicted by these problems. Such stories appeal more to the emotions than to the intellect. Complicated explanations are avoided. Stories that cannot be presented in this personalised frame are often simply not told. The consequence of this form of presentation can be predicted from the theory of framing. The framing of a story determines the causal understanding and attribution of blame for a particular problem.

Social problems are most likely blamed on individual persons when framed in a personalised manner. Since the deeper structural causes of the problems are seldom explained, the likely political consequence is scapegoating, but not solution of the problems. The incessant media focus on fear, danger, crime and disaster make people perceive the world as a gloomy and dangerous place. The psychological reaction to this perception may be predicted from the cultural r/k theory. If the entire nation, and not only individuals, are perceived as endangered, then this "mean world syndrome" will foster the kind of social climate that is commonly known as authoritarian.

The culture will become more punitive, intolerant, hierarchical and bellicose. Interestingly, framing theory leads to some of the same predictions, but based on a different mechanism. We thus have two different mechanisms leading in approximately the same direction. These two mechanisms are not mutually exclusive, but more likely to supplement each other. Cross-cultural comparisons show that the structure of the mass media may have a strong effect on political developments. The model outlined in figure 1 is an attempt to explain such effects by integrating contributions from the different scientific disciplines.

Economic factors determine the amount of journalistic investigation and cultural production that can be afforded. A highly competitive market with wasteful duplication of the most popular genres leaves few economic resources to spend on heightening the quality of each program. Economic considerations may force the media to deploy an attention-catching strategy by emphasising entertainment, emotional and personalised stories, sex, violence, gossip, etc. Economy determines the influence of advertisers and sponsors on the types of programs and stories that are being published. Sponsors also have an influence through sponsored cultural events and sports events that may not take place unless they are profitable to the sponsors.

The news are obtained from sources such as politicians, opinion leaders, experts, professionals, police, organisations, and ordinary people who happen to be involved in a newsworthy situation. These sources can influence the media, not only through the stories they tell, but also by rewarding or punishing certain media by providing or withholding desired information. The editors and journalists who produce stories obviously have an influence through their personal engagement as well as their professional, ideological and ethical principles.

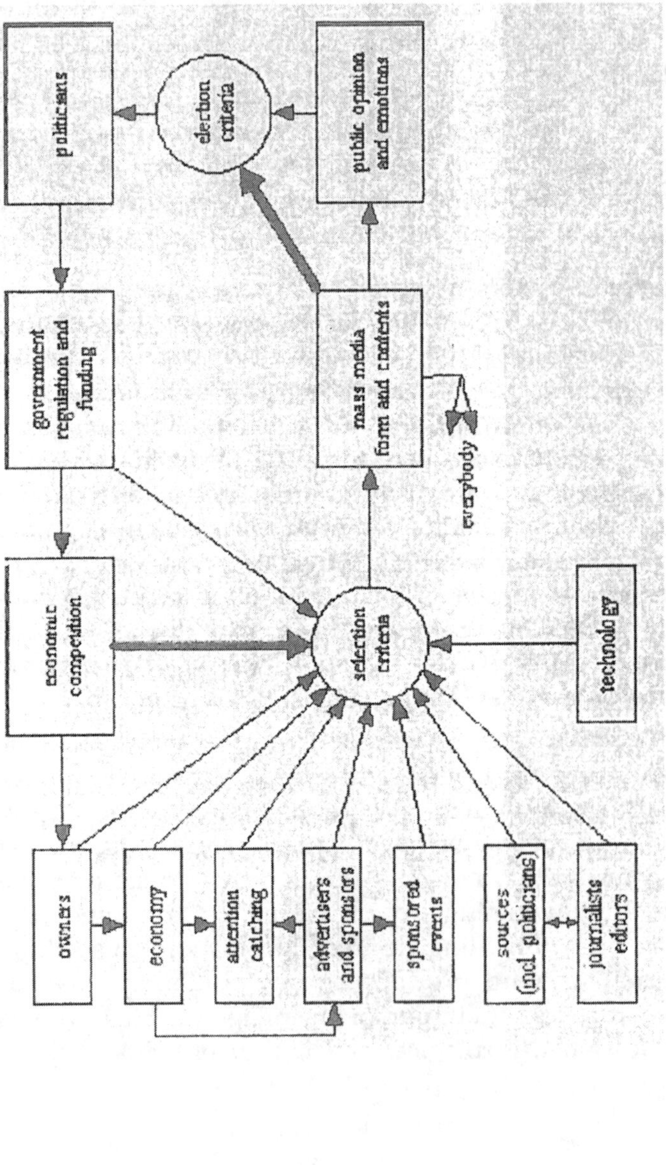

Figure 1. Integrated model showing the role of the mass media in a democratic society. The thick, gray arrows indicate meta-factors that determine the weight of other factors

All these factors influence the form and contents of the media products. However, the most important implication of the integrated model is that the degree of economic competition between the mass media is a meta-factor, which determines the weight of the other factors. A strongly competitive market situation may force the media producers to give more weight to considerations of attention-catching and to the wishes of the advertisers and less weight to ideology and ethics. Ideals of fairness, relevance, and thorough investigative journalism have little influence when fierce economic competition drains the media organisations of resources and forces them to compete on attention-catching stories and entertainment. Quality media that refuse to compete on these premises may simply perish unless they can rely on noncommercial sources of funding.

The media are conveying and influencing the public opinion, which in turn determines the democratic elections. The influence of the media works not only through voters' opinions. Everybody in society is influenced by the media, including politicians, opinion leaders, journalists, editors, and whoever may have the role of news sources. Furthermore, the media are influencing the criteria by which voters evaluate political candidates by means of agenda-setting, priming and framing.

7

Political Effects of Mass Communication

Mass media enhance citizens' abilities to scrutinise government actions. Media capture and hence the constraints on its capacity to perform a watchdog role. There is a host of reasons why governments are better informed than voters and, hence, act on the basis of privileged information. Politicians know more about their competence than those who vote for them. They have access to more policy advice and scenarios from a variety of sources. For example, if a bridge or dam is being built, then it is only through media scrutiny that citizens can ascertain whether proper attention has been paid to the relevant costs and benefits. Similarly when natural disasters strike an active mass media increases the ability of citizens to monitor their representatives have put in effort to protect the vulnerable. This is particularly important in low income countries where citizens rely so strongly on state action for social protection.

However, mass media enables citizens in all fifty villages to observe whether the government is responsive. This raises the incentive of politicians to respond since citizens in the other forty nine villages may use this information in their voting decisions. For information generated by the media to be valuable, it needs to elicit an appropriate collective response. Even in autocratic settings, this may be possible. However, clearly this is more likely to happen when there are democratic institutions such as free elections. In a democracy, citizens require information which they can use to select politicians that serve their needs and to punish those that do not. Otherwise formal democracy has no bite.

While most countries have media of some description, its mere existence is no guarantee that it is an effective vehicle for critical scrutiny of state actions. This requires that media outlets have real information about such actions which they are willing to print or broadcast. This will depend on the extent to which the media is regulated, captured or repressed. The latter is affected by a variety of government actions. These range from policy decisions affecting the regulation of entry and ownership of the media, through to explicit bribery or threats.

There are many countries which, while formally democratic, have limited amounts of press freedom. The "democracies" with low press freedom scores also tend to be low income countries. How the government treats the media industry affects the development of news media and the quantity and quality of news generated. What the raw data suggests it that there are huge variations in access to the media across the world.

Data from the World Development Indicators data for 1997 show a variation in circulation between 0.008 daily newspaper circulation per 1000 population in St Vincent and the Grenadines to 792 in Hong Kong. There are similarly broad variations in television ownership. The same data source shows a variation in television ownership per 1000 population varying from 0.1 in Rwanda to 850 in the United States. Not surprisingly, there are strong links between media development and other development indicators such as income per capita and literacy. After controlling for income per capita and regional dummy variables, there is also evidence that newspaper circulation and television ownership is lower in countries that have a larger fraction of state owned media using the data of Djankov et al.

Whether causal or not, there is also a strongly positive correlation between media penetration and measures of press freedom from Freedom House. Media penetration seems also to go hand in glove with indices of formal and real democracy. Using data from the Polity IV data base, countries that are rated as more democratic have higher levels of news media penetration as measured by newspaper circulation and television ownership.

Of course, the direction of causation is unclear. There is a similar positive correlation between media penetration and the weaker formal notion of democracy measured as whether a country has held an election in the past five years. What these raw correlations tell us is that there may be significant costs associated with having an underdeveloped media.

Moreover, underdevelopment of the media is often the result of decisions by governments to insulate themselves from scrutiny and criticism. Often this takes the form of government ownership, barriers to entry for private media companies and anti-defamation laws. While this may be in the interests of government officials, it is often less clear how it serves the public good. Deregulation of the media therefore stands out as a possible powerful policy lever that could be used to promote accountability in the underdeveloped world. How such deregulation could be implemented in the face of government opposition is a challenge that needs to be faced.

Political Agency Framework

A good framework in which to think about the role of the media is one in which citizens are imperfectly informed about the actions of government and the track records of their leaders. To the extent that politicians may behave opportunistically, and serve their own private agendas ahead of that of the public at large, then politics is a kind of principalagent problem. The principals are the citizens of the polity who finance government activities through taxes and are subject to various regulations, and the agents are the elected officials and bureaucrats who determine policy outcomes.

There are a couple of features of political agency which distinguish it from other agency relationships that economists have studied. First, the incentive schemes on offer are typically very crude. For example, with politicians, the only sanction typically available (except for cases of gross malfeasance) is not to re-elect. Monetary or other more nuanced incentive contracts are almost never observed. This has the consequence that incentives are mostly implicit, with politicians having to guess what the voters would like them to do, rather than the latter posting performance criteria in advance.

Even in the case of lobbying, it is very hard to imagine a very complete contract which specifies the details of what the principals (the lobbyists) desire. The second distinctive feature is multiplicity of principals. There are many citizens and other actors (such as corporations) who differ in countless ways. Thus even if the incentives could be made explicit, it might be very difficult for the principals to agree on the incentives that they will subject their agents to. Thus, we could easily find principals with diametrically opposed interests wishing to pull the actions of the agents in different directions.

Information availability is at the heart of this agency theoretic view of government and politics. When the principals try to influence policy either via the ballot box or by lobbying, then they do so with limited information about the agents whom they are lobbying. There are both problems of hidden action (moral hazard)—when an agent has discretion to make or take a bribe unbeknown to the citizens, and hidden type (adverse selection)—when the motivations and/or competence of the agent is unknown. Effective incentives would ideally punish incumbent politicians for bribe taking and/or incompetency. But if this cannot be widely observed, then doing so is difficult.

There are good reasons for believing that private information gathering exercises by the principals are unlikely to provide sufficient information. Anthony Downs argued that voters would be "rationally ignorant" about politics because they have significant costs of being informed and negligible benefits—they being only one out of a mass of voters. This rational ignorance comes on top of the usual free-riding problem in voting itself, when a single voter may not find the benefits of voting exceeding the cost. This might suggest great pessimism in the ability to find solutions to political agency problems.

However, there are at least a couple of reasons to be more optimistic. First, there can be significant private gains to becoming informed about policy. Consider the case of old-age pensions. Any rational individual planning for their retirement would have a significant private benefit from understanding the evolving public policy debate in this area. Second, the power of forces such as a civic duty may make private benefit a poor guide to what happens in practice.

The third reason for potential optimism is the primary focus here—the role of the media. Mass media can be a powerful source of information generation at low cost to citizens. By being bundled with other activities (such as sport or entertainment) many individuals may be induced to regard acquisition of information not as a chore, but as a pleasure, thus raising the general level of awareness about policy and public affairs. This, at least, is the rosy eyed view.

Here, we can use the framework of political agency to give a tighter specification of the issues. The effectiveness of the media can usefully be decomposed into two parts:

(i) the forces that enable a free and independent media to induce governments to better serve the public interest;

(ii) the forces that lead the government to successfully intervene to silence the media.

Media and Agency

There are three main routes by which non-captured media can affect political outcomes: sorting, discipline and policy salience. Each of these possibilities in turn and then what features of polities and media markets are likely to give the largest incentive to the media to perform this function. Sorting refers to the process by which politicians are selected to hold office.

The motivation of politicians is a potentially important issue for citizens—some politicians (albeit rarely) such as Gandhi and Nelson Mandela enjoy an almost saintly status while others are reviled. The practical ground is typically intermediate between these two. However, the kind of information provided in the media can potentially be important to voters who are deciding who to put in charge. This would include information about the previous track record of potential office holders.

Actions that they perform in office may also be an important source of information about their underlying motivation or competence. By printing news stories that responsibly cast light on this, the media can be a powerful force. To the extent that sorting is effective, ex post incentives are less necessary. The role of the media in achieving discipline is most relevant in situations of hidden action. Suppose that a politician is thinking of taking or making a bribe and that the probability that this will become public depends on the efficacy of the media in both discovering it and broadcasting it widely. Then the marginal cost of that action will tend to be higher, potentially deterring the individual from doing so. Thus, we would expect media development to be negatively correlated with such actions leading to better incumbent discipline.

The media can also have an effect on which issues are salient to voters. Timothy Besley and Robin Burgess considers the case of a vulnerable population in a developing country subject to shocks such as droughts and floods. Such populations are dependent on state action to mitigate the impact of these shocks but need political clout to get their interests on the political agenda. One way of achieving this is for politicians to find it worthwhile to develop reputations for being responsive in the event of shocks occurring. This requires that these groups are informed about actions of politicians and that, if they are informed, then the issue is salient among the many other characteristics of politicians that they care about.

Assuming that responsiveness of government to droughts or floods is a significant enough issue to these citizens, then more information enhances the salience of this issue at the ballot box and, thereby, creates incentives for politicians to build reputations for being responsive. Mass media can thus play a central role in enhancing responsiveness by providing information that citizens can use to decide whom to vote for. More generally, by publicizing politicians' stances on particular issues, the media can change the structure of salient issues in elections. This may mean that the media wields considerable influence. In some countries this can be less than benign, depending on the motives of newspaper owners -news stories can, for example, publicize events that enhance the salience of ethnic tensions leading to victimisation of these groups. All three of these effects rely on the media providing reliable information.

The quality of the news on offer to citizens depends on a number of factors. First, the transparency of the political system is important. In countries without traditions of free information flows, information will tend to be hard to obtain. The extent to which the media will print more speculative news will also be dependent on the legal environment in which the news media operate. For example, the United States allows a public figure defence in libel law and therefore makes it easier for news media to print stories without recourse to libel suits.

This contrasts with the UK where libel laws make publishing speculative news stories more difficult. Also important to news quality will be the methods and traditions of investigative journalism. This may depend on the training of journalists and the extent to which news editors reward investigative activity and allow journalists to devote time to it. It may also rest on some perception of how keen are the citizens of a particular country to be informed and hence the commercial value of breaking important news stories.

Political Capture of Media

The main obstacle of media effectiveness is the possibility of political capture. First, they want to reach a large audience. This is true both for newspapers because sale and advertising revenues are linked to circulation and for television stations because of advertising and, where applicable, cable fees. Competition for audience interest pushes the media to look for interesting news and to establish a reputation for reliability. While the desire to increase market share is common to most industries, there is also a second motivation that derives from the special role of media as political monitors.

Anytime someone is monitored, they may be tempted to ingratiate or threaten the monitor in order to get better coverage. In the case of the government and the media this takes a variety of forms. Some are very simple, like cash bribes offered to individual journalists, violent threats, or censorship. Some are more subtle and typically not illegal. The government can pass regulation that benefits the ultimate owner of a particular media outlet. For instance, if a newspaper is owned by an industrial conglomerate which also owns a car company, beneficial regulation can take the form of a tariff on car imports.

To ascertain which of the two motivations we should expect to prevail, Besley and Andrea Prat build a simple model of media capture. There are three classes of players: voters, politicians, and media. Voters are rational and, for simplicity, they have homogeneous preferences. Their problem is they cannot monitor their politicians directly. All the information they receive comes from the media. The political side of the model is represented by a standard two-period accountability problem. In the first period, a politician (the incumbent) is exogenously put in power. The type of the incumbent (good or bad) is not directly observable. At the end of the first period, an election is held in which voters can re-elect the incumbent or replace her with a challenger of random type. In the second period, the candidate who wins the election is in power.

The media industry is made up of n a priori identical outlets. With some probability, they receive verifiable news on the type of the politician, which they can report to the public. A media outlet cannot fabricate news and that an outlet that reports informative news has a higher audience than one that reports no news. Moreover, the audience share of an outlet that reports news is decreasing in the number of other outlets that report news. The best case for an outlet is to be the only one to break news.

We can assume that news can only be bad, that is one may have verifiable information that a politician is bad but not that she is good. This assumption is not restrictive for our purposes because the government would never want to suppress positive news. The important assumption is that news cannot be fabricated. Allowing for that—while keeping the assumption that voters are rational—would make the analysis very difficult. The credibility of media would arise as a result of a complex signalling game. The revenue of a media outlet has two components.

The first is an increasing function of audience. The second is a transfer from the government (which should be interpreted loosely as favourable regulation). The cost to the politician of making a transfer of a given value to the outlet depends on transaction costs. This is because some forms of transfer may be illegal or politically costly, while others can be disguised as normal policy making. More about transaction costs will be said later.

The timing of the game is as follows: (1) The media outlets receive or do not receive verifiable information about the incumbent; (2) The incumbent knows what information the media got and makes them transfer offers; (3) Each outlet chooses whether to accept or reject the offer; (4) The outlets that accept the offer suppress their information; the ones that reject it report their information to voters; (5) Voters re-elect the incumbent or replace her with a challenger.

In searching for the equilibrium of this game, the main question is whether the incumbent finds it profitable to buy off the media industry or not. If an outlet thinks that all the other outlets are going to be quiet, then its incentive to reject the incumbent's offer goes up because it would be the only one to break news to voters and it would gain a large audience. This means that, in an equilibrium in which all media sell out, the incumbent must pay each outlet as if it were the only one who could break news. Even if we keep the total industry potential revenues constant, increasing the number of media outlets makes it more expensive for the incumbent to buy their silence.

This is the sense in which media pluralism is good for media independence. Besides the number of outlets, the other parameters that determine whether media are captured or not in equilibrium are transaction costs and the amount of audience-related revenues. Both decrease the likelihood that the incumbent manages to silence media. Instead, the probability that media are informed does not affect media capture but of course it increases the probability that voters are informed. This model can be extended in a number of directions. Besides having a "type", the politician may choose the amount of rent extraction activity she carries out. The larger the rent, the higher the probability that the media are able to spot her.

Then, media monitoring does not only weed out bad politicians but has also a discipline effect because it makes dishonest politicians more likely to get caught. This creates a U-shaped relation between media effectiveness and political turnover. The probability that the incumbent is replaced is low both when the effectiveness is very low (because no politician is ever caught) and when the effectiveness is very high (because no politician dares to extract rent). Other possible extensions include ideological media, vertical differentiation, and endogenous entry.

The probability of media capture, and hence of bad political outcomes such as corruption, depends positively on the following variables: media industry concentration, transaction costs, and audience-related revenues. Transaction costs are particularly interesting. One should expect that they depend on media ownership. If the outlet is state-owned, the government may appoint the management and control the resources.

If it is owned by a family or has a controlling shareholder, the government can pass regulation favouring the interest of the owners. If it is a widely-held corporation, then the government cannot benefit the owners directly but has to do some direct transfer to the outlet. Finally, if the owner is a foreign entity transfers may become very difficult.

A prominent example is India which has a newspaper industry that is distinguished from the bulk of other low income countries by being both free and independent. In 1984, Amartya Sen has attributed a major role to this factor in explaining why India has not experienced any major famines in the post Independence era. He observes that "India has not had a famine since independence, and given the nature of Indian politics and society, it is not likely that India can have a famine even in years of great food problems. The government cannot afford to fail to take prompt action when large-scale starvation threatens. Newspapers play an important part in this, in making the facts known and forcing the challenge to be faced."

In contrast, the lack of democracy and of freedom of information have been pointed to as reasons behind why China experienced a major famine between 1958 and 1961 with excess mortality figures ranging between 16.5 and 29.5 million. Representative democracy and the media have also been identified as factors in African countries which have been successful in preventing famines. As the Sen statement makes clear media increases the salience of government performance in famine situations by providing information on the actions of politicians which citizens can use in their voting decisions.

Though suggestive the Sen analysis does not establish a robust link between development of mass media and government responsiveness. Analysis of the role of media in influencing government policy has recently been deepened by Besley and Burgess. Using panel data for Indian states for the 1958-1992 period, they look at two policy response systems. First, public distribution of food as a response to falls in food production associated with droughts. Second, spending on calamity relief as a response to crop damage caused by floods. They then examine how newspapers and politics affect how responsive state governments in India are to these shocks. They find that higher newspaper circulation is associated with government being more responsive to falls in food production and flood damage.

The magnitudes of the effects that they find is large—a 10% drop in food production is associated with a 1% increase in public food distribution in states which are at the median in terms of newspaper circulation per capita whereas for states that are in the 75% percentile a 10% drop in food production is associated with a 2.28% increase in public food distribution. Interestingly Besley and Burgess find that it is newspapers published in the regional languages that are driving their results. This makes sense—it is regional language news papers that report on localised shocks and are more likely to be read by local vulnerable groups and politicians.

In line with political agency theory it is the interplay between mass media and political institutions that determines government responsiveness. Besley and Burgess examine how various political factors influence government responsiveness. They find that political turnout increases how responsive state governments are to drought and flood shocks. Greater political competition is also associated with greater responsiveness. This makes sense as higher turnout and more intense political competition will increase the incentives for politicians to build reputations for being responsive to the needs of their citizens.

Table 1 is taken from Besley and Burgess and gives the rank of a measure of state level responsiveness in public food distribution in India along with rankings of other state characteristics. The responsiveness measure tells us how much food, on average, us publicly distributed as a response to food production changes in a given state. According to this measure, Kerala is the most responsive and Bihar the least responsive state. The striking feature of this ranking is how weakly this responsiveness measure relates to the income per capita ranking. However, the rank of newspaper circulation follows the responsiveness ranking quite closely.

These results along with those in Besley and Burgess are strongly supportive of the notion that mass media helps to solve political agency problems and make governments more accountable. The intuition of what is driving the results is simple—by making the actions of the politicians more transparent the media is providing information to citizens as to the likelihood that they will protected in the future.

Table 1. Ranking of sixteen Indian states in responsiveness and other variables (1 = Highest)

State name	Responsiveness	Per capita income	Per capita newspaper circulation
Kerala	1	13	1
Maharashtra	2	3	2
West Bengal	3	5	4
Tamil Nadu	4	8	3
Gujarat	5	4	6
Assam	6	10	15
Uttar Pradesh	7	11	8
Andhra Pradesh	8	9	10
Karnataka	9	6	7
Rajasthan	10	15	9
Punjab	11	1	5
Orissa	12	12	16
Haryana	13	2	13
Jammu & Kashmir	14	7	11
Madhya Pradesh	15	14	12
Bilhar	16	16	14

Citizens in turn are using this information in their voting decisions. Politicians realise this and this creates an incentive for politicians to be responsive to shocks. Note that this incentive is present even where politicians have no inherent interest in protecting citizens and are only doing so in the interests of garnering the votes of vulnerable citizens. Mass media thus affects responsiveness both by increasing the salience of the social protection issue and by affecting the selection of politicians via voting.

Citizen Participation in Politics

In some countries the introduction of citizens' rights to initiate laws, to call referenda and to be consulted on (mainly local and minor) decisions has gone some small way to compensate for these deficits of "representative" democracy. The ideal that all members of a community or "polis" should be able to participate in reaching common decisions has often been dismissed as impractical (especially where large populations are concerned, but also for other reasons). However, with modern technology it is theoretically possible to allow all citizens to inform themselves about public issues and to vote on them electronically. For the citizen, modern ICT (information and communication technology), especially computer networks such as the Internet, have vastly increased the speed and volume of communication, and the ease of access to information. Internet and Usenet discussion fora and the World Wide Web contain much political information and analysis.

There is much talk "onand off-line" about the chances of ICT to improve citizen participation in political life, which because of the new electronic media may assume new and surprising forms.

Several authors will be quoted, firstly a Czech who has lived for many years in western Germany, Jaroslav Langer, former Fellow of the Friedrich-Ebert Foundation, now retired.

> In its around 130 year history the modern party state has developed into an oligarchic system of rule, in which the parties have degenerated into para-democratic organisations which only feign representative procedures of decision-making. They are today no more than power-struggle associations designed to gain and maintain the greatest possible share of established political power, which in addition administer a state of permanent sociopolitical crisis. Their leading politicians, together with the lobby of power-holders in industry, finance and other interest groups together with the trade-unions, form a "political class" which usurps the authority and roles of the constitutional bodies, (translator: presumably "parliament" — Bundestag and "second chamber" — Bundesrat are meant) taking over their important sociopolitical decisions. (....)

He writes further:

> We need a new, democratic citizens' constitutional reality, for which there are already a selection of concepts worthy of serious consideration. These potentially realisable proposals, which have been published or presented at conferences, have been ignored or cautiously "silenced to death" by the political class, despite (their) frequent calls for new ideas and "visions". These proposals are in general ignored by the mass-media, which concentrate primarily on current events. They (translator: proposals, concepts for renewal of democracy) must therefore be brought to public attention from below, by citizens, by citizens' movements such as "More Democracy", through appeals of experts, and gradually introduced by this type of pressure.

Secondly, Dr. Christian Welzel of the interdisciplinary Science Centre, WZB Berlin. Welzel refers to "dramatic change" of FRG citizens' satisfaction with their democracy since the late 1980s.

> "The growing discontent by no means results only from a negative assessment of the economic and social achievements of the system, but arises from a discrepancy between the high value attached to democratic principles and the low level of

> their perceived fulfilment. In a 1997 survey, 78% reply that a "parliament, which represents the interests of citizens" has "much" to do with democracy but only 30% believe that this principle has been "very effectively" or "effectively" put into citizens in single political decisions": For 63%, direct participation of citizens is an important component of democracy, but only 24% are of the opinion that this component is strongly or very strongly available. Since the mid-1980s trust in institutions, especially institutions of political representation, has steadily fallen. This begins to strongly undermine the legitimation of the representation principle." He cites Walz whose data shows that, between 1984 and 1994, the proportion of "trusting" respondents fell from 56% to 23%." Welzel cites similar survey results for other countries of western Europe (although the surveys cited are not directly comparable with those from FRG).

From the 1998 report of The Democratic Audit of Sweden, by Olof Petersson, Jörgen Hermansson, Michele Micheletti, Jan Teorell and Anders Westholm

Voters give Swedish democracy a bad grade. Few citizens believe that the relationship between voters and their elected representatives within the European Union works well. Members of the public even consider popular government at the national level and in their own county councils as inadequate. Only municipal democracy receives a passing grade from voters. The SNS Democratic Audit discusses the problems facing democratic systems that are divided into different territorial levels. Because societal problems are becoming more internationalised, the political system is now forced to work across traditional territorial boundaries. The search is on for structures and institutions for internationalised democracy that citizens can view as legitimate. The contemporary debate on democracy is full of apprehensions. The optimism that characterised democracy's victory in Eastern Europe and in several developing countries has dampened. Some observers go so far as to wonder whether democracy will be able to survive its new challenges.

Numerous reasons are suggested by commentators, such as failure to deal with unemployment, and, in the Federal Republic of Germany, a so-called "Reformstau" (apparent failure to progress with numerous reforms, notably those of taxation and retirement pensions). Different factions of society with their own, special concerns and problems, have their correspondingly varied reasons for discontent. There are two broads groups of reasons why systems of democracy and governance, including the delegatory/representative and the direct-democratic, should be urgently reviewed and improved a) to improve collective problem-solving.

Problems referred to include the local, regional and global, the economic, ecological and political; illegitimate concentrations of and sometimes abuses of power, to give all people an opportunity to control more in their own lives, to allow the much bemoaned lack of social responsibility to be reduced by allowing more participation in public affairs, to give especially the young a valid impression that they will not spend their lives as passive bystanders and "election fodder". In the latter case, it is proposed here, much could be achieved to reduce the societal alienation and apparent nihilism seen among young people.

Role of ICTs

Many of the controversies have been re-activated because of developments in ICT. Firstly, the tension between representative and direct democracy. The term "delegatory democracy": delegates or elected groups may represent their electorate well or badly. It has often been asserted that in social groups which are or become larger than a village or small town that it is impractical, inefficient, not feasible or even impossible to design and operate a system in which every enfranchised person has the right to co-decide on issues of public concern, e.g. policy, laws, implementation of decisions. Before the emergence of ICT these arguments against participative democracy seemed more convincing, especially for very large units such as cities or states.

For instance, politicians in favour of innovations may judge that electronic voting and easier communication with voters would enable them to more readily raise a majority for their own personal campaign. Others, opposed to innovation, may fear for their autonomy of rule or that their failures may be revealed. Lobby organisations or populist politicians or political movements may believe that it would be easier to convince a broad public to support their cause, were it to be formally empowered in a direct form of democracy, than it would be to persuade parliamentarians or government ministers.

The delegatory model is by far the most prevalent. It appears that elites and publics, in many countries, quite unthinkingly, support a "representative" system as the only possible democratic form. Why is this? Often representative systems of governance arose in direct or indirect continuity with monopolies of power of one sort or another, which had been originally established (maybe centuries ago but in some cases recently) by violence, war and conquest, corruption, trickery, treachery or heredity (e.g. monarchies and aristocracies, juntas of one sort or another, leaderships of revolutionary parties). It may appear natural, having moved a little away from some type of dictatorship or other, and perhaps having struggled for more freedom and justice, to support a "new" system in which leaders may from time to time be rejected and replaced by popular vote. But have been taken over and accepted.

Critically seen, because parliaments are often weak, the party system in modern democracies may be regarded as a form of government in which the people are allowed to choose a ruling regime, effectively consisting of a few dozen, or less, prominent leaders (or, in those countries in which the parliamentary system works well, perhaps a few hundred leaders). Having been elected, this "regime" is often criticised for being mainly responsive to its "entourage" (in modern times the powerful financial, industrial, sometimes religious lobbies) with the voter having almost nothing to say, with no effective contact to government, parliament or political administration in the periods (during which all supposedly collective decisions are made) between infrequent elections.

Intra-governmental and parliamentary reform; relations between legislative and executive; informatisation of government and administration and implications for the citizen Capacity of parliament to control government, and the degree of independence of MPs from party discipline vary from country to country. Matters of intra-governmental and parliamentary reform, and relations between legislative and executive, will not be treated at all fully here. Suffice it to say that ICT may extensively change the ways in which government works, and may alter the relationship between elected representatives and administrations, as illustrated in a Finnish municipality.

Also, the "informatisation" of government and administration has considerable implications for the citizens who are the "consumers" and "owners" of these organisations. There may be some benefits in terms of ease of citizens' access to delegates, officials and to some forms of public information. There will also be increased difficulty for "outsiders" (most citizens) because of increasing complexity of the information and the ICT systems used to store and manage it. The "corridors of power", already locked to the ears and eyes of most citizens, perhaps "Kafkaesque", become increasingly "virtual". Also, this informatisation of government and public administration makes central control and manipulation of citizens and populations potentially much easier.

Effects of ICTs in Direct Democracy

Elements of direct democracy are already practised. The

rights of citizens to propose laws in parliaments, also to initiate and take part in referenda on local or national issues, and to be consulted about community planning etc. vary widely from country to country. Suffice to say that should the practice of calling referenda already exist then it would be relatively easy to introduce electronic voting and, in my opinion more importantly, also to enrich the processes of information, discussion and deliberation about the issue in question, during the run-up period to the referendum vote. Note that high barriers to referenda are often set, or they may be allowed only when called by the ruling group.

Consultation of constituents about policy and planning has usually only been possible in small units e.g. villages, towns, small districts, and both referenda and consultation are commonly limited to relatively minor issues (e.g. tax and financial questions may be excluded). Also, referenda and results of consultation may be only advisory, not mandatory on officials or delegates. It is of interest to note that in Bavaria, Federal Republic of Germany, a movement to introduce the citizens' right to call referenda organised a referendum (already allowed by the Bavarian constitution) on this question at federal state level. A law allowing community (city, town, district) referenda was successfully passed, against the wishes of the ruling political party. Secondly, although there are strong components of direct democracy in Switzerland, the Swiss government recently rejected a proposal to introduce the option to vote electronically in elections and referenda. The proposal was rejected because it was felt that security of voters' identity could not be guaranteed.

There is little to be said against trying to improve existing systems. But ICT appears to offer the chance for citizens to begin to take over more responsibility for collective decisions, so reducing the need for indirect representation and allowing decisions, whether they be delegated or taken directly, to reflect more closely the will of constituents. How exactly the new models of governance will look can only be surmised.

ICT Applications in Democracy and Politics

Functions of these applications may be classified as follows

a) Provision by parliaments, governments and public agencies of information for citizens, public and private institutions.

b) Enhanced interaction between parliamentarians and citizens.

c) Initiatives which aim to promote public debate and communication on matters of general concern, including ICT applications to citizen participation in governance and direct democracy.

"Ordinary" citizens can start political initiatives from scratch with the aid of ICT. A small group of California activists opposed a 1995 ballot initiative on immigration reform. Within three days of setting up an e-mail list service, the activists had 600 subscribers. Within a week, the list had grown to over 1,000, and within three weeks, there were 40 rallies being organised on college campuses around the country. It has been claimed that a world-wide information and lobby campaign led to delay of an international treaty, the proposed Multilateral Agreement on Investment MAI.

Using wide-area computer networks such as Internet and Usenet, citizens can set up theme-centred and/or geographically focussed "agora" (Greek: forum of citizens), linked to relevant information on-line and off-line. Such fora may help participants to clarify political views and to weigh the balance of arguments on issues of public concern. Policy proposals may emerge from the debates. An example of a local agora is Minnesota e-democracy (URL below), which combines e-mail with WWW to create a public forum. The rules of debate, resembling "netiquette", have been quite successful in avoiding conflicts and abuses. Substantial discussions on many topics have taken place and recently resulted in an organised political initiative (about public spending on sport), belying the reputation of political e-fora to be mere "talking shops".

Electronic town halls have been organised, and candidates for office and elected representatives have visited on-line to debate with citizens. Based in Germany, an initiative for democratic reform which successfully uses ICT is Mehr Demokratie. This group aims, with some success, to promote direct democracy such as citizens' law-proposals (for debate and voting in parliaments) and citizen-initiated referenda. They run an informative and educative WWW site, list-server discussion groups (one for members, one open to the public) and an on-line journal. A campaign to protect and nourish local democracy, showing benefits of applying new communication technology, is running successfully in Toronto, Canada. Some basic principles are:

1. Local government belongs to and should be responsible to the local citizens who elected it. Bill 103 imposes amalgamation on the cities in Metro Toronto, and must be opposed.

2. Citizens should have democratic control over education in local schools. Bill 104 imposes amalgamation of school boards in Metro Toronto, puts the control of local education until Year 2000 in the hands of be opposed. (unquote) E-mail has been used for building and co-ordination of citizens' efforts. Electronic fora have aided exchange of information, debate and decision-making. World Wide Web sites are being used to inform and educate about the issues and about how to organise change democratically.

Media and Election Campaigns

Polls can play an important role in democratic accountability by identifying the greatest concerns of voters that candidates should address and the policies that voters most want candidates to support. Polling can also contribute to democratic responsiveness between elections by helping incumbents to anticipate what voters expect. Dr. George Gallup, Sr., was among the most optimistic about the contributions of scientific polling to creating and sustaining a responsive democracy. Scientific survey research, it was hoped, would establish the consent of the governed. This optimistic portrayal of the contribution of polling to election campaigns and democratic government has faced a steady barrage of criticism.

Polls are blamed because elected officials overuse them. Responsible leadership, it is charged, should rely on independent judgment instead of following the public's preferences as divined in polling. This line of criticism reflects the doubts of Walter Lippmann, Joseph Schumpeter, and others about the basic competence of the public to possess the necessary knowledge, skills, and wisdom to identify their interests and the country's. Many of these critics forcefully argue for limiting the influence of ordinary Americans in order to expand the sway of experts and experienced statesmen who have the wisdom, knowledge, and training to guide the ship of state through an increasingly complex and threatening world.

Critics of the competency of citizens have been joined more recently by searing attacks on the methodology of modern scientific polling. Polling, it is charged, is incapable of providing accurate measures of voters' choices because of a series of intractable hurdles (from low response rates, to the growing use of cell phones, to an underrepresentation of younger voters). Flawed methods open the door to subjective, partisan bias, which enables pollsters to cook their data to favour their preferred candidates.

In short, polling is blamed for harming American public life on two fronts-polls encourage elected officials to abandon their responsibility for independent leadership, and they distribute flawed and biased information that fuels partisan fires. Polls and politicians are two elements of a complex process of political strategy and communication. The press is also a critical-or the critical-mediating element. What is the impact of the old and new media's large and ever-growing attention to polling? Does the press serve as a watchdog that ferrets out flawed polls and facilitates strong responsiveness to the public's concern? Or does it do something quite different?

In assembling this special issue, we were especially cognizant of the diversity of organizations and individuals that conduct, use, and publicly discuss scientific surveys or polls. In US, despite the public questioning of polling methodology, the preelection polls at the end of the 2004 presidential campaign were remarkably accurate. There are, without a doubt, a number of questions about samples and the development of new techniques for conducting interviews. These questions require serious attention, but the reactions of journalists, campaign officials, and uniformed observers have often been mistaken. In truth, the final preelection polls in 2004 were overwhelmingly correct in identifying George Bush as the winner and were also fairly close in estimating the margin of his victory. Michael Traugott demonstrates that preelection pollsters performed quite well in the face of extraordinary scrutiny and heated criticism.

For more than three decades, scientific surveys have relied on the telephone to conduct interviews and on the broadcast and print media to disseminate their results. The 2004 election appears to have marked a transition, as automated polls and Internet surveys expanded, and the Internet and its chat rooms opened up new horizons for the dissemination and public discussion of the polls. The 2004 election witnessed a significant new addition to the traditional practice of using random digit dialing telephone interviews-namely, the growth in the use of controversial fully "automated" telephone polling and Internet surveys. Automated and Internet surveys cost less money and may offer some advantages in terms of eliminating the distortions introduced by human interviewing.

New survey methods and modes of public discussion raise questions and challenges for future campaigns. The public dissemination of polling results is no longer controlled by well-known experts who enjoy wide credibility for the accuracy and integrity of their results, as was the case when the Gallup and a small number of other polling organisations dominated the field of public polling. Today, polls and pollsters have proliferated, and the level of scrutiny has intensified. It is now a standard part of the campaign consultants' playbook to attack polls that show their candidate lagging. The motivation is damage control, and the ever-vulnerable target is polling methodology.

Democratic Distortions

Dr. Gallup optimistically saw polls as allowing election candidates to respond to the concerns of a majority of voters, ushering in greater democratic representation. Election campaigns capitalise on polling to target subgroups of voters or harder-to-reach potential voters. The use of polls by modern campaigns has important implications. Instead of polling driving candidates to converge on the midpoint of public opinion, polls and other sources of information are being used to selectively mobilise support from targeted subgroups of voters. Polls are being used to narrow rather than widen the appeal of candidates.

What difference does the narrowcasting of election campaigns make to representative government? After all, a fundamental purpose of elections is to create institutional incentives for government officials to respond to the preferences of most Americans. Martin Gilens offers some compelling, albeit circumstantial, evidence that government officials are responsive to citizens but that it is a highly selective form of responsiveness. In particular, his findings suggest that elected government officials are most attentive to affluent rather than to middle-income and poor voters. The disparity in representation found by Gilens is consistent with a growing body of research. Larry Bartels has reported similarly distorted responsiveness based on income. Lawrence Jacobs and Benjamin Page show that the foreign policy preferences of U.S. government officials appear to be highly responsive to business elites, with less attention devoted to experts and little, if any, to the views of the mass public.

The narrowcasting of election campaigns on precisely targeted voters and the disparities in government representation stem from important changes in the incentive structure of American politics. For ambitious politicians, their primary focus is on avoiding the costs associated with compromising the core policy goals that are intensely supported by party activists, campaign contributors, and interest groups. To avoid the risk of electoral punishment, they turn to polls to craft appealing campaign messages and to microtarget voters.

The pioneers of scientific polling envisioned their work as promising rigorous precision, trustworthy information, and the expansion of democratic representation. That vision is threatened. The press has fuelled significant public doubt about the methods of polls by extensively reporting campaign smear tactics that have little grounding in scientific methods or the impressive track record of preelection polling. Candidates are using polls to select their voters and to fashion their policy choices. The overall effect is that the use and reporting of polls are distorting the process of democratic accountability and responsiveness that they were meant to support and strengthen.

8

Cultural Transformations in the Media-driven World

Different modernities are always and to a certain extent media-driven, because media of communication transform time and space conditions and they also provide interpretational frameworks for the new times. These transformations, technological and cultural, the media forming an integral part of them, trigger all kinds of reactions. Literary responses may reflect cultural panics and ontological insecurity, or, they are artistic innovations on a smaller or broader scale, as once, e.g., modernism and futurism. In mainstream (news) media texts these changes are very seldom problematised, since stable timespaces are the sine qua non of reporting.

Hence, the media tend to reproduce more or less archaic 'chronotopes', or traditional modernistic epistemologies in a radically transformed text, image and sound environment (digitalised images and virtuality, broadened access, Internet etc.). For problematisations of the media and thematisations of the communication order that they sustain we have to look somewhere else. The media themselves form part and parcel of modernity and, hence, various cultural responses/ expressions (in whatever media and generic forms) are at the same time reactions to the general, economic and technological modernisation process and to the media as such. To look at this complex from a place outside of the media—sometimes even outside of media research—might thus give fruitful vantage points, strongly under-exploited within media studies.

Such historical "reception studies" have convincingly shown, for instance, that the modern mass press of the late 19th century in several ways put its stamp on and shaped literary modernism. The argument sets out from David Harvey's, Steven Kern's and others' observations on the repercussions of changing time and space conditions upon cultural systems and forms of consciousness. Theoretical inspiration also comes from Immanuel Wallerstein and Mikhail Bakhtin. Historical and cross-cultural literary examples from Russia and Western Europe, and from different historical epochs, will be discussed, showing that cultural globalisation, closely linked to modernisation, evokes very different responses across media, genres and national cultures.

Two factors seem to be ubiquitous in the modernisation experience: timespace and media uncertainties. David Harvey, in his *The Condition of Postmodernity*, comments on the transformation of philosophical systems as a result of technological change affecting material time-space parameters of existence: it is typical in times of rapid technological transformation that the temporal and spatial foundations of the social order are threatened and, as a consequence, fundamental changes in the philosophical systems of reality representation occur. Thus, we would need some basic distinctions to develop further the analyses of transformed timespaces in media-driven modernities. Speaking of time (and it also applies to space), there is on the one hand, time as constituted in systems, and, on the other hand, time as social interpretation of reality. The media as technological forms intervene in both systems and collective interpretations.

Mikhail Bakhtin has made a similar distinction between what he termed 'real' vs. 'literary' chronotopes, the latter signifying the ways the literary genres assimilate "the real historical time and space": However forcefully the real and the represented world resist fusion, however immutable the presence of that categorical boundary line between them, they are nevertheless indissolubly tied up with each other and find themselves in continual mutual interaction. (..) The work and the world represented in it enter the real world and enrich it, and the real world enters the work and its world as part of the process of its creation... Timespace constructions, or chronotopes, will thus be foregrounded here, as one tool for the comparative study of socio-cultural change, the chronotope being "an optic for reading texts as x-rays of the forces at work in the cultural system from which they spring".

Chronotopic constructions and critical reflection on media performance can thus provide clues to social and cultural transformation, more than has so far been acknowledged. A number of basic assumptions can now be specified:

New timespace experiences are constitutive of modernity and they relate to changing communications conditions: The telegraph and, later, the telephone represented two important steps to the modern information or network society, the reason of course being that the necessary link between information transfer and physical transportation was broken. James Carey describes the cultural, or even philosophical implications: There were other technological marvels of the mid-nineteenth century, but the inscrutable nature of the telegraph made it seem more extraordinary than, and qualitatively different from, other inventions.

The key to the mystery was, of course, electricity—a force of great potency and yet invisible. It was this invisibility that made electricity and the telegraph powerful impetuses to idealist thought both in religious and philosophical terms. It presented the mystery of the mind-body dualism, and located vital energy in the realm of the mind, in the nonmaterial world. There are many accounts of new transportation and communication technologies' impact on mental and cultural levels. Wolfgang Schivelbusch, for instance, provides a rich documentation on the railroads and the ways railroad travel contributed to the "industrialisation of consciousness" by industrialising time and space and Stephen Kern did a similarly insightful study of the whole spectre of new technologies towards the end of the 19th century, all of them contributing to the rise of the modernist movement in art and literature. Cultural panics as well as artistic innovations flourished.

New timespaces (multiplicity, fragmentation, simultaneity, etc.) are often interpreted as typical of (global or universal) postmodernist culture, when, in fact, they were in place already in early modernity: Take any one of the traits often associated with postmodernism and you will find ample illustrations of how they appeared in the second half of the 19th century (some even earlier). For instance, leaving multiplicity till later, fragmentation was a characteristic of the early newspaper and of life in contemporary urban environments.

Also simultaneity belongs to the traits that are said to characterise modernitity as much as postmodernity. Kern sees this as a major cultural discovery already before World War I, and John B. Thompson notes the 'discovery of despatialised simultaneity', the way being paved by telecommunications. Of course this has to do with the fact that the material communications conditions (the telegraph etc.) were already around. Almost a century later Manuel Castells introduces the concept of "timeless time", a new experience produced by the, by now, even faster communication technologies (broadcsasting of moving images, digitalisation, etc.).

Also Lash and Urry have presented e concept, instantaneous time, which basically reflects the same cultural shock (related to post-Fordist production) experienced generations earlier. Kern comments on Appolinaire's poetry that it "sought to knit remote places and times into a single fabric of present experience—a zone between past and future, between near and remote...". Another example given by the same author is James Joyce and the way he used a "filmic" technique of montage in order to present his Dublin within "a slice of it out of time, spatially extended and embodying its entire past in a vast expanded present".

At the outbreak of the war, succession was replaced by simultaneity. Yeats describes the condition of modern life as "life of the moment". When Peter Sloterdijk writes about the present age of cynical reason, where an immense simultaneity has set its strong mark in our consciousness, this is obviously something that has been part of a cultural experience for more than a hundred years. Classical treatises of this experience in early modernity are found in Simmel's work: "The specifically modern experience of temporality finds it most succinct expression in Simmel's analysis (..)a consciousness of time, which can thematise the present only as a form of transition and nonduration".

These experiences look different among differently positioned actors and in different media, cultural forms and genres: In a criticism of Immanuel Wallerstein's timespace typology Göran Therborn notes that it exclusively refers to the way in which scholars (..) conceive of and use time in their studies. Actors' time, on the other hand, is the time orientation of all human actors... This neglect of actors' time, it may be argued, misses an important aspect of modernity and postmodernity.

One author who has explicitly addressed the timespaces of a variety of actors is Orlando Fals Borda, another sociologist: "For our purposes, people's SpaceTimes are concrete social configurations where diversity is part of normality, and where people 'weave the present into their particular thread of history'. Local affirmation, collective memory, and traditional practices are fundamental in such SpaceTimes". Not only do these experiences vary historically, across different social groups, genres and media, different timespaces may also co-exist in any given situation.

The multiplicity of timespaces (material/institutional as well as experiential) is itself reinforced by the global/national/local nexus: The timespaces of the nation state and of the traditional place may be overlayered or muted by global cultural elements. A multiple complexity of times bears on our lives simultaneously, says Barbara Adam. Of all juxtapositions and hybridities associated with the global, the co-presence of different temporal frames, and qualities of time, is perhaps the least observed, the reason being that spatialisation has taken theoretical precedence over temporalisation in postmodernist thinking.

The idea of "de-territorialisation" and "non-territorial" communication is a case in point, not least because of its centrality in many prevalent discourses on identity in the globalised world. It relates to the idea of 'non-places' being symptomatic of 'supermodernity', and implies that one specific spatio-temporal order has become dominant, at the expense of all others. But what is 'non-territoriality'? One interpretation is that geography, physical transportation and the location of the participants are rendered irrelevant (the thesis of extra-territoriality). Another interpetation has it that it is (inter)action not being confined to a given space or place. It is not within, but between territories (the thesis of expanded territoriality).

The first interpretation suggests that geography reigned till the advent of the modern media of communication, which is simply not true. Already writing losened the grip of geography. Second, what of interactions going on between territories? It is in the nature of communication as such that it surpasses distances in time and/or space, always involving the crossing of some kind of borders existing because of the different positions of the participants. And this communication may reduce or increase existing distances—produce sameness (identity) or difference as the case may be.

In spatial terms "(e)ven the most globalised and dematerialised business sectors, such as global finance, inhabit both physical and digital space. Such firms' activities are simultaneously partly deterritorialised and partly deeply territorialised; they span the globe, yet they are strategically concentrated in specific places...." As Barbara Adam Sassen sees time as multiple and she describes how "strategic economic projects have emerged in the play between two master/monster temporalities and spatialities. One of these—that of the national state as a historic institution, a master temporality often thought of as historic time—is a deteriorating spatiotemporality. Another, the global, is a spatiotemporal (dis)order in the making. As we have seen, also this is a phenomenon that can not be exclusive seen as a characteristc of late modernity.

In transitional periods the media are always at the centre of attention, not as allegories of something else, but in their own right: The ways the media are problematised bear witness of the more general experience of modernisation of which the media are an integral part, together with urbanisation and globalisation. What is this experience of modernisaton? Two related things have been apostrophised here: experiences of media(tions) and of transformed timespaces.

Experiences and artistic/literary works focussing media deal with the media, not necessarily allegorically, but as a constituing part of modernisation. A very different view is found in Fredric Jameson's writings, where the media seldom figure in their own right, but as allegories of the opaque world system and its dominant forces: "...our faulty representations of some immense communicational and computer network are themselves but a distorted figuration of something even deeper, namely, the whole world system of a present-day multinational capitalism".

Relation Between Postcommunism and postmodernity

How is postcommunism related to postmodernism, other than through the common prefix? Unless we postulate a sharp break, or a qualitative leap occuring more or less overnight (as some authors do), both between Soviet communism and what came after it and between the peculiar form of modernism that prevailed in Russia and whatever (recurring versions of robber or state capitalism) is supposed to have succeeded it, we must concede that the present system somehow is determined by its historical past.

In a certain sense "postcommunism" is a global cultural condition. Not least has the last decade witnessed widely mediated cultural and historical interpretations of the so-called post-cold war era, ranging from versions of the end-of-history thesis to postmodernistic celebrations of the breakdown of political and cultural borders and borderlines (or some mix of them: a situation beyond time, as it were).

On the one hand there are universalistic interpretations of "postcommunist culture" as just another instance of a global postmodern state, disregarding the kind of modernity that it has succeeded, as well as the media context. On the other hand, stress has been laid on the continuity of cultural traditions and conflicts with their roots far back in csarist Russia. In Post-Soviet Russia a great number of new novelists and poets have attracted a lot of attention, at home and abroad. Some of them have become cult figures in Russia and the object of a plentitude of literary analyses in the West.

The case of Viktor Pelevin, and his non-Russian literary interpretants, provide an entry into this strongly (contested) arena of political and cultural analysis. Pelevin is a controversial popular culture hero attracting thousands of visitors to web sites, news groups and fanzines. Is he a postmodernist writer and, as such, an exponent for a global cultural movement, or, is he rather to be read as a surrealistically bent commentator on contemporary Russia, following in the footsteps of quite a few renowned predecessors?

The following description of the modern self applies very much to Pelevin's world: "A subjective process of unlimited selfdevelopment, as traditional barriers of custom disintegrate—an experience necessarily lived at once as emancipation and ordeal, elation and despair, frightening and exhilarating. It is the momentum of this ceaselessly ongoing rush towards the uncharted frontiers of the psyche that assures the world-historical continuity of modernism.."

Finnish researchers have commented on the world of Pelevin that it is placed on the border, i.e. it is in a process of transformation or transition to something new, reminding us of Simmel "thematising the present only as a form of transition and non-duration". These authors also note that most of Pelevin's works is constructed of two realities, a multiple timespace which is pervasive also in, e.g., Vladimir Makanin's novel Underground. In Pelevin's most recent novel, Buddha's Little Finger, the co-existence of such these multiple realities, typical of transitional timesis thematised again, but now focussing the Stalinist period and its monolithic political and cultural apparatuses. In Babylon commercial media (most outpokenly television) make up the new monolith.

It is a world where television has a strong position as political, social and cultural centre and force. A theme of deep psychological impact echoes many of the commentators on the press towards the end of the 19th century, however different the historical contexts. The changes in the image produced by various technomodifications can be correlated with a virtual psychological process in which the observer is forced to switch his attention from one event to another and select the most interesting content from what is taking place—that is, to manage his own attention as the makers of the programme make it. This psychological process creates its own virtual subject, which for the duration of the television programme exists in place of the individual, fitting into his or her consciousness like a hand into a rubber glove.

But when a television is turned on, it is transformed from an object of the first type into an object of a second type. It becomes a phenomenon of an entirely different order. And although the person looking at the screen does not notice this customary transformation, it is truly immense. For the viewer the televison disappears as a material object that possesses weight, size and other physical properties. Instead of this the viewer has the sensation of being present in a different space, a sensation familiar to all who are assembled here.

Another theme, similarly reminiscent of modernist debates on the press, the mass effect: This is similar to the conditions of possession by a spirit. The difference lies in the fact that in this case the spirit does not exist; all that does exist are the symptoms of possession. This is a virtual spirit, but from the moment the viewer entrusts the programme-makers with redirecting his or her attention at will from object to object, he or she effectively becomes this spirit, and the spirit, which does not actually exist, possesses this viewer and millions of others.

The peculiar form of collectivity relating to media consumption finds its own interpretation here: What is taking place could appropriately be called the experience of collective non-existence, since the virtual subject that replaces the viewer's actual consciousness is absolutely nonexistent—it is merely an effect created by the collective efforts of editors, cameramen and producers. However, for the individual watching the television there is nothing more real than this virtual subject.

Deep impact and mass effect may be dependent on simultaneity, another theme: Furthermore, Lapsang Suchong of the Pu Er monastery believes that if a certain programme, for instance a football game, were to be watched simultaneously by more than four-fifths of the population of Earth, this virtual effect would become capable of displacing from the aggregate human consciousness the collective karmic vision of the human plane of existence, the consequences of which could be unpredictable. 'So then why do you turn it upside down?'

'That's the fourth Buddhist method. It's used when you really do need to watch the television after all. It's just that, when they read their text, there are several million people staring straight into their eyes, and as a rule they are very angry and dissatisfied with life. Just think about what kind of cumulative effect it generates when so many deceived consciousnesses come together in a single second at the same point.

Pelevin themes and literary techniques show many of the features generally regarded as constitutive of modernist writing: self-reflexiveness, simultaneity, juxtaposition, montage, epistemological ambiguity, and the fragmentation of the integrated individual subject. Valuable sources and analyses used so far include Alexandra Smith's study of the "postmodernist" image of Moscow in the works of Ludmilla Petruschevskaya and Viktor Pelevin (The clay machine-gun, Waterloo bridge, Life of insects). Another interesting piece of work is Nina Kolesnikoff's recent study of the narration of "postmodern time and place" in the works of Sasha Sokolov, Mikhail Berg, Viktor Erofeev, Arkadii Dragomoshchenko, Valeria Narbikova, Anastasiia Gosteva, Vladimir Sorokin and Andrei Bitov.

In a vein similar to Smith's Kolesnikoff identifies a whole range of literary strategies in the chosen novels that she finds typical of postmodernist writing in general. Especially she foregrounds the "chaotic" temporal structures and constructions, "leaving the reader in a bewildered state, because of the total absence of logical chains". Also, there are often several narratives going on at the same time, but rooted in different historical contexts.

Linda Hutcheon, "one of the main theorists of postmodernist literature", also believes that "postmodernism cannot simply be used as a synonym for the contemporary" and "it does not really describe an international cultural phenomenon, for it is primarily European and American (North and South)". There is, for instance, a cultural heritage to take into account here. Pelevin has himself mentioned his debt to Mikhail Bulgakov, writing in another tumultuous time, the 1920s.

In the international reception of Pelevin there are plenty of references to Buddhism, the romanticising of drugs, and many other global culture components. This is very problematic in many ways. For one thing, not a few literary theorists tend to overlook intertextual relations to other media than literature, not to speak of the general media context. One would also have to include in the analysis a number of concrete, contextual conditions to understand what is going on in today's Russian culture.

History can not be dismissed as easily as in some postmodernist writings, representing a version of the end-of-history thesis. History has not collapsed in Russia, as little as anywhere else on the planet. Neither are this country's writers blind to the structures now evolving. Julian Stallybrass has asked: "...how is it that culture is supposed to be fragmenting and diversifying when the ownership of the producers of culture is dramatically concentrating? How is it that all 'grand narratives'—accounts which seek to explain phenomena in terms of broad historical processes—are to be abandoned just at this moment of unsurpassed economic integration on a world scale?"

Colin Sparks concludes his perusal of the contemporary Russian media society thus: "The experience of Central and Eastern Europe highlights the fact that , in most of the world, there is a close relationship, and often interpenetration, between capital and politics". There is, in this literature, thematisations of oppression and resistance against the dictatorship of the postmodernist politico-commercial market.

Pelevin again: The rapid switching of a television from one channel to another, which is used to avoid watching the advertisments, is known as zapping. Bourgeois thought has investigated in considerable detail the psychological condition of the individual who engages in zapping, and the corresponding thought patterns, which are rapidly becoming the basic forms of the modern world. But the type of zapping that is considered by the researchers of this phenomenon corresponds only to switching between channels by the viewer.

The switching to and fro of the viewer that is controlled by the producer and cameraman (..) is a different type of zapping, a coercive form, study of which is prohibited in every country in the world except Bhutan, where television is forbidden. But coercive zapping, whereby the television is converted into a remote control for the viewer, is not simply one method among others of organising an image sequence; it is the very foundation of television broadcasting, the major means by which the advertising-informational field exerts its influence on consciousness. Assuming the condition of Homo Zapiens, the viewer becomes a remotely controlled television programme. And he or she spends a significant part of his life in this condition. Then, how can you ever resist or withdraw from this refined coercion?

There is only one, really effective way: "First you watch television with the sound turned off. About half an hour a day, your favourite programmes. When you get the idea they're saying something important and interesting on the television, you become aware of the thought at the moment it arises and so neutralise it. At first you are bound to give way and turn on the sound, but gradually you get used to it. The main thing is not to allow a feeling of guilt when you can't restrain yourself. It is like that for everybody at first, even for lamas. Then you start to watch the television with the sound switched on but the picture off. And finally you start watching the television completely switched off. Thats's actually the main technique and the first two are only preparatory. You watch all the news programmes, but you don't turn the television on. If you watch the television like that for ten years at least an hour a day, you come to understand the nature of television. And of everything else as well".

In one sense, postcommunism is a late form of modernity. In the 1920s, with Fordism and taylorism and the five year plans, time was accelerated, not for the sake of profit, but for ideological reasons, Castells argues. The collectivisation of agriculture also led to the breaking up of 'natural', cyclical time, favouring the linear time of modernity and industrialism.

Clock time came to dominate over space and society. In the 1990s the middle classes adopted the narrow vision of monetarised time and time and money became one. In that respect Russia became "westernised" at a moment when advanced capitalism were about to revolutionise its own temporal structure' (timeless time). In Russia the result has been an expressed mix of temporalities. This description of Castells could be taken further back, because multiple (system) timespaces and their concomitant literary chronotopes seem to have appeared much earlier, with the first industrial and early capitalism in Russia.

When capitalism got a foothold in Russia, Dostoyevsky, fascinated by the modern media (telegraphic news) of his time, was the first to epitomise on the cultural repercussions of the new order, in his "prosaics of simultaneity". Only such things as can conceivably be linked at a single point in time are essential and are incorporated into Dostoyevsky's world; according to Dostoyevsky, all is simultaneous, everything coexists. Thus there is no causality in Dostoevsky's novels, no explanations based on the past, on the influences of the environment or of upbringing and so forth. Every act a character commits is in the present.

Tere exist no genealogical or causal categories in Dostoyevsky's thought world, he almost never refers to history as such, every social or political issue is dealt with within the frames of the contemporary situation and this can not only be explained by his situation as a journalist. It should rather be seen as typical of his artistic vision and of his poetics—explaining his outspoken inclination towards journalism and his loving interest in the newspaper. He had a deep and subtle understanding of the newspaper page as a dynamic reflection of social conflicts as observed a particular day, the newspaper page offering big and small things juxtaposed to one another, thus unfolding a most contradictory material.

In contradistinction from so many of his contemporaries (e.g. Schopenhauer and Flaubert) he never distasted the newspaper, but rather studied their facts, 'at once real and remarkable', closely. He strived to compose a complete picture of the historical moment using the incoherent news fragments as building blocks, thereby exposing 'the links between the public and the private'.

9

Role of Media in Shaping Youth Culture

The influence of the media on the psycho-social development of children and youth is profound. The media has the potential to generate both positive and negative effects, and many studies have looked at the impact of media on society, particularly on children and adolescents. An individual child's developmental level is a critical factor in determining whether the medium will have positive or negative effects. Not all media programmes are bad, but data showing the negative effects of exposure to violence, inappropriate sexuality and offensive language are convincing.

An average child in a developed country watches nearly 14 hour of television each week. By his/her high school graduation, the average teen will have spent more time watching television than in the classroom. Studies show how time spent watching television varies between different age groups and cultures. This is especially relevant when studying the effects of excessive television exposure on disadvantaged populations. The amount of time that younger children currently spend watching television has not decreased significantly. A substantial number of children begin watching television at an earlier age and in greater amounts than what experts recommend. Evidence suggests that television's influence on children and adolescents is related to how much time they spend watching television. As a result, with prolonged viewing, the world shown on television becomes the real world.

Exposure to media frequently limits children's time for vital activities such as playing, reading, learning to talk, spending time with peers and family, storytelling, participating in regular exercise, and developing other necessary physical, mental and social skills. In addition to the amount of time spent for the media, other factors that influence the medium's effect on children include the child's developmental level, individual susceptibility and whether children watch television alone or with their parents.

Media can be a powerful teacher. Watching education and cultural programmes are examples of how toddlers can learn valuable lessons about racial harmony, cooperation, kindness, simple arithmetic and the alphabet through an educational television format. Some television programmes stimulate visits to the zoo, libraries, bookstores, museums and other active recreational settings, and educational videos can certainly serve as powerful pro-social teaching devices. In some disadvantaged settings, healthy television habits may actually be a beneficial teaching tool Still, watching television takes time away from reading and schoolwork. More recent and well-controlled studies show that even 1 hour to 2 hours of daily unsupervised television viewing by school-aged children has a significant deleterious effect on academic performance.

Media Violence and the Youth

For decades, researchers and professionals have argued about whether or not the portrayal of violence in the various media causes violence in society. Laboratory experiments, field research and correlational studies have all been used as investigative tools. Some studies have suggested that there is a direct causal relationship between violence in entertainment and violent behaviour, and others have concluded that there is no association whatsoever. Most studies have shown that there is some sort of relationship or association.

Most of these studies have focused on television violence and have concluded that there are some negative effects related to watching violent or aggressive behaviour on TV. They do not necessarily indicate a direct cause-and-effect relationship. Rather, they suggest that exposure to media depictions of violence enhances the risk that the viewer will engage in subsequent aggressive behaviour. The effects of exposure to violence in the media are by no means inevitable and may be amplified or reduced by a variety of other factors. Research into the effects of pornography and violent video/computer games, while less voluminous than television research, has begun to draw similar conclusions.

The relationship between media depictions of violence and subsequent violent behaviour is extremely complex. There are a number of interacting variables which play an important role in determining who will be affected, by what material, and in what way. The context in which the violence is portrayed and age of the viewer/player are the most important variables for determining the potential impact of violence. Also significant is the participant's ability to differentiate between fantasy and reality, and justified or unjustified use of force.

The following groups of children may be more vulnerable to violence on media:

— children from minority and immigrant groups;

— emotionally disturbed children;

— children with learning disabilities;

— children who are abused by their parents; and

— children in families in distress.

The effects of watching violence are influenced by the ability of individuals to discriminate between fantasy and reality, between justified and unjustified violence, and the capacity to critically evaluate the portrayal of violence within a social and moral framework.

There are a number of ways that on-screen violence can be portrayed which might influence viewers. These include:

— Perpetrators of violent acts who are rewarded or remain unpunished for their actions. To the vulnerable viewer, whether it be a child learning about the world or an already aggressive person, this could be interpreted to mean that violent behaviour is acceptable or even desirable;

— The aggressive action is seen by the viewer to be justified;

— There are few or no consequences portrayed, such as remorse, real emotional and physical pain, or legal consequences. The vulnerable viewer who is presented with a false impression of the reality of violence may be more likely to engage in violent behaviour, being unaware of the real consequences;

— The viewer identifies strongly with the perpetrator, or associates the cues for the violent behaviour with reallife cues, hence the violence appears to be more real. This can reinforce or justify the viewer's own behaviour;

— The viewer is predisposed to aggression. The violent images can act as a trigger to release these existing feelings;

— The violence leaves the viewer feeling aroused;

— Something or someone causes the viewer to be frustrated after watching violence;

— The on-screen violence actually pleases the viewer;

— The perpetrator's motivation is to cause harm or injury;

— There is a lack of critical commentary or non-violent balancing events.

Television is a unique form of entertainment in that almost every home in the western world has at least one television. Because television is a large part of everyday life for many people, images of violence could potentially affect a large proportion of the population, compared to videos and computer games which, while they are increasing in popularity, are watched or played by a smaller proportion of the population.

Television programming aims to satisfy the viewing requirements of all age-groups and all types of people and therefore broadcasts a wide range of material, whereas videos and computer games are individually classified and generally chosen according to that classification.

As with other forms of violence on television, there is concern that the reporting of suicides, homicides and violent and criminal events on the news, will result in imitation or "copy cat" action by some individuals. For example, some studies show that the number of suicide deaths recorded have increased after news reports of suicide, particularly where the reports detailed the method used by the victim. Many aspects of the mass murder in Hungerford in England in 1987 were remarkably similar to the Clifton Hill massacre in Australia, and it is thought that the reporting of the Australian tragedy may have triggered the events which took place in Hungerford ten days later. Similar copy cat hypotheses have been proposed linking the Port Arthur massacre in Tasmania with the mass murder in Dunblane in Scotland just weeks before.

Videos pose a greater problem than television due to the more explicit, violent material that they can contain within the regulatory guidelines and the fact that such material can be relatively easily accessed. Videos are available almost 24 hours per day and their content ranges from wholesome feel-good stories for the whole family, to "X" and "R" rated, violent and sexually explicit. Despite the classification system used, these films are readily available to persons in almost any age-group at any time.

The "copy cat" phenomenon as it applies to videos has been used by some people to explain such horrific events as, for example, the killing of a toddler in England by two ten-year-olds, who had apparently watched the movie Child's Play. Although such films might have an influence on the behaviour of some people, it must be emphasised that other factors also contribute to violent behaviour, and not all people who watch violent images exhibit violent behaviour as a result.

Most children have seen films intended for age-groups older than their own, and they want to see them because they are naturally curious. Children and adolescents are often unsupervised in their own homes or in friends' homes and can get access to these films. The children of parents who watch violent videos are more likely than other children to watch violent videos. It is difficult for parents or legislators to regulate access to videos, but parents in particular must be made aware of the possibility that their children may have access to this material.

Pornographic films, especially those containing violence, can contribute to callous sexual behaviour and violence towards women. This can be due to the manner in which women are portrayed in these films—often either as promiscuous or submissive. The images portrayed of women as objects to be used by men for sex, are potentially damaging in the social messages which they present.

In their meta-analysis of the available data, Paik and Comstock found that erotica had a potentially negative effect on the attitude of men towards women, even without incorporating violence. However, as with other research findings about the effect of viewing violent or erotic material, it is important to remember that there are other variables which influence the behaviour of any particular viewer. The context in which this material is portrayed is important, as is the psychological state of the viewer and whether or not they are predisposed to behaving aggressively. The same complex issues which surround the debate about the effects of violence also apply to the effects of pornography.

Many video/computer games contain some level of violence (although most of these contain "low level" violence), often requiring the player to fight other characters in some sort of battle, injuring or killing them in order to proceed to the next level of the game. Some of the more explicit games have sexual themes, and some have sexually violent themes. The concern expressed about such games is due to the level of interactivity involved. It is as if the player is actively participating in the violence.

As with television or video violence, there is increasing concern that players will become more aggressive as a result of violent games, or will become desensitised to the violence. There is, as yet, little evidence to suggest that a direct causal relationship exists between playing violent video/computer games and becoming violent in real-life.

Although there is now a classification system for video/computer games, the real concern with this type of electronic entertainment is that this material can be easily accessed and downloaded through the internet. As the internet cannot be effectively regulated at present, this is extremely difficult if not impossible to avoid, and therefore causes a great deal of concern for parents.

There is some software which can be used to limit access to some parts of the internet but some parents may find this difficult, particularly as the children may be more multimedia information-technology literate than they are. As the pace of technological development increases, the potential for future games is that they will be extremely realistic, as virtual reality has already demonstrated. These games may give players the sensation of actually injuring or killing people. It remains to be seen whether this would lead to an increase or decrease in violent behaviour or homicide rates.

Media Influence on Teen Sexual Culture

Today, media has become a leading sex educator. Television exposes children to adult sexual behaviours in ways that portray these actions as normal and risk-free, sending the message that because these behaviours are frequent, 'everybody does it'. A study in Canada shows that sex between unmarried partners is shown 24 times more often than sex between spouses, while sexually transmitted infections and unwanted pregnancy are rarely mentioned. Teens rank the media as the leading source of information about sex, second only to school sex education programmes. Numerous studies document adolescents' susceptibility to the media's influence on their sexual attitudes, values and beliefs.

The physical, emotional, and social consequences of teen sexual activity include high rates of teen pregnancy, and sexually transmitted diseases including AIDS. Each year thousands of sexually active teenagers contract a sexually transmitted diseases (STD), and the younger a female is when she first has sex, the more likely it is that she will have "involuntary or forced" sex.

Many health professionals believe that mass media content depicting casual sex with no consequences has resulted in a host of negative behaviours among teens who may be persuaded that teen sexual activity is "both acceptable and wide spread". Child healthcare providers are being encouraged to assess patients' media use because of its potential association with unhealthy behaviours. Although parents and educators try to promote abstinence or condom use, teens are increasingly exposed to media sexual content that does not provide information about health risks and personal responsibility. Both negative and positive advertising messages have been shown to influence young people, according to a pediatric medical association that calls on the mass media to promote responsible sex, and healthy behaviours.

In addition to modelling unhealthy sexual behaviours, entertainment may negatively influence other aspects of teens' physical and psychological well-being. Research suggests that media portrayals of unrealistic body images negatively impact teens' self-esteem. Teens, especially young females, become discontent with their bodies and may develop unhealthy eating behaviours in an attempt to achieve media-ideal body types. Although family and social relationships also have an influence, teens learn about society and sexual relationships from visual media images portraying body types, clothing, and other cultural norms.

Sexual content in mass media has a "profound real-life effect" according to researchers who point to the co-evolution of media messages and sexual culture in society. Mass media can either reinforce norms or offer insights into alternative ways of thinking. Entertainment content depicting sexual norms, stereotypes, double-standards, and sexual roles may have a profound influence on teens' perceptions about sex, body image, and social norms.

Teens often seek social and sexual information from mass media sources rather than their parents or other adults. These teens may be attracted to programmes with sexual content. In a study of prime-time television shows popular among young viewers, sexual references accounted for as much as 50% of character interactions. These programmes typically depicted sex as a "recreational" pursuit rather than something pertaining to relationships or reproduction, and the sexual content reinforced gender stereotypes of men as aggressors, and women as sexual objects who are valued for their physical appearances.

Recent researches on children and media show that teens who watch sexual content on television are more likely to engage in sex; teens who watch a lot of television tend to have negative attitudes about being a virgin; and teens who see sexual content as being more real are more impacted by the sexual content. Age and gender may also influence how teens select media, according to one study that found older teens were more likely to tune in to sexual content, and that females were more likely to learn about sex and relationships from sexual content in the media.

Music Television (MTV) is an example of electronic media programming that barrages teens with sexual messages. From the beginning, MTV transformed music into television programming by using fast-paced visuals to grab the attention of a very specific youthful audience -a new generation that had been raised with television and had different ways of processing information. In order to make the aural and visual elements fit together, music video producers and directors, rather than entertainers and writers, control visual images that may have nothing to do with the musicians' or artists' original concepts. MTV became a programmer's dream of non-stop commercial television that changed the way people hear popular music and how they see the meanings that are embedded in the music content.

Teens report that they watch MTV because it helps them to understand the songs better, and to understand what the music is about. However, the content that the teens are tuning into is more than 75% sexual, with stereotypical portrayals of males and females. MTV uses sexual images of women through "short, sharp, shots of intense visual pleasure" to encourage viewers to watch closely and stay focused so that they do not miss anything.

Camera angles and other production techniques in MTV videos depict women in violent scenes and women giving ambiguous yes/no signals. Visual images in videos are sexual even when the lyrics are not, according to researchers who say that "sex sells, in music videos and elsewhere". Some media effects researchers believe MTV sexual content influences how viewers perceive sex and sexual behaviours in society. Music videos that depict gender stereotypes and recreational sex without consequences influence teens' identity formation by modelling the world through these images.

In controlled research studies it was found that males who were shown pornographic sex without violence had more negative attitudes toward rape than males who were shown violence without sex. These findings directly relate to teens, and others, who typically watch television and non-X-rated movies. The prevalence of violence—even without sex—in mass media entertainment, according to the researchers, can contribute to more sexually aggressive attitudes among viewers.

Despite myriad concerns over entertainment's influence on teens, some researchers argue that there is insufficient evidence of a causal relationship. They assert that studies demonstrating a correlation between sexual content in entertainment and teen sexual behaviours do not prove whether sexually active teens watch more sex or whether watching more sex encourages teens to be sexually active. These researchers take a broader perspective of media influence on teen sexual culture, going beyond content and effects, to see how individual characteristics of ethnicity, gender, developmental stage, and socio-economic class influence teens' media use and the incorporation of media ideas into teens' daily lives. These researchers situate media influence on teen sexuality in the context of family, friends, school and other social situations that provide information and influence teens' sexual perceptions. For example, early sexual experience is associated with lack of parental involvement, and beliefs that other teens are sexually active, while mitigating factors include parental involvement and teen participation in social activities that do not provide sexual opportunities. This interactive association is further influenced by individual predictive factors such as onset of physical maturity. According to these researchers, teens select and use media messages either to socially reproduce media images by following the status quo, or to socially resist media images by finding and following examples of alternative behaviour.

While many parents, educators, activists, and health professionals are working on solutions based on the perception that media sexual content influences teen audiences, researchers who view media influence in this complicated, contextualised perspective call for long-term media use studies to determine the actual influence of media on teen sexual culture. Academic researchers provide multiple perspectives, theories, and data that contribute to this media influence debate, sometimes facilitating progress, and sometimes the opposite.

Media and Food Culture

Because television takes time away from play and exercise activities, children who watch a lot of television are less physically fit and more likely to eat high fat and high energy snack foods. Television viewing makes a substantial contribution to obesity because prime time commercials promote unhealthy dietary practices.

The fat content of advertised products exceeds the current average diet and nutritional recommendations, and most food advertising is for high calorie foods such as fast foods, candy and pre-sweetened cereals. Commercials for healthy food make up only 4% of the food advertisements shown during children's viewing time. The number of hours of television viewing also corresponds with an increased relative risk of higher cholesterol levels in children.

Television can also contribute to eating disorders in teenage girls, who may emulate the thin role models seen on television. Eating meals while watching television should be discouraged because it may lead to less meaningful communication and, arguably, poorer eating habits.

Media's Influence on Alcoholism and Smoking Behaviour

Alcohol and cigarette companies are spending millions of dollars for their advertisement each year. Children and teenagers regularly see beer commercials carrying the message that 'real' men drink beer. Convincing data suggest that advertising increases beer consumption, and in countries such as Sweden, a ban on alcohol advertising has led to a decline in alcohol consumption.

Tobacco products are not advertised directly on television in many countries. However, passive promotion occurs when, for example, a soap opera star lights a cigarette in a 'macho' act, a Formula One race car has cigarette advertising on it or sporting events carry the names of tobacco companies. There is evidence that passive advertising, which glamorises smoking, has increased over the past few years.

Television is not the only way that children learn about tobacco and alcohol use; the concern is that the consequences of these behaviours are not accurately depicted on television. One-half of the G-rated animated feature films available on videocassette, as well as many music videos, show alcohol and tobacco use as normative behaviour without conveying the long term consequences of this use.

Influence of Advertising

Advertising can have positive effects on children's behaviour. For example, some alcohol manufacturers spend 10% of their budget on advertisements warning about the dangers of drinking and driving. In addition, although some health care professionals disagree about the health benefits of appropriate milk use, milk consumption has increased as a result of print and broadcast advertisements.

The developmental stage of a child plays a role in the effect of commercials. Young children do not understand the concept of a sales pitch. They tend to believe what they are told and may even assume that they are deprived if they do not have advertised products. Most preschool children do not understand the difference between a programme designed to entertain and a commercial designed to sell. A number of studies have documented that children under the age of eight years are developmentally unable to understand the difference between advertising and regular programming.

The average child sees more than 20,000 commercials each year. More than 60% of commercials promote sugared cereals, candy, fatty foods and toys. Cartoon programmes based on toy products are especially attractive. Advertisements targeting adolescents are profoundly influential, particularly on cigarette use. The question of whether children are more resilient to the influence of television is debated frequently. Most studies show that the more time children spend watching television, the more they are influenced by it. Earlier studies have shown that boys may be more susceptible than girls to television violence.

Cyber Media Technologies and Changing Youth Culture

We are living in a hyper-interconnected world, a global society of communicative interactions and exchanges that stimulates profound cultural transformations and realignments. The changing global media landscape is shaping the socialisation processes, values, and beliefs of young people, and influencing young people's decisions, in areas such as educational choice, employment, leisure, and life in general. New technologies offer a culture of information, pleasure and relative autonomy, all of which are of particular appeal to society's youth. This has implications not only for young people themselves but also for their relationships within the family and between generations.

The advent of globalisation has meant, for many young people, the sphere of experience has become global and local at once. Young people are often among the first to take advantage of their introduction. Subsequently, the challenge is to give culturally valid meaning to the use of new technologies.

New technologies have continued to make significant inroads into the inner workings of society, this holds true for youth as well. "As new technology becomes increasingly embedded in everyday niches, it is common for youth to interact with dozens of digital devices throughout a typical day, and many spend hour-upon-hour learning about and manipulating computer devices such as laptop computers, handheld computers, game consoles, cell phones, pagers, and audio players".

The concept of youth culture and new media technologies is a relatively new term, however the rate at which technology has moved into the lives of the young is historically unprecedented. Growth within this area began in August 1981 when IBM released the IBM PC (personal computer). From here the industry continued to grow with Apple in 1983 releasing 'Lisa' their then latest project. 'Lisa' contained many ground-breaking functions such as a mouse, drop down menus, icons, folders, windows and copy and paste abilities among other features.

Following the establishment of home PC's the 1980's also bought with it the introduction of video games; items which were soon to dominate the toy market. Video games were one of the first mediums to combine visuals and active participation for children and youths, they are a form interactive multimedia used as entertainment.

The next major development following this was the internet, which was established in the 1990's. It has been described as the combination of "the interactivity of video games, the information of computers, and the images of MTV" and thus the internet "created an entirely new means of social interaction".

In countries where there are high rates of boradband connectivity many of their youth are able to play online games together. The players are not physically located in the space, they are often involved in socialising together by connecting domestic spaces and time zones through online gaming communities. These activities can have a large impact on the broader youth culture.

Presently computers, the internet, mobile phones, television and VCR's are competing with one and other in the ever growing electronic arena. More recently as a result of considerable technological advances there has been the convergence of individual technologies. An example of this is the convergence of mobile phone technologies with that of the internet. Young people today can now communicate to other youths around the world as well as access information from the internet via their mobile phone.

In developed world, almost 80 per cent of people aged 14-24 access the internet at least once a month, more than a third said they cannot live without a mobile phone and 44 per cent believed computers and technology have given them more control over their lives. The networked generation's trend towards online activities and interactive media has also resulted in a dramatic decline in traditional activities such as newspaper readership. The digital revolution means the world is literally at your fingertips.

New media technologies are increasingly becoming more than just a simple way to pass the time. In fact, some academics suggest that technology is at the very cultural heart of the current generation of young people. "For the new culture, a trip into virtual reality is far more significant than remembering Proust,". Technology, such as the internet, mobile phones, PDA's and iPods to name a bare few, provide young people with unlimited access to opportunity. It has revolutionised the way we communicate and interact with each other. "Technology generates opportunities: new things to explain; new ways of expression; new media of communications; and creates new forms of destruction,".

Young people's access to new technologies at home, at school, in the work place, even at the local McDonald's restaurant, allows for constant connectivity to the networked world. Youth are plugged into every possible outlet, 100 per cent of the time, partly because they want to be and partly because they need to be in order to be competitive and play participatory role in today's world. As youth use the new technologies, they produce the substance of every day and making the meaning of their culture.

However, the technical and social convergence brought about as a result of developments in technology is already creating interaction problems, in particular in the younger users. Cyberbullying is a disturbing new trend among young people abusing the technology. The implication is that in an arena where the law is largely not applicable, socially agreed upon values and boundaries must be upheld and respected in order for us to make full use of the technology available.

New technologies have had an influencing impact within society, affecting the way in which people, largely the younger populace, interact, socialise and work. Though since the introduction of new technologies there has been many issues that have arisen by the public and the scholars as to the impact new technologies has over youths of society.

One of the key issues that have arisen from youth culture and new technologies is the growing dependency of such technologies as the internet among the youth of society. Arguments have arisen over the addiction and over reliance some youths have towards new technologies especially the internet and the various online communities it provides, particularly online chat and online gaming programmes. Among the issues that have been addressed are the adverse impacts of Cyberspace addiction, and the displacement between reality and virtual reality, and its impacts on real world social relationships, Health and communication skills. Further more issues have stirred over privacy issues of internet content as well as the unrestricted filtering of information that youths are able to gain access to.

New technologies have over time branched into the various spheres in society and have been implicated within the educational systems of many nations. The development of technologies and the innovation of communication tools have enhanced various learning aspects. Advancements in particular ICT's have improved the standards of vocational education and distance education for youth within various sections of the globe. "ICT crept through the side door into education with promises of time saving, efficiency and improvements in learning". Many see new technologies as a deconstruction of barriers between the physical spaces, as communication technologies have enabled users to communicate directly from various sections across the globe.

The increase in new technologies has made way for industrial convergence, leading to the deconstruction of local centres of powers, as industries move towards a global market place. This has created several central issues for youths, including the ability to adapt to the emerging technological advancements and the global market place, "information can now be obtained from several points and young people must know how to access this information if they are to enter the workplace and communicate effectively" The loss of national identity through youths due to a global presence is also another issue raised by academics.

Computer technologies have developed into more and more important tools in everyday niches. It is common today for children to interact with different types of digital devices throughout a day, additionally many of them spend hours and hours in learning about and operating computer devices such as laptop computers, handheld computers, game consoles and other digital devices.

Benefits and Risks of Internet

Parents may feel outsmarted or overwhelmed by their children's computer and internet abilities, or they may not appreciate that the 'new medium' is an essential component of the new literacy, something in which their children need to be fluent. These feelings of inadequacy or confusion should not prevent them from discovering the internet's benefits. The dangers inherent in this relatively uncontrolled 'wired' world are many and varied, but often hidden. These dangers must be unmasked and a wise parent will learn how to protect their children by immersing themselves in the medium and taking advice from the many resources aimed at protecting children while allowing them to reap the rich benefits in a safe environment.

The internet has a significant potential for providing children and youth with access to educational information, and can be compared with a huge home library. However, the lack of editorial standards limits the internet's credibility as a source of information. There are other concerns as well. The amount of time spent watching television and sitting in front of computers can affect a child's development. Excessive amounts of time at a computer can contribute to obesity, undeveloped social skills and a form of addictive behaviour. Although rare, some children with seizure disorders are more prone to attacks brought on by a flickering television or computer screen. No data suggest that television viewing causes weakness of the eyes. It may be different when a child is closely exposed to a computer screen for long periods, although there are no definitive references to support this.

Other concerns include pedophiles who use the internet to lure young people into relationships. There is also the potential for children to be exposed to pornographic material. Parents can use technology that blocks access to pornography and sex talk on the internet, but must be aware that this technology does not replace their supervision or guidance.

Table 1. Benefits and risks of internet use by children and youth

Benefits

- Near limitless information resource
- High degree of availability and affordability in most communities in the western world
- An asset for research or homework
- A communication tool for teachers and university professors with their students
- Rapid and inexpensive communication via e-mail and video linkage
- Access by the disabled to much that may otherwise be unavailable:
- Through technology that makes computer use possible
- By taking advantage of communication with peers that does not require that their disability be visible
- Source of entertainment

Risks

- The internet, by its interactive nature, is prone to use for excessive periods of time. 'internet addiction', also known as pathological
- Internet use or internet addiction disorder, is a known problem among adults and is no less a problem with children whose usage may be unlimited
- Instant messaging and e-mail may interfere with legitimate work (schoolwork and in the workplace)
- Excessive time spent on the internet may interfere with normal socialisation between child and peers, and with family
- Excessive use fosters inactivity and, potentially, obesity

Misinformation

- Lack of monitoring for appropriateness or accuracy of information
- Health risks posed from following incorrect information
- Fostering inappropriate ideas for children and teenagers such as the following:
- Encouraging inappropriate weight loss and diets.
- Generating a sense of need to acquire material goods
- False advertising or scams typically spread by e-mail
- Temptation to acquire credit cards to pay for online services

Adverse effects on values

- Pornography: Underage children may accidentally or by design access pornographic sites
- Predators have access to minors through unsupervised use of chat rooms and e-mail
- Loss of inhibitions normally experienced when face-to-face, promoting sexual exchanges and promiscuity
- Online gambling
- Potential for plagiarism in school work
- Promotion of hatred or violence through web sites targeting a specific group, such as women, homosexuals, and religious or ethnic groups
- Violence through video games, song lyrics and online bullying, access to hazardous materials or information on making weapons.

There is a wealth of information on coping with the vast resources of the web, both good and bad. Above all, parents should be encouraged to appreciate that there is potential for more good than bad, as long as one has the knowledge to tell the difference. Youth claim the internet as a defining part of their culture and an integral part of their daily lives. Teachers and parents alike must be armed and ready to face that challenge and ensure that they reap the potential benefits as safely as possible.

Importance of Regulating Youth's Exposure to Media

The public is beginning to recognise the potential risk that the portrayal of violence in the media poses, especially for children. The shift appears as psychologists, media industry professionals and other researchers argue about causality, while policy makers search for some evidence which will form the basis for sound policy decisions. The consideration then for policy formulators would be how much to reflect public opinion, the wishes, unscientific commonsense and moral views expressed by ordinary people in society.

In a recent Morgan poll in Australia, 85 per cent of respondents thought that the media concentrated too much on sensationalist reporting of sex and violence, while 80 per cent thought that the media did not care about people's feelings and rights to privacy. Forty-two per cent thought that television ought to be censored in some way.

Another study conducted by the Australian Broadcasting Tribunal (ABT), into TV violence in Australia, documents countless submissions received from the public and worried parents about television news coverage, and the effect that it might have on children. A number of submissions suggested that the news be broadcast at 9 pm or later, instead of the earlier prime-time slot that it currently occupies. The study also found that 60 per cent of adults thought there was too much violence on television, and 72 per cent thought that TV violence would have an effect on children.

There is some evidence to suggest that the level of violence in television programmes, films, newscasts and crime programmes may have led to an increase in fear that society is more dangerous than is actually the case. The viewer who identifies strongly with the victim can have increased fear about being attacked, which reinforces the view that society is dangerous for that person.

Acknowledging the potential impact that watching violent scenes on television or video has on individuals and society, yet noting that different people will respond differently to similar stimuli, the policy challenge is twofold: first, to enhance media violence awareness and responsibility amongst the public; and second, to avoid mechanisms which could trigger unacceptable behaviour in susceptible individuals.

This is best achieved by intersectional collaboration, balancing censorship and regulation which have limitations in the extent to which they can control what people see and do; by new technology which can empower individuals to control what information is received or accessed in their own homes; by public health and health promotion campaigns which inform people of the potential harmful effects; and by education campaigns to teach children and adults the discriminatory skills necessary for healthy use of the entertainment and information media.

Censorship is generally not a satisfactory option when it involves limiting access to information which a substantial proportion of the public claims it has a right to access. Censorship may also lead to the "forbidden fruit" phenomenon and the development of black markets.

Regulation of broadcasters has similar limitations but self-regulation in response to public demand and opinion, could go some way towards reducing the potential effects, if it can be practised in a truly effective manner. Classification and advisory systems are already informing viewers about the nature of programme content, and together with responsible scheduling, can help lessen the impact of on-screen violence. One positive action which broadcasters should consider is to ensure that there is a balance of "pro-social" programmes showing healthy cooperative behaviour, counteracting the harmful, antisocial messages of violent, aggressive images.

Most of the committees which have investigated this issue have recommended that public health education campaigns, directed particularly at parents, are necessary in order to inform people about the potential detrimental impact that television and video violence can have, especially on children. It is well known that parental influence can be a major factor in reducing the impact that TV/video violence will have on children.

Media literacy education for children in all primary and secondary schools is necessary in order to teach children how to critically evaluate the images which are presented to them on an everyday basis, in all forms of electronic entertainment, including video and computer games and the internet. This could take a similar format to traditional literature classes, or drug and sex education classes, as it is another part of modern life which can be potentially damaging if approached with a lack of relevant knowledge. Education such as this is already occurring in and the lesson plans are even available on the internet.

The new technologies, which are developing rapidly, are constantly stretching the limits of our imagination and the types of material which we can access. Technological advances such as the "v-chip" (violence chip) can be programmed to block out unwanted programmes from television broadcasts. Blocking and filtering software such as "Net Nanny" and "Surf Watch" can similarly be used to limit internet access. It remains to be determined whether such blocking mechanisms are used responsibly.

As with censorship, new technology relies on parental involvement. It requires parents to be aware of what their children are watching or gaining access to. Parents have to monitor and control their children's viewing habits. Studies show that parents play an important role in their children's social learning, but if a parent's views are not discussed explicitly with children, the medium may teach and influence by default.

10

Mass Media in a Multicultural Society

The media are capable of fulfilling various important functions such as providing information, serving as a platform for public discourse within the democratic state, and entertaining. It can also fulfil an important task in cultural matters. First, media contents must reflect and express the culture of the society in which the media operate, and when it comes to multi cultural societies they must reflect all cultures in the society. When the media convey contents which relate to minority culture, individual members of the minority group are exposed to their culture and it is passed on to them. Exposure to minorities' cultures is also enriching for the majority and increases awareness of other cultures which exist within the state.

Second, the media should encourage cultural creativity and originality and promote the production of cultural contents, thereby providing support for the development of the various cultures within the multi-cultural society. The point concerning the development of cultures relates to the fact that cultures should not be perceived as being static. A culture should not be regarded as a museum of particular traditions. Instead, a dynamic conception of culture is desirable, whereby culture is seen as changing and evolving, the outcome of a process of examination and debate amongst members of the cultural group. Such a conception of culture and culture-forming debate stems from the liberal outlook which values culture because of its capacity to facilitate individual autonomy.

Perceptions of the social reality are heavily influenced by the media. People's perceptions of minority groups, including cultural minorities, are influenced to a great extent by what they are exposed to in the media. Often, different social groups live in separate areas from one another. This physical separation prevents direct contact between individuals from the different groups and their conceptions of other groups are consequently informed largely by what they absorb via the media. It is therefore important that cultural minorities and their cultures will not be absent from the media and hence from public attention. It is also important that the media present cultural minorities in an appropriate manner, not by stereotypes and certainly not by means of negative stereotypes. The proper presentation of cultural minorities in the media is important for its effects both on the majority and the minority.

As to the effects on the minority, absence from the media creates within individual members of the minority group the feeling that there are not many others like them in society. Conversely, media representation of minorities has an empowering effect on the minorities. Also, negative media representation clearly weakens minorities. The frequency and manner in which minorities are presented in the media affects minorities' capacity to retain their identity as a separate cultural group and avoid assimilation into the majority.

Giles et al. introduced the concept of group vitality. Vitality is "that which makes a group likely to behave as a distinctive and collective entity within the inter-group context." "They suggest that the higher the vitality of a group the more it is likely to survive and thrive in an inter-group context. According to vitality theorists, the higher the vitality individuals believe their group has, the more likely they will be to invest energy in preserving the group's identity. Group members' appraisals of relative vitality are based on their experiences in a variety of contexts. The manner in which groups are presented and portrayed in the media is of great importance, since the media is the most common source of information. Abrams et al. argue that television "has the ability to tell us stories about people, places, and ideas that we would otherwise be unable to experience. In so doing, television instructs us on power, inequality, and fate. It is a medium that can empower as well as disempower."

Regarding the effects on the majority, minorities' absence from the media can create among individuals from the majority the impression that there are no minorities, that there are no cultures other than their own, and that there are no groups with different interests and conceptions. Such lack of awareness as to the existence of other sectors and cultures leads to the deprivation of minority groups, since these groups will be absent from public discourse and, as a result, their interests and conceptions will not be taken into account.

Media and Public Discourse

During the last two decades political theorists have been re-debating the meaning of democracy. Habermas suggested that it is important that there be a sphere in which to conduct public discourse. Such discourse is important because laws and policies gain increased legitimacy when they are the outcome of a discussion in which all those whom they are likely to affect were allowed to participate. When legislators and policy makers are attuned to public discourse and when their decisions are influenced by it, the democratic ideal of self-rule by the people is better realised. Habermas stressed that such discourse must relate to the good of the entire public, rather than personal or group interests, and that it must be conducted in rational terms.

In modern states, with their large populations, the venue for public discourse on issues of public concern is, of course, the media. Thus, the realisation of the ideal depicted by Habermas mandates that the media provide a stage for public discourse on current affairs and allow all those likely to be affected by the issue to participate in such discourse.

Habermas has been criticised by Nancy Fraser and by Iris Young. They argue that his approach contains no regard for the need to assure that the public discourse would enable all to participate. Habermas, they argue, ignores the possibility that certain groups will be excluded from the discourse. Their concern stems from the observation that in today's world certain groups, such as women, blacks, homosexuals and the handicapped, are not sufficiently included in the public discourse, if at all. They argue that the implementation of Habermas' assertion that one must speak in terms of the general good is a recipe for the advancement of the good of the elites. Young says that the ideal of impartiality in the public sphere conceals the fact that what is actually being advanced is the good of white men. It is further argued that Habermas' insistence that discourse must be conducted in rational terms works to the advantage of the groups who express themselves in such manner and to the disadvantage of groups who deploy emotive forms of expression.

The ideal endorsed by Fraser and Young is of public discourse in which all groups are given ample opportunity to participate, where there are no preconditions concerning the nature of the discourse and in which it is permissible to speak in terms of the good of the group and not necessarily that of the public in general. In addition, Fraser and Young argue that each group should to be able to conduct public discourse in which only group members participate. This is because the dominance of social elites may bias the discourse conducted in the public sphere common to all groups to the disadvantage of minority groups. Discourse within the group allows group members to speak freely and to jointly discuss their group identity and group interests. Once their views and demands have thus been formed it will be easier for the group members to present them in the public discourse common to all groups.

The arguments of Habermas, Fraser and Young concern what true Democracy demands in relation to groups in general. Implicit in these arguments, however, are also conclusions relating to the matter at hand — the treatment of cultural minorities. They speak of equality in discourse and its significance for groups' capacity to promote their own interests. For present purposes, cultural minorities' participation in public discourse will assist them in promoting their interest in preserving their culture and their continued existence as a distinct group. For example, they can influence decisions to allocate resources for the preservation of their culture by means of the funding of museums, theaters and cultural contents via the media. Second, they can exercise influence to obtain exemptions, adaptations, etc. which would assist them in maintaining their cultural identity.

Language of Media

The language in which the media operate has an important effect on groups' capacity to maintain their culture. Language is a central element of cultural identity, and the disappearance of the language which distinguishes a cultural group severely impairs its ability to maintain its cultural uniqueness. The language in which the media operate is therefore a matter of much importance in states consisting of cultural groups speaking different languages. For each group it would, of course, be ideal if the media operated in its language. In practice, however, it is impossible to manage the state's institutions, economic life and public discourse in more than one language.

Thus it would seem that cultural minorities whose language differs from that of the majority do not have a right that the state's institutions and economic life will be conducted in languages other than the language of the majority. Similarly, it would appear that they do not have a right that the media operate in other languages. However, when a minority with a different language is concentrated in a particular region of the state and constitutes a majority in that region, it is reasonable to accept that minority's demand that state institutions and the media operate in its language within the region.

With regards to cultural minorities who do not constitute a majority in a certain region, one should distinguish between native and immigrant minorities. Native minorities should have a right to preserve their language by various means, although they do not have a right for public life to be conducted in their language. For example, such native minorities have a right that their children will be taught at school in their own language.

In this context there seems to be a certain clash of interests. On the one hand, teaching in the minority's language threatens to undermine the state's interest to avoid a tower of Babylon effect and ensure that people know the language in which public institutions and the economy are conducted. On the other hand, minorities have a strong interest that their children learn in their language, since this contributes to the preservation of the language, which is a fundamental cultural element perceived as part of their identity. However, this clash is largely illusory.

One should not forget that minorities are usually strongly motivated to know the majority's language so as to become integrated into society and succeed economically. Not knowing the majority's language limits their prospects. Minorities can therefore be expected to know both languages. In Israel, for example, Arab citizens are schooled in Arabic and just about all can speak both Hebrew and Arabic. In order to secure the state's interest, it is possible to determine that native minority students will be required to learn the majority's language as a second tongue during the course of their schooling.

The media can be used in a similar manner so as to assist native minorities who do not constitute a majority in a given region to preserve their language. First, it is possible to add to the TV broadcasts of non-group media subtitles in the minorities' languages. This accommodation would not be very expensive. Second, group media operating in minority languages can contribute to the preservation of the languages, and hence the cultures, of minorities. As opposed to native minorities, immigrants do not have a right that the state undertakes measures to assist them in the preservation of their language. Emigrants choose to leave their country and settle in a state which is run by a different language. They are of course free to take initiative to preserve their language, but they cannot demand that the state assist them in these endeavours.

In light of what has been said thus far it emerges that if one wishes the media to enable cultural minorities to maintain their identity and culture the following conclusions should be observed:

— Group media are desirable, both because they allow the cultural minority to discuss its interests without the distorting effects produced by the domineering presence of elites. In addition, such media facilitate dialogue between group members thus enabling the cultural group to determine which parts of its culture to retain and which parts to change.

— Non-group media should present a reality in which cultural minorities are present and must avoid under-representation as well as stereotypical representation of such minorities.

— Non-group media should strive to establish conditions in which cultural minorities have an opportunity to present their views and demands through discourse in the public sphere common to all groups.

— Whether designated for specific groups or not, the media should allocate time for discussions of public issues, i.e. provide a platform on which public discourse can take place.

— Even non-group media must provide contents which reflect the cultures of minorities.

— Non-group media must be conducted in the majority's language; however, native minorities are entitled to subtitles in their language. Media operating in the minority's language will assist the minority in maintaining its language, and hence also its culture.

— Non-group media should provide a platform for group members to debate their culture, innovations and changes.

Group media are desirable. However one may wish to consider the extent to which such media are harmful and therefore problematic. The existence of separate media catering for different groups could have the practical consequence of creating a separation between different segments of society. With each group viewing only its own media, there would be no familiarity between groups. Such lack of inter-group contact could cause animosity between different groups, with people's views of other groups continuing to be informed by negative stereotypes. Moreover, unfamiliarity with other groups will lead to a lack of awareness anal misunderstanding of those groups' interests and of the need to act in consideration of them.

The argument against group media is therefore that they reinforce processes of fragmentation and impair the social cohesion necessary to maintain the state's stability. Furthermore, such media cause each group to be concerned with its own interests rather than to seek the common good. Sunstein relies on findings in social psychology which reveal that when discourse occurs in a homogeneous group it causes participants to adopt more extreme views than the views they held at the outset of the discourse. In light of this, there is a danger that discourse conducted in group-designated channels will produce more extreme views amongst group members.

Concerns regarding group channels can be significantly reduced when minorities are given adequate treatment in non-group-designated channels. When such conditions pertain, members of the minority group can be expected to watch not only the broadcasts of their group's channel but also those of channels which are not group-designated. Moreover, viewers who belong to the majority will be exposed to minorities, their needs and their cultures. Thus, the drawbacks of group media would be largely dispersed of if channels which are not group designated would treat cultural minorities and their culture befittingly.

The approach advocated here is that there ought to be group media of cultural minorities as well as equitable treatment of minorities and their cultures within non-group media. This approach can be justified as providing the best of both worlds. Each of the two options, that of group channels and that of including minority cultures in non-group-designated channels, has both advantages and disadvantages.

When both options are realised simultaneously the disadvantages of each are to some extent cancelled out. Thus concerns that group media might generate fragmentation, alienation and extremism are dispelled when non-group-designated channels present minorities befittingly. The disadvantage of presenting minorities and their culture in non-group media relates to concerns that the contents will not be sufficiently authentic. However, the existence of group channels should ensure that cultural minorities would be able to find enough authentic material.

Two problems that are likely to arise with regards to group media are:

1. The question of how the state ought to treat group media which reinforce inter-group hostility, racism and superciliousness;
2. How should the state respond to situations in which group media do not allow individuals from a certain group within the minority to participate in the discourse it conducts.

Media and Cultural Minorities

While realities certainly differ from one country to another, in recent years there have, nevertheless, been similar trends in the media systems of many Western states. First, the media have, for the most part, come under private ownership. Public media is either gradually disappearing or receives such limited funding that it is forced to adopt commercial practices in order to generate an income. Second, due to the scarcity of electronic frequencies in the past, these frequencies were perceived as a public resource which the government should distribute so as to safeguard the public interest in information, culture, democratic discourse, etc.

Consequently, it was thought that the electronic media ought to be subjected to an obligation to provide certain contents, such as a certain amount of airtime dedicated to news broadcasts, coverage of important public issues, presenting a range of opinions with regards to such issues, broadcasting qualitative programs for children, etc. This produced a legal dichotomy — while newspapers were not subjected to state intervention, substantial intervention was exercised upon the electronic media. The dichotomy was preserved even after the emergence of new cable and satellite technologies which rendered the scarcity of frequencies irrelevant.

However, in the United States and Western Europe there is currently a trend towards de-regulation of the media so that the non-intervention approach is being increasingly extended to electronic media. The supporters of this approach consider media content to be a product no different from other products and therefore they think that the free market is the mechanism that will best ensure that people get what they want Third, currently the media is not only privately owned. Ownership is increasingly held by giant corporations rather than families, parties, social organisations or local entities. As a result, the media is increasingly guided by considerations of profit and not by ideals of good journalism or concern for the public good.

In order to understand the operational logic guiding present day media it is important to note that very frequently a large part of the media's income comes not from readers or viewers but from advertisers. If at first it appears that what the media does is produce content for readers or viewers, a more thorough observation reveals that often the media is in fact selling audiences, or the means of access to them. The purchases of this product are advertisers. When considered in this light media content appears to be a means by which the media attracts the attention of readers or viewers to the advertiser's message.

Since the mass media can convey messages to many people simultaneously, advertisers are prepared to pay the media large sums of money for advertisements. The amount of money which the media can demand in return for broadcasting advertisements is, at first sight, a function of the amount of viewers who are expected to be exposed to the advertisement, i.e. a function of the rating of the program in which the advertisements are included.

Accordingly, the media can be expected to be guided by the concern to transmit content which is likely to attract as many viewers as possible. In many instances this is indeed the media's objective. Pursuing this objective has the following constraining effects on the nature of media content:

— Content should not be too challenging or serious because it would then deter viewers;

— Content must not annoy some of the viewers or bore them.

As a result of these constraints, there is a multiplicity of entertainment and sports programs as well as sensational news broadcasts reporting on crime. By contrast, serious content such as non-entertaining news, debates on disputed public issues and 'high' culture programs appear insufficiently. In addition, there is a tendency not to portray non-mainstream points of view or material which is of interest only to small segments of the population, and contents are consequently of limited diversity. However, the size of the viewing audience is not the only factor which advertisers consider. They are also interested in the identity of the audience. Not all audiences are of equal market value. Because of their limited purchasing power, poor viewers are not particularly important to advertisers. Accordingly, advertisers will tend not to fund a program with high ratings if most of the viewers of that program are poor. The result of the funding of the media by advertisements is therefore that programming which is of interest to poor groups will be under-produced, whilst programming of interest to groups with purchasing power will be subsidized by advertisers.

With regards to quality cultural contents the fact that they appear insufficiently in the media also stems from the relatively high production costs they entail. This leads broadcasters to favour programs that maintain ratings, but cost less to produce. There are therefore two reasons why the media does not provide enough cultural contents:

— Concern that part of the viewership will be lost because it is bored by such contents;

— Media operators' attempts to reduce expenses.

What has been said above has the following implications for the matter at hand: first, the media do not provide sufficient cultural contents, and this is true both with respect to minority cultures and the culture of the majority. However, the absence of sufficient cultural content in the media is particularly disturbing with respect to cultural minorities, who are in a vulnerable as regards their ability to preserve their identity from cultural assimilation. Second, the provision of minority culture is even more limited than that of majority culture, since it involves materials which are of interest only to a small part of the viewing population. Third, if a certain cultural minority is poor, contents of interest to it will not be broadcasted.

We have observed that as far as commercial media are concerned, media content is a means of production utilised to produce the product — audiences for advertisers. We have also observed that in order to maximise viewers and readers the media strive to provide contents which accord with popular taste.

To the extent that it is possible to identify correlations between the characteristics of audience segments and between the types of contents they prefer, it might be profitable to produce newspapers or channels whose contents are adapted to the tastes and interests of particular segments of the public, such as a particular racial or ethnic group. Such segment-specific media might be successful in raising funds from advertisers, particularly from advertisers whose products are desired by the group in question. The technological developments which introduced cable and satellite television some 15-20 years ago, have made it possible to create new television channels for specific audience segments, provided it is economically viable to do so.

There is evidence indicating that different racial and ethnic groups have different preferences with respect to media content. For example, whites and African-Americans have different preferences with respect to television content. Surveys asking viewers from these groups to rate their favourite programs revealed that only very few programs were preferred by viewers from both groups.

Indeed, there are some broadcasting networks which emphasise content that is of interest to African Americans. The most noticeable of these is United Paramount Network (UPN). Seven of the ten most viewed prime-time programs in African-American homes are aired by this network. African-Americas constitute more than 70% of the viewership of six of these seven programs. In addition, there are cable television stations which focus on this minority.

Commercial enterprises have such interest in African-American viewers because they form the largest minority segment of the U.S. television household population, comprising approximately 13%. The second largest segment is that of the Hispanic-Americans who comprise approximately 10% of the U.S. television household population. Interest in this segment also derives from the fact that its part in the general population has greatly increased and its birth rate is a few times greater than the U.S. average. In addition, this audience segment is concentrated in a few large urban centers, and therefore the cost of reaching it is relatively small. During the 2004-5 season 46% of Hispanic-American homes spoke only or mainly in Spanish More than 600 local television stations are affiliated with the Spanish-language network

It appears that presently only these two minorities interest commercial enterprisers enough to convince them to fund programs and television channels designated for them. Smaller minorities are insufficiently attractive for advertisers and it is therefore difficult to find television channels designated for Chinese-Americans or for native-Americans. If a general conclusion can be derived from this it is that only minorities that are sufficiently attractive for advertisers will have media that are designated for them.

The sums which are required for operating newspapers are relatively low in comparison to those required for operating television broadcasts. Minorities may therefore be less severely disadvantaged when it comes to their ability to maintain newspapers of their own.

One may well wonder to what extent commercial television channels catering for specific groups can be expected to fulfil the function of assisting in the preservation and development of culture and in creating a public sphere for deliberation and transmission of cultural content. It is reasonable to expect that contents on such channels, whose object is to attract the members of a particular group, will address matters of interest to the members of the relevant group. It is therefore reasonable to expect such channels to portray the group's culture.

Equally though, one can expect that the owners' commercial incentives would have an impact, so what was aforesaid with regards to non-group media is also true here: concern about deterring viewers will prevent the airing of programming perceived as being too serious. Thus, contents will tend to be entertainment orientated and content addressing 'high' culture and discourse within the group will be sparingly provided. It also seems that the more clearly a group's identity is formed and the more unique its culture the more interest its members will have in cultural contents, and it is possible that this will be reflected in the contents portrayed in the media designated for the group.

Role of Stereotypes

Due to commercial considerations, the media must take care to assure that minorities are not absent from their programs and that they are not portrayed in a negative stereotypical manner, since this might cause members of the group to choose other media, in which they are favourably portrayed. Because of this line of reasoning and as a result of minority groups' criticism of television networks whom they accused of under-representation and stereotypical representation, there have been some positive changes in this matter.

Early research concerning television in the United States revealed that most characters featured were white middle class males. Non-dominant groups such as ethnic minorities, women, poor people and the elderly suffered from under-representation and from stereotypical representation. Later research indicates that certain improvements have taken place. African-Americans not only do not suffer from under-representation, but are in fact over-represented in prime-time television. While they constitute approximately 12% of the population it has been found that they play 16% of the main and minor roles in prime-time television. However, the situation is less optimal with regards to other minorities. There is an under-representation of Hispanic-Americans, Asian-Americans and Native Americans.

Furthermore, research continues to indicate ethnic stereotyping, although there has been an improvement in media representation of minorities. For example, it has been found that Hispanic-Americans portrayed in prime-time television had the same income, intelligence and cleanliness levels as their white counterparts. This stands in stark contrast to past findings which revealed that Hispanics were portrayed as stupid and dirty. Similarly, it was found that 11% of African-Americans portrayed in prime-time programs had professional, white-collar positions, compared to 10% of Whites. However, with regards to television news reports of crime, African-Americans were found to be over-represented as perpetrators of crime. A similar finding was reached with regards to reality-based police shows on television. So that at least in some regards American television can still be said to portray these minorities in a negative stereotypical manner.

With regards to women, research reveals that male characters appear more frequently than female characters and that certain depictions of women in television remain stereotypical. Nevertheless, there has clearly been an advance in women's television representation during recent decades. They appear more frequently, and more women are presented outside the home and in lucrative positions.

The Manner of Intervening

In the above sections we observed the importance of culture for individuals — it is a context in which they can choose and realise their autonomy, it is crucial for individuals' identity and for their sense of worth and self-respect: In light of this, we noted the need to recognise a right to culture. Furthermore, we noted that a commitment to equality between individuals necessitates that this right be granted to different individuals in equal measure.

Cultural minorities are often in a disadvantaged position in the cultural marketplace, where their cultures are exposed to gradual erosion, and that the state should therefore take measures to assist them in preserving their cultures. The challenges facing these minorities are apparent in the context of the media — the cultural contents which they value are inadequately provided, they may be absent from the media or they or their culture may be stereotypically presented, they are insufficiently included in public discourse, etc. This implies that where the media is concerned —there is a lack of equality between cultural minorities and the majority.

What is the correct interpretation of equality in this context? A possible interpretation is that every citizen is entitled to the same amount of money with which to attempt to satisfy her media-related needs. Another interpretation is that equality requires that every person receive the media contents that are important to her. The first interpretation requires only equal opportunities for individuals, whereas the second requires equality of outcomes.

The media tend to produce materials that interest the majority and relate to its culture, and to under-produce materials designated to cultural minorities. Thus, making do with equality of opportunity between individuals will, in most instances, lead to inequality of outcome between the majority and cultural minorities. In order to attain equality of outcome, society would have to invest more resources in securing the interest of an individual belonging to a cultural minority in receiving the media content she values than it invests in securing such interest for an individual from the majority.

When deliberating which interpretation ought to be adopted, it is worth recalling that cultural media content promotes the ability of individuals to obtain things which are fundamental, such as autonomy, the formation of personal identity, a sense of worth and self esteem, and a sense of security. Kymlicka argues that membership in a vibrant cultural community ought to be considered a Rawlsian 'primary good'. If membership in a cultural community is indeed a primary good, then it should be distributed equally, just like all other Rawlsian primary goods. Similarly, Habermas states that a liberal approach must secure 'strict equal treatment, directed by the citizens themselves, of the life contexts that safeguard their identities' . Thus, it would appear that the inequality caused by the media — which provide minorities with too little of the cultural contents so pertinent to the realisation of their right to culture — merits corrective intervention.

Furthermore, when the workings of the media market lead to insufficient inclusion of cultural minorities in public discourse, citizens' capacity to influence decision making in the democratic state is rendered less equal. In Harper v. Virginia Board of Elections the Supreme Court of the U.S. struck down a poll tax, on the grounds that charging everyone the same amount burdened the poor more than the rich and thus violated equality. Harper seems to imply that a democracy should act to ensure that cultural minorities will be included in the public discourse taking place in the media. For if this were not the case then citizens would not have an equal capacity to influence decisions. In addition, when cultural minorities are not included in the public discourse in the media, then their freedom of expression is, of course, more restricted than that of the majority.

However, state intervention with the media on behalf of cultural minorities is a sensitive issue, since it has ramifications concerning the scope of the freedom of expression and the freedom of the press. It is common wisdom that when it comes to these freedoms state intervention ought to be constrained, so that the state will not abuse its power to silence opinions. Conversely, we have observed that when intervention is lacking crucial interests are impaired. The desirable solution to this dilemma contains a number of elements.

First, a distinction has been made between the printed press and between electronic media. While the First Amendment prohibition on infringing the freedom of the press has been strictly interpreted with regards to printed press, electronic media were perceived as public resource thus entitling the state to condition the issuing of licenses for the operation of such media on the fulfilment of certain requirements designed to safeguard public interest concerning the provision of information, discourse on public affairs, cultural and educational contents, etc.

The advantage of such a legal duality is that it allows for the best of both worlds. On the one hand, the capacity to intervene when it comes to electronic media allows the state to secure public interests that are inadequately served when the market is left to its own devices. On the other hand, concern that the state's authority to interfere with the media will be abused is considerably diminished when the printed press is granted unqualified freedom. The state should intervene on behalf of cultural minorities but that this should be done only in relation to electronic media. A 'hands off approach should be applied to the printed press.

Second, it is necessary to distinguish between two types of intervention that can be applied to electronic media:

— Suppression, i.e. prohibiting the transmission of 'bad' content, e.g. prohibiting stereotypical portrayal of cultural minorities or of other minorities.

— Measures designed to induce 'positive' contents in the media.

If is better to avoid suppression, because if it is used the government is likely to abuse the authority to exercise suppressive measures in order to suppress contents it views unfavourably. The damage which such measures entail is therefore likely to outweigh the advantage of preventing the transmission of 'bad' contents. Moreover, respect for people's autonomy mandates that the government allow them to hear speech even when this might cause them to adopt problematic views or harmful behaviour. By contrast, measures designed to cause the media to broadcast content which serves the public interest are worthy forms of intervention.

It is possible to conceive of three types of intervention to promote positive content:

1. *Conditioning the issue of a license* to operate electronic media on the satisfaction of certain requirements set out by the state concerning the transmission of content which serves the public interest.

2. *Structural regulation*. Creating structural changes in the media, designed to influence the media to broadcast contents which serve the public interest. This option refers to state's attempts to influence the media ownership structure, or the control structure with regards to decisions concerning media content. A principal example is the legislation common to many states which seeks to promote content diversity by prohibiting excessive concentration of ownership in the media.
3. *Subsides*. Granting subsidies or other financial incentives for the media to produce and broadcast content which serves the public interest.

It should be emphasised that the justification for these three forms of intervention must not be that they are required in order to prevent the broadcast of certain contents. However, it must be recognised that the use of such measures in order to promote certain contents comes at the expense of other contents that would have been broadcasted if not for the intervention. To give an extreme example, if the state required channels to broadcast certain contents 24 hours a day the result would be complete suppression of the freedom of the press and the freedom of expression. However, one senses that no such form of suppression occurs when the state requires that educational programs for children be broadcasted for 3 hours per-week.

It might be argued that state intervention to promote the broadcast of certain content is objectionable because it offends the principle of the freedom of the press. According to this approach the function of the press is to serve as a watchdog protecting the people of the democratic state from their government. The press' task is to expose corruption or incompetence amongst political leaders in order to deter them or to alert the public of the need to replace them in the next elections. The press must therefore be an entirely independent institution so that the government has no capacity to interfere with contents.

This approach, however, is too narrow, because the press has other roles within a democratic, multi-cultural State: to provide a forum for public discourse affecting politicians' decision making; to provide the public with information enabling it to form enlightened opinions on public issues; to allow minorities to participate in the public discourse so that they will have equal opportunity to influence decisions; to reflect the cultures of the different groups; to provide minority groups with a public sphere of their own in which to express themselves freely and develop their identity and culture, etc.

The critical question is whether it is possible to rely on the media market to provide us with the press which the people of a democratic multi-cultural state require. When it comes to cultural minorities the answer to this question is, in no small part, negative. In light of this, the worthy approach is one which allows the state to intervene so as to promote the appearance in the media of the contents necessary in a multi-cultural democracy.

The state ought to be permitted to create legislation which intervenes, mainly by means of subsidies and structural regulation, to improve the manner in which the media fulfil their roles in a multicultural democracy. Having said this, concern for infringement of the independence of the press should not be treated lightly. Because of this concern, suppression of content should not be permitted and that there should be sparse use of conditionality in the issue of licenses for media operators. Additionally, intervention in order to induce the media to disseminate certain content should not be permitted in relation to the printed press. Both the existence of group media catering specifically for cultural minorities and the representation and inclusion of cultural minorities in the non-group media are important.

Non-group Media and Cultural Minorities

The objectives with regard to non-group media are as follows: representation of cultural minorities in the media, non-stereotypical representation, transmission of content which addresses minority culture, providing a platform for public discourse in which cultural minorities are adequately represented. Possible means for obtaining these objectives include:

1. State grants provided by government bodies for the creation of art and cultural materials. Such subsidies reduce the cost of cultural contents thus increasing the chances that media operators will broadcast them. A state committed to multiculturalism will take care to assure that such grants are provided in a manner which does not disadvantage minority cultures.

2. Affirmative action in acceptance to schools of journalism, and scholarships for minority members wishing to study journalism. Subsidies for media employing journalists from cultural minority groups. The idea behind these suggested structural changes is that an increase in the amount of journalists who belong to cultural minorities will facilitate media content which is more sensitive to minorities' cultures and needs. Thus 'Unity: Journalists of Colour', a large and fast-growing professional association of journalists, is committed to: increasing the numbers of journalists of colour to better reflect the actual composition of the American population and improving the 'representation' of people of colour in the news.

   Nevertheless, one may well question to what extent journalists belonging to minority groups will manage to avoid being co-opted into the perspective typical of non-group media, whose first and foremost target audience is the majority. Moreover, there is good reason for concern that journalists from minority groups will have difficulty withstanding pressure from media owners guided by commercial considerations. These structural changes must therefore be part of a broader structural change that will afford editors and journalists more power vis-a-vis owners than they currently posses.

3. Financial incentives for broadcasters who:
   - broadcast content that deals with minority cultures;
   - provide proportional representation of minority characters and avoid stereotypical representation;
   - broadcast content which includes cultural minorities in public discourse.

   The state can determine that state authorities will only advertise on channels which meet these criteria, or that such channels will receive tax benefits or subsidies.

4. Subsidies might prove a problematic means, because they entail expenditure of funds derived from taxpayers and are thus often ill received. In the United States, for example, suggestions to spend more on educational television programs for children repeatedly encountered objection. Hence, instead of subsidizing media operators, it may be preferable to determine that the conditions for licensing such operators will include a requirement to broadcast a minimum weekly quota of content concerning cultural minorities and their cultures.

5. A number of measures may be undertaken to ensure that the media provide a platform for public discourse and adequately include cultural minorities in the public discourse. First, it is possible to implement a policy which was practiced and subsequently cancelled. Thus electronic media will be required to dedicate a reasonable amount of airtime to programs concerning important public issues and to encourage and grant an opportunity to present a variety of views on controversial issues. Second, certain organisations recognised as the representatives of cultural minorities may be given a right of access to the media, so that media operators will be obliged to broadcast their views on issues relating to the relevant minorities and their cultures. In some European states there is a right of access to the media for political parties, social organisations, religious associations, etc.

Another possible measure is to require the media to accept paid editorial advertisements from social groups.

Group media and Cultural Minorities

We have observed that the following objectives apply to media designated for cultural minorities: to encourage the formation of such media; to encourage the transmission of media content concerning the group's culture so that it will be handed down to the younger generation; to ensure that group designated media function as a platform for discourse within the group enabling the group to develop its identity and culture and to increase group members' awareness of their interests. When group media function as a platform for discourse within the minority group, it is important that the discourse will be open to all group members who wish to participate in it. I.e., it is important that there will not be a minority within the minority which is prevented from participation.

Minorities must not be prevented from establishing media of their own. In many states would-be electronic media operators are required to obtain a license. A commitment to multiculturalism implies that the state's authority to issue such licenses must not be used as a means to prevent the establishment of minority-designated media in an effort to assimilate cultural minorities. This may sound patently obvious, however Israeli authorities decided some years ago that radio broadcasts would be allocated on an area, rather than a group, basis. It appears that this decision was motivated by apprehensions concerning the contents which might be transmitted by the Arab minority's media. Since this decision prevented certain groups within Israel from obtaining the media services they required, it led to the formation of pirate radio stations

One can expect the media market to produce channels catering for large minorities that are sufficiently attractive for advertisers, but not channels for more marginal minority groups. In view of the aforementioned importance of group designated channels, the state ought to assist minorities in establishing media channels of their own.

It is possible to introduce structural changes which will increase the number of media channels owned by members of minority groups. In the United States, for example, the Federal Communications Committee (FCC), having concluded that minority viewpoints were inadequately represented in the media, implemented a policy of preferential treatment in favour of minorities in 1978, which was designed to enhance minority ownership and management of broadcast media. In accordance with this policy, when the FCC conducts a hearing in order to determine which of a number of competing entities will be granted a license to operate a broadcasting channel, one of the factors it must consider is minority ownership or management. Accordingly, if the candidates are equal in all of the other six factors that must be considered, then the candidate which is owned or managed by minorities is the one that must be selected. The U.S. Supreme Court upheld the constitutionality of this policy in the 1990 case of Metro Broadcasting, Inc. v. FCC. Two years later the United States Circuit Court of Appeals for the District of Columbia Circuit invalidated a similar FCC policy giving preference to women.

This policy is grounded on the assumption that the identity of the owner is a good proxy of the nature of the media content which will be broadcasted. The Justices who formed the majority in the Metro case thought that there was sufficient evidence to support this assumption, whereas the dissenting Justices rejected this conclusion and argued that it does not give sufficient account of the impact that commercial considerations have on the formation of media content.

In the economically competitive reality in which the media operate, the owners' identity is likely to have only a limited effect on the nature of media content. Because of commercial considerations media operators will tend to provide contents which the majority finds interesting and valuable, whilst neglecting minorities. However, commercial considerations will also lead to the creation of channels specially catering for groups who are of sufficient value for advertisers, and these channels will broadcast content of interest to minorities.

The nature of media content depends mainly on the owner's decision whether the channel is designated for the population in general or whether it will instead strive to target a specific minority market. Thus, for example, a white owner will broadcast contents of interest to blacks if her channel is designated for blacks, and a black owner will broadcast content which interests the white majority if her channel is designated for the population at large. This point is illustrated by the fact that in the year 1995 203 radio stations in the United States were owned by African-Americans, but these represented only a fraction of all radio stations whose target audience were African-Americans. Thus, Channels addressing African-Americans were, for the most part, owned by whites. Still, most of the 203 stations owned by African-Americans were designated for the African-American community, a fact which demonstrates that there is nevertheless some connection between the identity of the owner and the content.

It also seems that the FCC's policy cannot produce substantial change, since it applies only in the few instances in which there is nothing in the other six factors to separate between candidates. It is now commonly accepted that the implementation of this policy failed to produce the desired change. A substantial financial stumbling block to acquiring ownership in the media is the large sum of money which needs to be raised in order to operate a media channel. This poses a problem for cultural minorities who are in a weaker socio-economical position. This, is the principal reason why minorities own so little of the media in the United States. Here, it is worth noting that while it is very costly to operate a television channel, the cost of running a newspaper is relatively low. On the other hand, one must also recall that television is now the medium which draws most attention, whereas newspaper readership is constantly declining.

One may question to what extent a group channel will actually achieve the objectives outlined here for such channels. This question appears particularly pertinent when the commercial considerations guiding channel owners are given due account. Clearly, a group-designated channel will present content which corresponds to the tastes of group members far more than a non-group channel, which strives to appeal to the majority of viewers, would do. However, it is likely that the commercial considerations guiding owners will produce the same problems as would occur in non-group channels —a tendency to concentrate on entertainment and avoid serious content in pursuit of high ratings benefiting advertisers. It is therefore reasonable to expect that even on the channels of cultural groups there will not be sufficient discourse on public issues of concern to the group and qualitative cultural contents will be inadequately provided.

The mistake in policies such as that of the FCC lies in the assumption that the owner's identity as a member of a minority group will make a substantial difference. So long as the commercial considerations guiding the owners of group designated channels remain the same, the content problem will remain, even when owners are members of the group. A better solution is to be found in a structural change of media ownership that places more of the media under the ownership of non-profit orientated group associations. When profit is not the motivation, there is a greater chance that qualitative cultural content will be broadcasted and that a platform for group discourse will be provided. In order to achieve such structural change the state can provide tax exemptions or subsidies to non-profit associations which operate channels. Such associations could also be given preference in acquiring ownership.

It is also possible to provide financial incentives to group channels owned by commercial entities to induce them to broadcast 'positive' contents. However, as was already explained with regards to the similar suggestion made in relation to non-group channels, one cannot rely too heavily on subsides since taxpayers are prone to object to them. Consequently, the central method of promoting the formation of group channels providing the desired contents is to encourage ownership by non-profit associations.

Above, it was suggested that a right of access to non-group media should be granted to associations representing cultural groups. However, when it comes to group media it is important that non-group members will not be given a right of access. Affording non-members a right of access might hinder the group-designated media's capacity to fulfil its function as a forum for the group, reducing its capacity to serve as a source for the group's identity and cultural formation and as a place to confidently converse in terms other than those of the majority group.

Access to Group Media

It is desirable that there be group designated channels and that the state should act to promote the creation and operation of such channels. However, a cultural group may itself contain sub-groups with conflicting interests and outlooks and there is reason to fear that those in control of the group's media will deny access to certain factions within the group. For example, the Israeli ultra-orthodox community denies its female members access to the media.

How should the state respond when minority factions within a cultural minority group are denied access to the group's designated media? It may be argued that there is no room for state intervention in favour of these minority factions, because this would entail the imposition of liberal values on non-liberal cultures. Within Haredi circles, for example, it is held that a woman's dignity necessitates that she refrain from participating in the public sphere.

The argument here is that state intervention endangers the integrity of illiberal minority cultures and may lead to their erosion and eventual disappearance. According to this approach, when a group's culture is non-egalitarian and infringes an individual's rights that individual must decide whether to consent to the infringement or leave the group and, as long as members are free to leave the group, no problem arises. Such an approach is expressed in the Canadian Supreme Court's decision in Hofer v. Hofer, where the court accepted the Hutterite church's argument that the freedom of religion protects religious groups' right to live in accordance with their religious principles even when this entails an infringement of the rights of individual members of the group.

However, does the majority in a cultural group have the right to prevent minorities within the group from trying to change the group's cultural perceptions and practices? Culture should not be seen as a museum for unalterable traditions. It is unrealistic to perceive cultures as being static and homogeneous. Cultures are by nature dynamic, complex and multi-faceted. The present contents of a given culture are the outcome of past struggles between different elements within the cultural group, each of whom strived to mould the culture in accordance with its own tastes and interests.

Challenges from minorities within the cultural group are a regular fixture of cultural life. For this reason, the majority in a cultural group does not have a right to prevent minorities in the group from attempting to change the existing cultural understandings of the group. The right to culture of the individuals who form the majority of the group does not include a right to prevent other group members from trying to promote changes.

The importance of group-designated media is in the fact that they provide a space for group members to conduct discourse in which they jointly shape their culture. Depriving some members of the group of access to the group's public discourse thwarts those members' capacity to participate in the formation of the group's culture. It is reasonable to assume that such denial of access is motivated by a desire to secure the interests of the majority of group members at the expense of the minority.

Earlier, we observed why it is important that cultural minorities be included in the public discourse within non-group media. Without such inclusion, minorities are denied the opportunity to influence public discourse and the ensuing decision-making. As a result, they and their interests are likely to be ignored during the decision-making process. By analogy, when a group channel does not provide access to a segment of group members, these members' capacity to promote their beliefs and interests is impaired. Just as we protect the interests and culture of cultural minorities from disregard and erosion by the majority and its culture, so too should the minority within the cultural minority be protected.

So long as the majority within a cultural group can prevent access to the group's media it cannot legitimately contend to minority members that if they do not accept the existing culture they may leave the group. Conversely, when all elements within the group are included in discourse and given an opportunity to influence the formation of the group's culture, then it is more legitimate to tell those who remain in the minority to "either accept or leave". Having said that it is wrong for the majority to prevent minorities within the cultural group from having access to the group's media, one must not forget that this issue has bearings on the freedom of expression and the freedom of the press.

There is cause for concern that regulatory authority in this area will be abused to silence opinions. When it comes to regulation of media designated for cultural minorities this concern is even more pronounced. The regulator should not have the authority to deny a licence to group media operators-on account of their failure to provide access to minorities within the group. Regulation should instead focus on providing incentives to group media that allow access for minorities within the group and on denying incentives when such access is not provided.

11

Internet and Cyberculture

The Internet is more than just a massive digital library waiting to be harvested, processed, stored, and retrieved. It is an environment with high quality material on the virtual shelf alongside low quality and often illegal materials. The physical and the virtual worlds are often contrasted, with the virtual world and its cyberculture viewed as uniquely different from 'realworld culture'. While it is true there are characteristics of cyberculture that set it apart from more traditional measures of culture, the boundary between the two worlds has never been precise; the evolution of virtual social, information, and economic spaces has demonstrated this with remarkable clarity.

Digital technologies could influence mass public opinion in different ways, and this process can be understood using the four-fold schema illustrated in Figure 1. The participation hypothesis holds that the opportunities for information, networking, and communication via digital technologies might affect patterns of civic engagement, either reinforcing those citizens who are already most active through traditional channels, or mobilising new participants who are currently disengaged from the political process, for example by energising younger voters who pay little attention to newspapers and TV news, or by stimulating community activists.

Mobilization Thesis / Participation Thesis	Traditional Groups	New Groups
Traditional Values	*Reinforcement*	*Mobilization*
New Values	*Cultural Change*	*Transformation*

Figure 1. The potential impact of the Internet upon public opinion

Alternatively the cultural hypothesis holds that the rise of the Internet will influence the predominant values and attitudes within society, such as strengthening the values of individualism and cosmopolitanism, or heightening concerns about environmentalism or globalisation. If politics on the Internet affects both new groups and new values then this has the potential for the greatest transformation of public opinion, and this is what commentators frequently assume when searching for the impact of cyberdemocracy. But any of the four functions can be understood as important effects upon the body politic.

The cultural approach aims to understand the impact of the Internet by examining whether the predominant values, attitudes and beliefs found within the online world are distinctive from the broader political culture. Many have speculated that the free-wheeling, individualistic and somewhat irreverent spirit that appears to be characteristic of the World Wide Web, captured by many of the quirkier dot.com ads and webzines, may help shape a distinctive cyberculture, as well as altering ascribed social identities such as those of gender and race.

Moreover cyberculture is not one culture it is many-it is the world of the scholar, the average citizen, and the deviant. The Web is a cultural asset that we must manage and it is its intellectual capital that we must selectively harvest and pass to future generations. Before we begin to tackle the problem of digital preservation of the content of the Internet and in particular that of the Web we must tackle the problem of objectives.

Why do we wish to preserve Internet-based information and to what purposes will it be put in the future? The problem is how will we study cyberculture and its by-products, and what information will we need to capture from the Internet to document our culture effectively. The dynamic nature of the Internet makes it difficult to document and often what you capture is not there in the future, even a few days later, or as in the case of Internet news services it may be gone within a matter of minutes or hours. This fluidity makes the scientific study of the Internet difficult. The experiments necessary to study it can rarely be repeated and the information it contains and its shape is always changing. Herein lies a parallel between the study of the Internet and its cyberculture and the work of anthropologists documenting 'real-world cultures.' In considering the issue of preserving the cultural assets that exist in cyberspace we need to examine:

— the unique qualities of cyberculture and net-based e-materials (e.g. web pages, images, text);

— the problems of selecting (e.g. whether based on prioritised criteria or harvest everything), accessioning, and describing or cataloguing Internet derived e-materials (e.g. web pages);

— legal issues (e.g. copyright, privacy, data protection, national security, trademarks, patents);

— the growing complexity of collecting the web (e.g. caused by the increasing use of dynamic web pages served from underlying databases);

— the difficulties inherent in preserving and providing long-term access to and ensuring the usability of Internet-derived e-materials; and,

— the need for methods for studying these materials where they can be preserved.

What is different about cyberculture and Internet-based information resources from traditional materials? Essentially two kinds of information exist in the net-based environment:

1. information that we can classify as a by-product of 'real communities'; and,
2. information that can be classified as a by-product of virtual communities.

The by-products of real-world communities include electronic publications such as e-journals, e-books and web pages, and the electronic records of institutions and their transactions, such as databases, the emails exchanged by Heads of State and their ministers and other Heads of State, which private networks or the Internet have been used to distribute. The by-products of virtual communities also include emails and web pages, but they include the records of newsgroups, listservs, MUDs, and chatrooms. Some of these latter 'by-products', like conversations between two strangers in the street, go unrecorded (e.g. chatroom interactions).

The theory of post-materialism and post-modernisation associated with the work of Ronald Inglehart provides perhaps the most developed theoretical argument for value change. If this theory is applied to the online community it suggests that, given the typical age and educational profile of Internet users, we might expect to find a cyberculture that is particularly sympathetic towards post-materialist values of freedom of expression, and tolerance of diversity, social egalitarianism, secularism, internationalism, self-expression and participatory democracy.

Cyber-society is a place of choice par excellence so that where people go and what they do is likely to be strongly channelled by their prior preferences and interests: it can be expected that music lovers will gravitate towards Napster and its equivalent, financial analysts will download stock-market tickers, and political sites will primarily attract activists. In this sense, as many commentators have argued, in the short-term the experience of going online can be expected to reinforce rather than alter individual attitudes and values.

But could digital technologies still have a more diffuse and enduring impact upon the political culture? The central hypothesis examined here is that the online community is likely to display an ideological orientation that is particularly sympathetic towards postmaterialist values. If we establish that a distinctive cyberculture does predominate, then this could affect the political system in many different ways.

If the cyberculture reflects post-materialist values this could provide a sympathetic environment for alternative social movements and transnational advocacy networks sympathetic towards these values. Moreover in the longer-term, the impact of the Internet culture may be expected to shape the values and attitudes of the youngest generation of users, including children who are growing up surrounded by this technology in their homes and schools, contributing towards the process of value change in postindustrial societies, and the transmission of this culture globally could also be expected to accelerate the process of value change in traditional societies.

The Theory of Post-Materialism

The theory suggests that economic and technological development produces profound transformations in the social and economic system and that these, in turn, lead towards fundamental shifts in underlying social and political values. In the industrialised world, Inglehart suggests, the younger generation growing up in the post-war era experienced conditions of unprecedented affluence and security. Based on analysis of the World Values survey, Inglehart demonstrates that important generational differences in basic priorities are evident across industrialised societies, with the younger generation giving greater emphasis to quality of life issues such as concern for environmental protection rather than economic growth, sexual equality rather than traditional roles within the family, secular rather than religious values, and the importance of individual freedom, self-expression, internationalism and participatory democracy.

The counterculture new social movement of the 1960s and 1970s exemplifies the political expression of these values, along with the development of new parties. In contrast Inglehart shows that the older generation, whose formative youthful experiences occurred amidst the insecurities caused by the era of the great depression, as well as the two world wars, prioritises more traditional bread-and-butter issues such as basic economic growth, jobs, low inflation, and national security, the class politics of economic redistribution and the welfare state, as well as displaying more deferential attitudes towards bureaucratic and political authorities.

Rather than support for cosmopolitanism, surveys show that the older generation remains nationalistic in orientation. Postmaterialist theory suggests that the long-term process of value change through generational turnover and societal modernisation has produced more secular cultures in postindustrial societies, with declining support for traditional moral values associated with respect for hierarchical institutions including government, the army and the Church.

"In the Postmodern shift, values that played a key role in the emergence of industrial society—economic achievement motivation, economic growth, economic rationality—have faded in salience. At the societal level, there is a radical shift from the priorities of early industrialisation, and a growing tendency for emphasis on economic growth to become subordinate to concern for its impact on the environment. At the individual level, maximising economic gains is gradually fading from top priority: self-expression and the desire for meaningful work are becoming even more crucial for a growing segment of the population."

Although remaining controversial, the evidence for this thesis has been examined in more than sixty countries through successive waves of the Eurobarometer survey since the early 1970s, and the World Values Study since the early 1980s. Inglehart's work provides a plausible account of the flowering of alternative social movements in postwar America and Western Europe, as well as providing insights into some of the major contrasts between traditional and secular moralities found among rich and poor countries worldwide.

This theoretical framework poses many intriguing questions that could be applied to understand the ways in which the online community differs from the audience for the traditional mass media. A number of reasons would lead us to suspect that we should find a distinctive culture on the web, particularly one sympathetic towards post-materialist values. First, we know that the online community is disproportionately young, affluent and well educated, as well as being clustered in richer societies, and therefore the population fits the exact profile that should prove most sympathetic towards post-material values.

The generational gap among Internet population has been established in hundreds of surveys; the 1999 Eurobarometer, for example, shows that about one third of the under-25s use the Internet, ten times more than among the retired population. In contrast, in Europe the regular audience for television news and readers of the daily press are disproportionately found among older age groups, a wellestablished pattern that has been evident for decades, suggesting that this is largely a byproduct of life-style choices and more sedentary leisure patterns as people age.

Similar generational divisions in the use of the traditional and digital media are also well established in the United States. If the typical demographic profile of the online community is reflected in the contents and activities on the web, then an egalitarian and secular culture should flourish on the Web. The available survey research in America does provide some limited support for the claim that a distinctive culture can be found online, although the previous evidence remains scattered. Davis and Owen found that in the mid-1990s the online US population (defined as those who went online at least once every few weeks) tended to be slightly more liberal towards equal rights, less supportive of traditional lifestyles and families, more interested in government and public affairs, with stronger than average levels of political efficacy, although Internet users proved indistinguishable from the general public in terms of their partisan identification and trust in government.

Another study of the American online community in the mid-1990s by Hill and Hughes also reported that Internet political activists were consistently more liberal than the general public on issues such as censorship and homosexuality, as well as being slightly more anti-government in orientation than the rest of society, although the survey results were somewhat mixed and inconsistent. These studies are suggestive but these attitudes may reflect the early profile of the Internet population rather than the typical user today, as the pioneering and cooperative spirit of alternative politics characteristic of the chat-rooms, bulletin boards and MUDs found in the university community of online users in the early 1990s may have been overtaken by a more commercially-dominant corporate-interest shopping-mall web of E-Bay and Amazon.com today.

It also remains unclear how far it is possible to generalise more widely from the American cyberculture to other countries, and more systematic crossnational evidence is needed to support the claim of a distinctive cyberculture around the world. The limitations of the sources of existing survey data means that unfortunately it is not yet possible to compare the political attitudes of the Internet population across a wide range of developing societies and consolidating democracies, an issue that will have to await further research.

Systematic social surveys or official Census measures monitoring the Internet community have not yet become widely available in most poor countries, and the evidence that is available from market research is often based on unrepresentative samples, biased by respondent self-selection. Where the Internet population is limited, surveys representative of the general population usually provide too few users to allow analysis of the attitudes and behaviour of this group.

Political Culture on Internet

The evidence confirms that, there is a distinctive cyberculture found among the most enthusiastic members of the online community in the United States. American Internet enthusiasts are far more supportive of progressive new social movements, such as the gay rights movement, the pro-choice movement favouring reproductive rights, the women's movement, and the environmental movement. American Internet enthusiasts were also more likely to be self-described liberals. Internet enthusiasts also proved slightly less supportive of 'new right' causes like the National Rifle Association and the pro-Life abortion lobby.

Moreover this pattern is not simply a by-product of the younger and well-educated population found online, since the difference between groups remains significant in regression models even with the introduction of prior social controls. The defining feature is less whether someone is online per se than how they feel about digital technologies: those who see themselves most strongly as Internet enthusiasts are also most likely to sympathise with the alternative social movements. Yet at the same time on the economy there is a different pattern, since Internet enthusiasts are also more likely to be pro-business, as well as describing themselves as being personally well off.

They are also slightly more likely to be self-identified Republicans, although this difference fades in significance once social controls are introduced. Clearly rather than a single left-right dimension, Internet enthusiasts display a more complex set of identities, suggesting an orientation sympathetic towards a range of alternative movements on the social agenda but also a free-market perspective towards the economy.

Cultural Values on the Internet

Does other evidence, values and beliefs of the online population, confirm the existence of a distinctive cyberculture? To explore this in more detail the Pew survey included 4-point Likert-type scales where respondents were invited to express agreement or disagreement with a series of value statements. These items covered multiple cultural dimensions and principle components factor analysis was employed to identify the underlying dimensions. Sixteen items were eventually selected as falling into two distinct scales: support for traditional religious or secular moral values, such as the belief in God, the importance of prayer, and traditional attitudes towards marriage and the family; support for left-right economic values including attitudes towards business corporations, labour unions and the government's role in welfare.

Each of these proved highly inter-correlated dimensions in public opinion and they formed consistent value scales. Although lacking the classic Inglehart measure of support for post-materialist values, these represent some of the traditional ideological cleavages that have long divided public opinion and party politics in Western democracies, and a post-materialist orientation should be indicated in support for secular morality. The analysis compared the proportion agreeing with these statements among Internet users and non-users.

The first model shows the simple correlation between use of the Internet and support for these values. To help explain this pattern, the second model presents the results of the regression coefficients after introducing the standard demographic controls for age, sex, race, education and income. The findings confirm the existence of a distinctive cyberculture in America, even after controlling for their social characteristics. Moreover the results broadly reflect the pattern already observed concerning the identities of Internet enthusiasts, lending greater confidence to the conclusions.

Internet users are also more tolerant towards alternative lifestyles like homosexuality, less supportive of traditional ideas about marriage and the family, and less approving of censorship. Most importantly, these contrasts are not simply the byproduct of the younger age and higher education of the online population, since the difference in moral values remains significant across all items even after introducing demographic controls. This evidence supports the idea that there is an alternative cyberculture, and one that is more secular in orientation than non-virtual Americans.

Many of the core components underlying the theory of a post-materialist culture are reflected in these values of social tolerance and rationalism. At the same time this is not just a simple matter of a more liberal or 'new left' cyberculture across the board, since Internet users proved significantly more rightwing than non-users concerning the role of the welfare state and government regulation of business and the economy.

The online community displays a more free-market orientation towards these issues, for example twice as many non-users than Internet users agreed with the value statements that 'business corporations make too much profit' and 'it is the responsibility of government to take care of people who can't help themselves', a pattern broadly consistent with that already observed concerning economic identities.

The online community proves more laissez-faire towards the role of state, expressing lower support for government intervention to alleviate poverty. Interestingly, on the issue of the environment, in contrast to the expectations of the post-materialism researches, Internet users are less supportive of government regulation. Recent research evidences suggest that the cyberculture sympathises with the values of openness, freedom and tolerance, on both the social and economic agenda, perhaps reflecting the broader ethos of individualism and alternative lifestyles that seems to flourish online.

12

Cultural Institutions in Digital Age

In the late twentieth and early twenty first century, the development of a critical mass of media and their impact on society presented such complex institutional challenges, particularly in cultural institutions. The rise of social communication has been pre-empted by the mutual remediation of telephone, television and computer. In that light, community cocreation could be considered the convergence of memory, community, narrative and interaction. As audiences are given agency, their experiences with the interfaces of new media achieve new forms of interaction with the virtualised and dematerialised physical world.

Community cocreation provides audiences with an agency where their individual experiences can bring together the social communication which relays the connections between memory, community, narrative and interaction. New media were defined as those forms which combined computing, communications and content through the process of convergence. While some of the questions of new media revolved around opportunities in representation — hence the rise of visualisation — the contribution of new media would become their ability to produce new and otherwise unrealisable outcomes for social communication.

Shifts in entertainment and cultural tourism continue to impact upon the cultural sector. Global access to mass broadcast media; cyberspace and virtual reality technologies; video and interactive games, mobile technologies, the web, synchronous and asynchronous communication increasingly play significant roles in the consumption of cultural media. While these technologically based media continue to proliferate, 'sitespecific' experiences which resemble museums — for instance, interpretive centers and theme parks — present challenges to the ways in which the museum and its audience conceptualise their experiences. These media use immersion in technology in an abstracted way by using mediated realities as a mechanism for drawing audiences into their knowledge base.

Less information comes to us via sensory, bodily experience while far more arrives in mediated, representational forms. The relation between visual experience and cognition then becomes increasingly crucial as a means of understanding the places available to the subject in this heavily technologised and electronically mediated culture. The separation of the visual and the haptic can sometimes result in an overemphasis on the former: visually based toys, displays and environments appeared, as if to compensate for the diminished role played by the senses. Although vision becomes detached from the body, it is reattached to an illusory body, that being the figure at the centre of the immersive experience — the one who enjoys the view.

The challenge for the contemporary cultural institution is to ensure that cultural content is not abandoned and that the value and durability of context is presented as much as the artifact itself. One of the reasons that immersion can be so deceptive in the cultural environment is that it limits the possibility for communities to partner with institutions. While they are engaged in effective and immersive interaction, this replaces effective communication of values or intention on the part of the audience. Witcomb suggests that — increasingly — the museum's role is one of translator and mediator and proposes that it see itself as involved in the production of cultural identity.

The relationship between institution, e-community and audience can be illustrated by borrowing from Peirce's language of semiotics. The community becomes the 'sign', the institution is the 'object of representation' and the audience becomes the 'interpretant'. Cultural 'experience' is a relative construct of the triadic relationship between these entities, represented in figure 1.

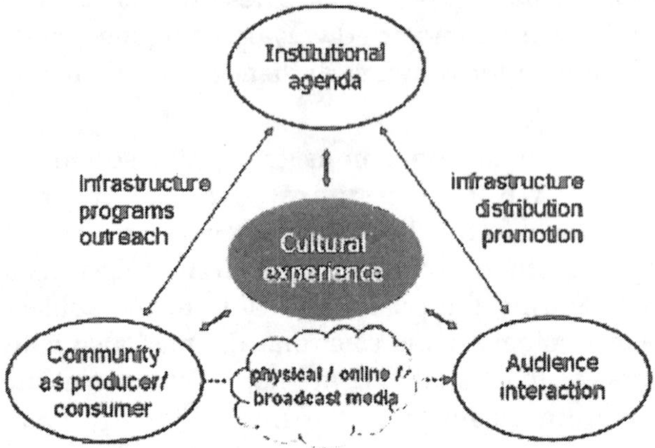

Figure 1: Semiotic representation of cultural experience as a construct of the triadic relationship between community, institution and audience.

By using the semiotic structure, we can reappraise the role of the community in cultural communication. The community can go beyond being a stakeholder of an institutional exhibition: new media and information literacy allows the community to both produce and consume its own original cultural content, in the form of narratives, wikis, blogs, vlogs or any other medium which is supported by the institution and connects to the audience. The institution ceases to be the sole custodian of cultural experience; instead it provides cocreative infrastructure for the community and distributes original cultural content to the audience via multiple platforms—physical, online and broadcast.

This semiotic model of the institution community audience relationship is a virtuous one to the extent that all parties benefit. The institution achieves community engagement as well as original cultural content to offer to a more distributed audience across multiple platforms. The community benefits from information literacy training by the institution, as well as a platform and audience for cocreative production. The audience has access to new and innovative cultural experiences co-created by the institution and community.

Knowledge Transmission in Digital Age

Throughout the modern age, cultural institutions created public spaces, buildings, collections and disciplines which presented mediated social narratives. These narratives were often conveyed as part of broader political, social and cultural discourses. Vested with such authority, cultural institutions came to dominate the transmission of cultural knowledge in the public sector.

This power came about in part due to relations between society and technology as they stood in the late eighteenth century. At that time, scientific culture (which was heralded as the discipline of the new age) relied on the discussion of visions in the populace through such mediums as public lectures, books and philosophical societies.

At the heart of these technological and social practices was the edict to transmit knowledge to the public. From the late nineteenth century onwards, museums used a variety of built and technological mediums to deliver this cultural knowledge. Museum exhibitions were used as a communicative form to transmit universal laws. Such presentations enforced the institutional position of authority over their audiences.

The didacticism of the early modernist museum resulted in the transmission of knowledge as patterns communicated by emerging scientific systems of representation such as evolution. Evolutionary display sought to present 'universal scientific truths' by recording and displaying species which, when collected and presented in a series, would tutor the masses in both the specific object, and the family (whether natural or cultural) from which it came. The evolutionary display method tended to reduce cultural artifacts to specimens of natural science.

This method of knowledge transmission was supported by technologies such as panoramas and dioramas etc. Perhaps one of the most visually arresting uses of technology at this time was Mr. Wyld's Great Model of the Globe 1851. This immersive structure included viewing galleries connected by staircases, surrounded by a ground level circular corridor housing Wyld's maps, models and plans. Wyld's Model of the Globe used a number of technologies to transmit knowledge about the world: whilst being analog, it shares a common theme with many of today's seemingly accessible cultural experiences — that of immersion in technology. Immersion in technology has been used extensively in "museumlike" organisations, particularly interpretative centers and theme parks.

Cultural Institutions in New Media Environment

Since the beginning of the modern cultural institution, community objects and stories have been collected and in the process, social relations have become cultural capital where "the politics and poetics of collecting are the politics and poetics of us all; and its messages are messages for us all". In that environment, the commodification of cultural content brought with it the possibility for institutions to control the valuechain of information.

Possibly the most significant difference between these early symbolic conquests and the convergent new media environment is that within the modern cultural institution, collecting cultural artifacts suggested a form of "cultural violence" This came about primarily due to the ways in which community information was acquired. The 'real' artifacts enabled abstract ideas to be sustained, positioning people, nations and territories and constructing boundaries to social and cultural processes. These conquests were drawn together to map out the limits of the known.

In the new media environment, communities, individuals and—to a growing extent—broadcasters and institutions are working together to present cultural information. When communities and individuals have the means of production at their fingertips -such as wikis and blogs—their knowledge and access to information becomes a powerful medium through which others can consume cultural knowledge.

Beginning with the advent of broadcasting and increasing with the internet, cultural institutions have faced critical challenges which include drawing audiences into their physical spaces and providing cultural interactive experiences which are both novel and entertaining. Cultural institutions not only hold major collections, they often have state of the art resources which can be utilised to deliver their messages to a broad audience.

For instance, the Singapore National Library has just reopened on a new site with a mandate to become the premier site for the research needs of Singapore and SouthEast Asia . The National Museum of Australia has one of the few fully functional broadcast studios in any museum worldwide and is currently utilising these resources to stage a "Talkback Classroom International United Nations forum" which provides students from Australia and the USA with a forum to discuss issues in a broadcast recorded at the UN Headquarters in New York. China and the Association of the Southeast Asian Nations (ASEAN) Library have recently signed with a regional bloc to promote awareness, understanding and appreciation of each others' arts and culture through artistic collaboration and exchange, joint research and study, exchange of information and people-to-people exchange and interaction. The bloc will support the conservation, protection and promotion of tangible and intangible cultural heritage through programs in cultural heritage management, protection of intellectual property rights and networking and exchange among cultural heritage agencies and organisations.

Each of these examples points to a growing phenomenon whereby cultural institutions have adopted the internet as a distribution medium for their collections and public programs. Few have come to terms with the profound shift in contemporary society from 'passive' media consumption to audience interaction with content: that is, few have established distribution models which not only provide access but display and allow interaction with the products of community cocreated content. The value of this content can be considered within the historical framework of cultural institutions and the ways in which they present and represent collective memory.

Cultural Broadcasting

In the late nineteenth century, memory, consciousness and time were considered to contribute to the development of a collective memory where reality was reinterpreted through a 'collection of things'. This representation became problematic when individuals lost the ability to discern that representation was derived of recollection and perception Bergson suggested that as we become conscious of an act we detach ourselves from the present and replace ourselves in the past, metaphorically and more specifically within particular sites and spaces.

This transportation from actual to "virtual" time and place enabled communities to create and recreate experiences either personal of collective. In the 1920s and 1930s, Halbwachs claimed that collective memory was rooted in concrete social experiences and associated with temporal and spatial frameworks, therefore it could be constructed by recollecting places and situating ideas or images in patterns of thought belonging to specific social groups.

In the Victorian period, cultural institutions such as museums and libraries began to emerge as instruments of the ruling classes with a mission to educate. The communication strategies which they adopted were used to tell the story of the institution. In the contemporary media environment, instead of communities being defined by geographic or joint interest, the internet enables "communities of practice" which engage in a joint enterprise via mutual engagement.

Agre proposes that the interactions which emerge in this mediated environment engage in some degree of collective cognition where individuals learn from others' experiences, set common strategies, develop a shared vocabulary and evolve a distinctive and shared way of thinking. The local museum, library or gallery is an example of this collective cognition at work. As the communities find ways of displaying their own stories, they often draw on nostalgic memory to create 'a past' which will generate a touristic impulse.

This collective nostalgia renders the present familiar and validates and affirms present attitudes and actions in respect to past ones. Cultural institutions have become a meeting ground for both official versions of the past and the individual or collective accounts of reflective personal experiences. Just as Wallace suggests that visitors bring a well-stocked memory of film narratives into the cultural institution, they also bring their life histories and memories.

Cultural institutions in Asia, Australia and the UK are often state-sponsored and act as custodians of cultural information. The USA operates under a different economic model where only the largest organisations are state-sponsored whilst the bulk operates in the not-for profit sector. This key economic difference affects the ways in which museums work with their communities and see their role in relation to their donors.

The cultural institution can now evolve from meeting ground to media distributor, using the life histories and personal experiences of visitors as a source of unique cultural content, thereby enabling community cocreation and providing information literacy. In contemporary media environments, cultural institutions can use new media to broaden audiences, create cultural interactive experiences and achieve broader distribution of content.

The term 'new media' includes not simply interactive digital artifacts, but also new ways of consuming and producing such artifacts. Standardised internet technologies allow non professional content creators to display and distribute new media artifacts by offering much lower 'barriers of entry' and greater immediacy than the traditional mass visual medium of television.

This means that nonprofessional community-based creators can produce distinctive cultural content for broader audiences. Wood illustrates key points of new media in relation to broadcasting:

— New media forms should be designed around the way people live and interact with each other, rather than around the technology.

— New media provides opportunities to use the archives of media material which illustrate our past lives and cultures.

— Audiences need reliable information from trustworthy sources; therefore the context from which material is distributed is important.

— The context of audiences must be taken into account when preparing content.

Wood's summary points to the convergence of a number of resources and disciplines to explore both the narratives and experiences which result from audience engagement and interaction with content. It suggests that to create the environment for audience engagement, innovative methods will need to be developed to enable the cocreation of meaning and the generation of new content for wider audiences.

Convergent information and communication technology (ICT) has promised the delivery of multi channel, multi-platform content where choice is in the hands of the consumer. This can described as shifting consumption patterns and empowering audiences by enabling access to content on their own terms—i.e. where, when and how they choose. New media has not delivered the demise of traditional media but has propelled many media companies into powerful conglomerates with stakes all along the media value chain.

Convergent ICT is being used by broadcasters for the repurposing of content across multiple platforms and to facilitate greater cross-media collaboration. In terms of outcomes, the multi-channel, multi-platform challenge brings a commercial focus to the possibilities of repurposing content for online distribution as well as describing a technology-oriented initiative to rationalise TV broadcast formats as part of digital TV developments. This initiative is consistent with the concerns of cultural institutions, particularly in the implementation of cross-platform cultural knowledge where the development of media and their impact on society have challenged both commercial and cultural organisations.

By reconfiguring relations between systems and audiences through institutions and cultural networks, new models of production, distribution and learning can be developed. Media distributors have identified a need to move beyond information archiving and display and into content generation and more porous community interface. Examining the possibilities and limitations for digital cocreation within these established, culturally rich environments will ultimately inform a model for effective lowcost digital content that will develop out of consumer led creativity across public, community and commercial sites.

The coevolution of broadcasted, customised and community-created media can be described as a paradigm within which active individuals and communities use computer-mediated networking to tell and exchange their stories and to enhance the interaction among member and their peers in other groups. This form of community cocreation can both develop new paths for community knowledge and simultaneously enhance community life. Institutions which represent distributed cultural constituencies may have to work harder for audience share, and digital community cocreation programs can help the institution to the extent that such programs not only empower ground-up digital cultural creation, they also create new community audiences.

The balance of distribution between professionally produced and community cocreated content is explored by J.R Marinho who suggests that the differing concerns of each bring its own problematic. Content distribution channels are services and tools (commodities) while social communication is the content (cultural asset) which travels along these channels and is of strategic value to both parties. When communities are engaged in the process of creating content, there is less of an opportunity for telecommunications companies to control both distribution and social communication.

Marinho's concerns stem from a belief that the convergence of media and telecommunications could create the control of the entire value chain including production of content, packaging and programming and distribution. He contends that in the process of continued and unregulated cultural convergence, cultural assets are increasingly dominated by communication companies who are often restricted in their capacity to distribute their products.

Digital cultural communication seeks to circumvent this potential bottleneck in the cultural distribution process by offering cultural institutions as alternate channels. For example: Australian Museums OnLine links collections across the country while the ASEAN network provides a useful example of how community knowledge can be collected and distributed across Asia. These examples provide content management systems where audiences can access cultural information from reputable sources. Institutions can promote their new partnerships by introducing communities to tools and methods for digital cocreation. The next step in the cocreation process is to ensure that community created content can be "broadcast" across the multiple platforms which the convergent new media environment allows.

Issues of Ownership

Issues of ownership become increasing complex when audiences partner with cultural institutions, not least because of existing restrictions on appropriate usage of content, but because institutions need to develop protocols which take into account the creative ownership of digital artifacts. Copyright laws are difficult to comprehend as categories for ownership can span multiple users. In the not-for-profit sector, this is particularly complex because museums often have different policies regarding the sale of work and leasing to commercial entities.

Copyright serves the purpose of encouraging creativity and innovation by those who create by helping to ensure that they benefit financially from their ideas for a finite period before those ideas' utility is further exploited by their joining the unprotected 'commons'. As innovation is often a product of inspiration from existing creative works, copyright protections which are too rigid can limit creativity.

One way of approaching this is to consider restricted peer-to-peer networks as alternatives to unrestricted file-sharing. By approaching copyright in this way, the institution again provides a leadership role by encouraging their community to connect with the institutions and create content while providing mutually beneficial conditions of fair use for content. By encouraging innovation and allowing access by a wide audience, cultural institutions can again provide the infrastructure to enable the development of e-communities.

A more generalised approach to intellectual property issues has been termed the Creative Commons. Creative Commons enables copyright holders to grant some of their rights to the public while retaining others through a variety of licensing and contract schemes including dedication to the public domain or open content licensing terms (http://creativecommons.org). An excellent example of the way in which Creative Commons can be achieved within cultural institutions can be found in the development of the British Broadcasting Corporation's Creative Archive (Dean 2004). While many issues have arisen in the development of the Archive, there are some consistent problems which will be addressed throughout the development of this approach. This includes broadening the cultural debate to ensure that intellectual property decisions have a cultural dimension. Cultural identity and investment in culture are increasingly part of the creative workforce and the new economy. How we provide access to this content in democratic ways and ensure that audiences can both consume and produce creative works remain at the heart of intellectual property issues in this sector.

Information Literacy in Australia

The Digital Cultural Communication method has successfully informed the authors' recent design consultancies for a number of multi-platform cultural projects in Australia, including an end-to-end community co-creation and cultural e-community program for the State Library of Queensland (Watkins and Russo 2005a), and the online expansion of a physical exhibition by the Museum of Brisbane and Brisbane Institute to connect with e-communities (Watkins and Russo 2005b).

The State Library of Queensland's Queensland Stories initiative is an end-to-end program designed to enable community members to partner with a cultural institution in the preservation and represen-tation of cultural identity. Queensland Stories offers an opportunity for active, participating and creative individuals and communities to explore shared history through narrative, photo-graphy, audio and video. This growth of active content producing communities has required new and different tools to facilitate interaction among communities. The State Library of Queensland has provided a mobile multimedia "laboratory" which is made available for community narrative projects in regional areas of Australia. This information literacy training has powerful cultural outcomes: the community is empowered to create its own "digital stories", short multimedia narratives constructed from personal photographs and memories.

The Queensland Stories website provides a streaming media display platform for the multimedia narratives produced within the information literacies workshops. The design approach has considered the current library systems which require new audience literacies to enable consumption and production of content. By defining the characteristics of particular existing systems, information literacy architecture demonstrates how communities and institutions can describe the value of particular ICT products in the development of audience-focused outcomes. The information literacy architecture (table 1) illustrates how new media technologies can be used to enable cost-effective content creation and distribution.

Table 1: An information literacy architecture

Architecture characteristics	ICT product/service	Enabler
Access	Telco infrastructure	Cost-effective distribution
Publication	Podcasting	Community protocols, IP/copyright, censorship, privacy
Evolution	Blogs	Users contribute content, systems encourage evolution
Interaction	Wikis	Capture, display and distribution of content
Collaboration	CSCW	Community participation and audience feedback
Platforms	CMS	Common technology and protocols

Table 1 demonstrates some of the relationships between the types of programs or themes which the institution can proactively develop (architecture characteristics) and matches these to the types of ICT products and services which enable information literacy. The enablers illustrate the types of outcomes which can be achieved by linking institutional themes with ICT products towards common creative ends. It also seeks to define the types of information literacy which would be required to support these outcomes.

Many challenges remain within the Queensland Stories project, primarily a scarcity of workshop facilitators with the necessary information literacy to transfer skills in narrative and new media to the community. Furthermore, the limited telecommunications infrastructure within the vast yet sparsely populated state of Queensland limits many regional and remote communities to low-band dial-up internet access which prevents a satisfactory online audience experience of the digital story collection. These issues remain the focus of ongoing research and consultancy by the authors.

Blogging in South Korea

The commercial environment continues to spawn a myriad of sprawling e-communities. A particularly successful example is South Korea's "Cyworld", a personal diary-style website which features commentary, pictures and links to other sites (www.cyworld.com). Cyworld is an advanced blogging site which interconnects personal homepages, encouraging users to form a network with friends or colleagues. This network is now an e-society with 13 million residents and visitors - more than a quarter of South Korea's population. There is certainly nothing new about personal home page product – for example, the Yahoo! search engine has been offering portal personalization for years.

But Cyworld could be of interest to the cultural institution wishing to extend the quality of its online experience to audiences because the concept combines interactivity, personal creativity and audience reach. In this regard, Cyworld provides a number of lessons from the commercial sector which may be of use to the cultural ecommunity.

Firstly, the site targets a specific audience segment—the information literate twenty-something market. Cyworld has been enormously successful at drawing together a huge proportion of the South Korean youth market towards the creation, support and maintenance of a viable and highly creative ecommunity.

Secondly, Cyworld provides an appropriate technical infrastructure for the audience segment. Its developers have constructed an online space where audiences can create their own content, browse other user's blogs and link to relevant external pages. Cyworld is extending its services into Taiwan, Hong Kong and Singapore and in order to accomplish greater interaction and wider distribution, the developers are currently assessing how local relevance can be realised in each country. By providing an infrastructure specific to the needs of a particular community, Cyworld will graft diverse cultural identities to their sites to produce a localised product for each new country of distribution. This strategic approach demonstrates the proactive role that an organisation can take in the development and representation of cultural identity. Importantly, it demonstrates how cultural institutions could reconsider their resources to support diverse cultural e-communities.

The third lesson from Cyworld is the use of interaction design which encourages the ecommunity to cocreate personal content. Cyworld features its own currency, slang and particular social pressures. Cyworld community members inhabit an address or a "mini-hompy" (or mini homepage). The mini-hompy is represented by an empty virtual room which the inhabitant then "decorates" to construct a distinctive online personality. Unlike e-communities which use blogs to further political, social or historic causes, Cyworld audiences use this site to publish their own creative efforts and to explore the possibilities of community cocreation. In so doing, Cyworld as a whole creates new media artifacts and new types of interaction which in turn strengthen the organisational impetus to support and maintain the community.

Cultural Web Portals

While blogs and wikis provide up-to-date nonprofessional media for individuals to create content, Content Management Systems (CMS) offer opportunities for decentralised and community-oriented modes of publishing whereby media organisations and cultural institutions evolve from gatekeepers to mediators between communities. Cultural institutions can facilitate this exchange by supporting the interchange of content and ideas while providing new tools for digital cultural communication.

Cultural institutions which position themselves as community providers are bound to benefit as they extend their audiences and opportunities for advertising and commerce. By providing infrastructure which includes training, institutions are in an enviable position; they own the content and manage the method of distribution. If they are able to creatively combine community creativity with customised services in innovative ways, they can extend their programs to meet the needs of individuals and small communities.

The relationship between institution, community and audience which underpins digital cultural communication can be seen in a number of examples from smaller cultural institutions around the world. For example, the Ban Jalae Hill Life Tribe and Culture Center in Thailand provides a rare case study of a privately funded, community-run multi-platform cultural portal comprising:

— A solar-powered physical center.
— An online museum.
— An end-to-end community cocreation program. A community TV initiative.

The Mirror Art Group which runs the Cultural Center is made up almost entirely from community members. It operates on the tenet that technology can help preserve and document a vanishing way of life, especially in communities which do not rely on written language. Most hill tribes have only developed a written script within recent generations and literacy remains extremely low. The Mirror Art Group captures cultural knowledge throughout the Northern Thai tribes in a number of ways: digital storytelling, folk music recordings, community interviews and documentation of traditional festivals.

For example, working with village elders, the Mirror Art Group has begun creating a video record of genealogical lines in surrounding Akha villages. By recording the elders reciting their genealogy and producing video compact discs, the Mirror Art Group are both documenting cultural heritage and attempting to revitalise traditional customs by broadcasting cultural content to the world, thus encouraging Akha youth to see themselves and their identities as valued within modern society. The cultural portal incorporates traditional music, videos, transcripts of genealogies as well as still images, stories and general interest for the mutual benefit of community members and broader audiences. Furthermore, the Center features a community TV initiative which keeps abreast of relevant local issues and provides positive media images to the hill tribe youth community, as well as addressing a lack of knowledge in the wider community about the hill tribes of modern Thailand.

The cultural portal www.hilltribe.org is supported by the institutional funding but is created by the community and maintains a strong link to the dispersed communities throughout the region. The Center also provides digital literacy outreach programs to community members with a diverse range of media products which are displayed at either the physical site, the online museum of the community TV broadcast. This represents an innovative approach to cultural representation in both sitespecific (Center) and distributed (website) cultural content. In many ways, the Center's approach is similar to Cyworld:

— Infrastructure is provided to develop and maintain the community.

— Community cocreated content is at the heart of the interaction.

— A specific audience is targeted.

Unlike a number of institutionally supported cultural portals, the online museum does not describe itself as an arts portal and is therefore not restricted to displaying higher art forms. Neither does it emulate other indigenous cultural portals, which focus on institutional or governance matters. Therefore the Center presents itself as a viable and interesting case study for the ways in which cultural institutions can partner with communities and audiences to create meaningful cultural interactive experiences while broadening the distribution of cultural knowledge and utilising media technologies to the mutual benefit of all partners.

13

Media Literacy and Modern Culture

The term 'media literacy' refers to the knowledge, skills and competencies that are required in order to use and interpret media. Yet defining media literacy is far from straightforward. Yet for some, the analogy with written language—and hence the term 'media literacy'—is simply too imprecise, if not positively misleading. Some scholars of literacy, for example, caution against this rather loose and metaphorical use of the term, arguing that it blurs necessary distinctions between written language and other modes of communication.

Meanwhile, some media analysts reject the idea that our understanding of visual communication is based on a mastery of cultural conventions like those that apply in language. On the contrary, they suggest that we understand visual and audio-visual representations using the same skills that we use to interpret the everyday world around us. Ultimately, the value of the literacy analogy depends on the level at which we decide to locate it. As Paul Messaris suggests, the basic conventions of 'film language' do have to be learned; but they are learned comparatively easily and quickly, not least because they mimic familiar processes of perception and comprehension. Interpreting a zoom or a dissolve, for example, is relatively straightforward if one takes account of contextual information.

In fact, attempts to develop a theory of 'film language' have been fraught with difficulty: it is very hard to find analogies between the 'small elements' of film (shots or camera movements, for example) and the equivalent elements in verbal language (the word or the phoneme), let alone aspects such as tenses or negatives. Several analysts conclude that film does not in fact possess a syntax, which would enable us to distinguish between 'grammatical' and 'ungrammatical' statements. Likewise, psychologists' attempts to identify the component skills that make up 'television literacy' have been fraught with difficulty.

At least in principle, it should be possible to break down what a competent viewer needs to do in order to 'understand' a piece of television; yet this does not necessarily correspond to the ways in which meanings are actually produced. Particular formal features of television do not carry fixed meanings, which can be objectively defined. A camera zoom, for example, may 'mean' different things at different times; and it may on certain occasions 'mean' the same thing as a tracking shot or a cut to close-up. Such apparently basic elements of media language cannot be said to be processed automatically.

However momentarily, viewers have to make active choices about their meaning. Nevertheless, it is important to distinguish here between interpretation at this 'micro' level and the 'macro' level of textual meaning. How we interpret a film, for example, does not depend only on how we 'read' particular shots or sequences. It also depends on how the text as a whole is organised and structured, for example via narrative; on how it relates to other texts we may have seen (intertextuality), or genres with which we are familiar; on how the text refers to, and makes claims about, aspects of reality with which we are more or less familiar (representation); and on the expectations we bring to it, for example as a result of the ways in which it has been publicised and distributed.

Understanding these different elements might also be seen as forms of 'literacy', in the sense that they involve the production of meaning and pleasure from a range of textual signs. Thus, the 'literacy' that is generally referred to in the case of 'media literacy' is clearly more than simply a functional literacy—the ability to make sense of a TV programme, for example, or to operate a camera. Literacy is not seen here merely as a kind of cognitive 'tool kit' that enables people to understand and use media. And media education is thus rather more than a kind of training course or proficiency test in media-related skills.

For want of a better term, media literacy is a form of critical literacy. It involves analysis, evaluation and critical reflection. It entails the acquisition of a 'meta-language'—that is, a means of describing the forms and structures of different modes of communication; and it involves a broader understanding of the social, economic and institutional contexts of communication, and how these affect people's experiences and practices. Media literacy certainly includes the ability to use and interpret media; but it also involves a much broader analytical understanding.

For the advocates of 'multiliteracies', and for others in this field, this emphasis on the plurality of literacies is not just about multiple modes (or media) of communication. It is also to do with the inherently social nature of literacy—and hence with the diverse forms that literacy takes in different cultures, and indeed within the increasingly multicultural societies in which we live. Research on print literacy clearly shows that different social groups define, acquire and use literacy in very different ways; and that the consequences of literacy depend upon the social contexts and social purposes for which it is used.

It is for this reason that such researchers tend to refer to 'literacy practices' or 'literacy events' rather than merely to 'literacy' per se: in other words, they regard reading and writing as social activities, rather than as manifestations of a set of disembodied cognitive skills. From this perspective, therefore, literacy cannot be considered separately from the social and institutional structures in which it is situated. This is a social theory, which effectively dispenses with a singular notion of literacy and replaces it with a notion of plural literacies, that are defined by the meanings they produce and the social interests they serve.

It implies that individuals do not create meanings in isolation, but through their involvement in social networks, or 'interpretive communities', which promote and value particular forms of literacy. The study of literacy should thus necessarily address questions about the economic and institutional contexts of communication—for example, how different social groups have different kinds of access to literacy, and how access and distribution are related to broader inequalities within society. This approach also implies that acquiring literacy (in whatever form) makes possible particular forms of social action. It enables people to do things, whether in their occupations, in their private lives or in civil society; and the forms it takes depend on what it is that is being done.

Social action is inevitably related to the operation of power within society; and so we might say that literacy is about the production of symbolic meanings, which in turn embody and enact particular relationships of power. In the case of 'media literacy', therefore, this approach suggests that we cannot regard—or indeed, teach—literacy as a set of cognitive abilities which individuals somehow come to 'possess' once and for all. We would need to begin by acknowledging that the media are an integral part of the texture of children's daily lives, and that they are embedded within their social relationships.

We would need to recognise that the competencies that are involved in making sense of the media are socially distributed, and that different social groups have different orientations towards the media, and will use them in diverse ways. In this sense, we should expect that children will have different 'media literacies'—or different modalities of literacy—that are required by the different social situations they encounter, and that will in turn have different social functions and consequences. And we should acknowledge that individuals have 'histories' of media experiences that may be activated in particular ways in particular social contexts, or by particular 'literacy events'.

Media Literacy Mapping

There have been various attempts to define the components of 'media literacy', and to prescribe how these might be taught to children at different ages. The British Film Institute's model of 'cineliteracy', first proposed in the Report Making Movies Matter, is one example. The BFI's model refers specifically to moving images, although most of the aspects identified can also apply to other media, including print; and there is no compelling logic for considering moving images in isolation.

The BFI model breaks down the field into three 'conceptual areas': 'the language of moving images', 'producers and audiences' and 'messages and values'. The document seeks to provide a model of 'learning progression' that will inform teaching about the moving image at different ages and stages of children's school careers. In addition to defining the 'experiences and activities' students should be able to engage in at each stage, it also defines the 'outcomes' that are to be expected, and the 'key words' that suggest 'the areas and types of knowledge that each stage might involve'.

For babies, television must appear as simply a random selection of shapes, colours and sounds, However, as they develop the ability to identify three-dimensional shapes, and come to understand the functions of language, children begin to develop hypotheses about the relationship between television and the real world. To begin with, television may be perceived as a kind of 'magic window', or alternatively as a magic box in which tiny people are living. Yet by the time they are about two, children seem to have understood that television is a medium that represents events which are taking place (or have taken place) elsewhere.

Through the experience of video, they also come to understand that television can be recorded and replayed, and that it is not necessarily 'live'. From the age of two, children are also developing an understanding of the 'language' of television. They learn that it follows rules or conventions which are different from those of real life. Thus, they learn that a zoom in to close-up does not mean that an object has got bigger, and that a cutaway to another object does not mean that the first object has disappeared. They learn to 'fill the gaps' which have been left in editing, for example when a character leaves a room and is next seen walking down the street. They learn to recognise the beginnings and endings of programmes, and to perceive the differences between programmes and advertisements. Between the ages of three and five, the distinction between television and real life gradually becomes more flexible.

While very young children appear to believe that all television is real, slightly older children may express precisely the opposite view; yet by around the age of five, children generally give more considered responses, suggesting that television is sometimes real, sometimes not. Between about five and seven, they also begin to distinguish between different kinds of programmes according to how realistic they are perceived to be. For example, they are likely to distinguish between cartoons, puppet animation and live action, and may well find events portrayed in live action drama or news much more frightening than similar events shown in cartoons. These relationships are often worked through in their television-related play, where children are actively experimenting with the differences between 'real life' and 'just pretend'.

By middle childhood (age 8-9), children are becoming more aware of the possible motivations of television producers—and indeed often quite cynical about them. For example, they will discuss how the narrative of a soap opera is organised in an attempt to keep us watching, or how advertisements attempt to persuade us to buy. They are also keenly interested in how programmes are produced, and (by the age of ten or eleven) are offering increasingly 'critical' judgments about the quality of the acting or the realism of the décor.

In both respects, they are much more likely to regard television as an artefact, and much less likely to see it as simply a 'slice of life'. Between middle childhood and early adolescence (between nine and twelve), children are also increasingly bringing more general social understandings to bear in their judgment of television, noting what is absent as well as questioning what is present. They may compare their own experience of family life, for example, with the representations provided on television, judging them to be less realistic as a result. Yet they may also acknowledge that in many cases, and for many reasons, television may not seek to be realistic in the first place, and that the need for plausibility has to be balanced against the need to amuse or entertain.

Similarly, while a particular scene may be perceived as unrealistic on an empirical level—for example, in genres like science fiction or melodrama—it may also be seen to express an 'emotional realism' which children may recognise and find moving. Finally, from the age of about eleven or twelve upwards, children may begin to speculate about the ideological impact of television, and the potential effects of 'positive' or 'negative' images of particular groups on audiences, even hypothetical ones. They begin to become aware of the process of 'stereotyping', both in real life and in the media. They may also come to perceive the differences between different styles of 'realism', and develop an aesthetic appreciation of the various ways in which the illusion of reality is created by television.

Explicitly or implicitly, television as a medium teaches the competencies that are required to make sense of it, just as books teach children how to read, and what reading means. A good deal of children's television, for example, is concerned to 'demystify' the medium, by demonstrating how programmes are produced, and by playing with the distinctions between television and real life—even if its attempts to do this are sometimes contradictory. Furthermore, parents and peers are also informally teaching children as they watch television together.

By confirming or questioning the accuracy of television representations, explaining and supplementing what is shown, and offering advice about whether television should be taken as a model of real-life behaviour, they are helping children to develop a more complex and nuanced understanding of the relationships between the medium and the real world. Nevertheless, there are several problems that might be raised with such an acccount, and with psychological research of this kind more broadly. The sequence identified here can easily be mapped on to a Piagetian model of cognitive development; and as such, it runs the risk of being reduced to a mechanical sequence of 'ages and stages'.

Critics of psychological research also suggest that it tends to adopt a rationalistic notion of child development as a steady progression towards adult maturity and rationality. In the case of work on children and the media, this developmentalist approach inevitably privileges certain kinds of judgments (particularly rational, 'critical' judgments) at the expense of others. Thus, a distanced critique of the implausibility of television is taken as a sign of 'maturity'; and in the process, any expression of pleasure or enjoyment may come to appear positively naïve.

Perhaps more significantly, this kind of account runs the risk of neglecting the social dimensions of children's engagements with television. In the context of group discussion, condemning programmes as 'unrealistic' provides a powerful means of defining one's own tastes, and thus of claiming a particular social identity. For example, girls' frequent complaints about the 'unrealistic' storylines or events in action-adventure cartoons often reflect a desire to distance themselves from what are seen as boys' 'childish' tastes, and thereby to proclaim their own (gendered) maturity. On the other hand, boys' rejection of the 'unrealistic' muscle-bound men in a programme like Baywatch may reflect anxieties about the fragility of their own masculine identity. Boys' rejection of melodrama or girls' rejection of violent action movies can thus be seen as rather more than the mechanical application of fixed judgments of taste: on the contrary, they represent an active claim to a particular social position—a claim which is sometimes tentative and uncertain, and in many cases open to challenge by others.

There is undoubtedly a considerable pleasure in this kind of critical talk: mocking the 'unrealistic' nature of television, speculating about 'how it's done', and playing with the relationship between television and reality would seem to be important aspects of most viewers' everyday interaction with the medium. Yet this kind of talk clearly does rely to some extent on disavowing one's own pleasure—or indeed displeasure—at the moment of viewing. Drawing attention to the special effects in horror movies, or laughing at the over-acting in soap operas, seems to offer a sense of power and control over experiences that might have been frightening or moving at the time, and thus provides a pleasurable sense of security.

However, it is important to stress that this kind of critical talk also serves particular functions in the context of dialogue with others. Most children know that many adults disapprove of them watching 'too much' television, and they are familiar with at least some of the arguments about its negative effects upon them. In some instances, these arguments are addressed directly, although children are generally keen to exempt themselves from such charges: while their younger siblings might copy what they watch, such accusations certainly do not apply to them.

Just as adults appear to displace the 'effects' of television onto children—thereby implying that they themselves are not at risk—so children tend to suggest that these arguments only apply to those much younger than themselves. In a sense, judgments about the 'unreality' of television could be seen to serve a similar function, albeit in a more indirect way. They enable the speaker to present him- or herself as a sophisticated viewer, who is able to 'see through' the illusions television provides.

Judgments about the reality of television are much more of a preoccupation for middle-class children. Both quantitatively and qualitatively, their judgments appear more complex and sophisticated than those of the majority of their working-class counterparts. Yet these arguments should not be seen to support any simplistic conclusions about the levels of 'media literacy' in different social classes. Rather, it would seem that these critical discourses serve particular social functions for these children, which are at least partly to do with defining their own class position. They provide a powerful means whereby middle-class children can demonstrate their own critical authority, and thereby distinguish themselves from those invisible 'others'—the 'mass' audience—who are, by implication, more at risk of suffering the harmful effects of television.

Limits of Assessment

This detour into research about children and television illustrates several broader issues that are directly relevant to media education. On one level, it suggests that a socialscientific concept such as 'representation' is not some kind of alien academic imposition on students. On the contrary, it shows how children's understanding of this issue derives (at least initially) from their everyday attempts to make sense of the medium, which begin in early childhood. However, it also suggests that judgments about representation or realism are frequently very complex.

Children use a range of different types of knowledge in making such judgments, which include their developing knowledge about the processes of media production, their knowledge of the 'language' of media, and their knowledge of the real world. As this implies, judgments of reality are almost bound to be a focus of tension and debate. Some people (such as teachers in classrooms) may assume the power to impose particular definitions or versions of reality; and 'reality' is often seen here as a matter of what children ought to think, rather than how things are. As such, these definitions are very likely to be resisted. This should at least caution us against the difficulties of attempting to enlighten children about the 'inaccuracies' and 'distortions' of the media—an approach which still informs many media education curricula.

The key point here, however, is that children's judgments about the reality of what they watch on television cannot be seen as a purely cognitive or intellectual process, or as a merely individual one. On the contrary, it is through making 'critical' judgments of this kind that children seek to define their social identities, both in relation to their peers and in relation to adults. Likewise, assertions about the 'effects' of the media—whether explicit or implicit—inevitably reflect broader claims about one's own position. What we believe to be 'real' also depends to a large extent on what we want to be real, and hence on the pleasures that particular representations may offer us.

The classroom is not a neutral space of dispassionate scientific enquiry, in which objective 'truth' can be easily established. On the contrary, it is a social arena in which students and teachers engage in an ongoing struggle over the right to define meaning and identity. Making sense of the media is not simply a matter of what goes on inside children's heads: it is an interpersonal phenomenon, in which social interests and identities are unavoidably at stake. In this sense, a model like the British Film Institute's map of 'cineliteracy' is inevitably very reductive.

It encourages us to assess 'outcomes' against normative statements of particular stages—defined, at least partly, through students' ability to employ particular 'key words' (from 'zoom' through 'stereotype' to 'hegemony'). It does not particularly help us to know how we might intervene in order to move particular students onwards in their understanding; nor does it acknowledge the social dynamics of learning in the classroom. Ultimately, it is not so much a model of 'learning progression' as a model of assessment.

The notion of 'media literacy' is far from unproblematic. Yet it firmly situates the study of media within a broader analysis of communication; and in doing so, it implicitly questions the continuing dominance of print culture within education. Media education directly challenges many of the assumptions and practices that characterise the teaching of language and literature in schools. It represents a call for a more inclusive and relevant—but also more coherent and rigorous—approach to teaching about culture and communication. In particular, the social theory of literacy outlined here implicitly challenges the textual emphasis of much literature teaching—and indeed, a good deal of media education as well.

Media literacy necessarily entails a systematic understanding of the formal strategies and conventions of communication—and as such, media education is bound to entail close textual analysis. Yet texts are only part of the picture. Media literacy obviously entails 'a capacity to decipher, appreciate, criticise and compose'; but it also requires a broader understanding of the social, economic and historical contexts in which texts are produced, distributed and used by audiences. At the same time, the emphasis on literacy reminds us of an element that is often neglected in media education. For literacy clearly involves both reading and writing; and as such, media literacy must necessarily entail both the interpretation and the production of media.

14

Ownership and Control of Media

Ownership is an important element of media dependence, it is far from the only method government uses to manipulate the media where it is unfree. State ownership of newspapers, radio and television stations may not be the most important determinant of media manipulation.

Media Manipulation

There are four specific avenues through which government manipulates media in this environment:

1) direct control via outlet ownership,
2) indirect control via infrastructure ownership,
3) indirect control via financial pressure, and
4) indirect control via entry regulation.

Direct Control via Outlet Ownership

The state owned media outlets is not difficult to imagine how government influences media provided information. These outlets are financed entirely by the state and consequently do not rely upon consumers to remain afloat. Since they are beholden to the state for funding, state owned media outlets have a strong incentive to avoid being critical of the current government. Furthermore, as state owned enterprises, these outlets are run exclusively by government appointed directors who determine both the stories that will be covered as well as the light in which these stories will be conveyed. Politicians in power thus choose directors and editors that will do their bidding, creating heavily biased news.

Although the outlets are technically in the hands of private owners, they are not acquired and operated for the purposes of profit, but instead to manipulate information reaching the outlet's audience. In many instances these outlets are not even self-sustaining but are instead cross subsidized by their owners' other businesses that generate profits. Politicians find it worthwhile to keep these media sources operating despite the fact that they often generate monetary losses because of their ability to control information reaching the public. Berlusconisation is most pervasive on the local scale in less urban areas where local newspapers and radio stations are struggling financially.

Indirect Control via Infrastructure Ownership

The American journalist A. J. Liebling once said: "Freedom of the press is guaranteed only to those who own one." Liebling's remark is an insightful one because it highlights the importance of who owns the inputs used in media production. If media outlets are privately owned but vital means of production and distribution are monopolised in the hands of the state, government's control over the media remains strong.

For example, in Romania, state ownership of media related infrastructure is one indirect method government uses to manipulate the media. Similarly, the distribution network for printed media in Romania, Rodipet, is state-owned. Rodipet functions as one of government's strongest structural controls over the printed media industry. The state is able to use its monopoly position over distribution in much the same way that it was able to use its former monopoly position over newsprint to indirectly control what information reaches the public.

Indirect Control via Financial Pressure

There is great truth in the old adage that one should not bite the hand that feeds them. Where media is independent of government this means avoiding the ire of its customers. Where media outlets rely upon government to remain afloat, however, it means staying on the good side of those who wield political power. By creating an environment in which most private media outlets depend financially upon the state.

Many private media outlets also rely heavily upon state-purchased advertisements to remain in business. Government uses this financial power to pressure media sources to 17 bias reported information such that it favours the governing party. The State Ownership Fund (FPS) decides with which media outlets various state-owned enterprises will contract for advertisements. As a government institution the FPS is able to effectively wield this power to influence media sources in need of advertisement revenue. For instance, the FPS may agree to purchase advertisement space in a newspaper if the newspaper agrees to favour the governing party in its coverage.

Government illegally withholds information that might reveal "hidden relationships" between itself and private outlets. Such withholding is technically illegal under the Freedom of Information Act passed in late 2001. However, when the state's interest is at stake the act is typically not enforced. Regulation forms another important method of financial pressure that government uses to manipulate the media. These regulations empower politicians to find real or imaginary financial and operational violations by media outlets that refuse to do their bidding. Alleged violations are then used to financially or operationally strangle unfriendly media sources via hefty fines, raising the cost of compliance so high as to prevent profitability, or outright foreclosure of outlets. Government can also use the threat of infraction to blackmail[18] media sources into biasing news coverage. Likewise, ambiguous and constantly changing regulation creates a guise for politicos to "inspect" unfriendly media outlets to obtain sensitive financial and customer information that is then used to squeeze these outlets' private sources of revenue.

Indirect Control via Entry Regulation

As Djankov et al point out, politicians benefit by regulating firms' entry into particular industries. In the case of the media industry this is particularly true. By acting as the gatekeeper to the media industry, government can keep out potential media providers who might be hostile towards their policies and throw out existing media producers who do not serve its ends. In this way entry regulation gives government a powerful method of indirectly manipulating mass media.

For example, the Romanian government regulates media entry through licensure. The National Council of Broadcasting (CNA), a council composed of eleven members appointed by the president, government, and parliament, makes licensing decisions for television and radio broadcasting. The CNA, which was established in 1992, has monopoly power to grant or revoke an outlet's permission to broadcast at any time. In addition, once an aspiring media broadcaster has been granted a license by the CNA it must obtain operating authorisation from the Ministry of Communications and Information Technology, which constitutes another politically determined hurdle to entering the broadcasting industry. Through this power to determine what media outlets may and may not enter the media business, government is able to influence information conveyed via broadcast media. For instance, Omega TV was recently shut down by the[20] CNA after a guest appearing on one of its programs was critical of the Romanian government.

Media Manipulation in Economic Performance

Napoleon once said: "If I were to give liberty to the press, my power could not last three days." Clearly he understood the power of media in checking the abuses of political rulers. Furthermore, Napoleon's remark suggests that a free media would have made a difference for France's economy. If he were correct, an independent media would have forced him to change his policies or be thrown from power. This policy difference would in turn have generated a markedly different French economy. As this line of reasoning indicates, media manipulation primarily affects economic performance indirectly through its impact on which policies are adopted. What policies are adopted is in turn a function of the behaviour of those in political power. In transitioning countries like Romania, policy adoption refers specifically to economic reforms.

Policies broadly tend to serve one of two interests: public interests or private ones. Policies that serve public interests are those that generally raise the long run living standard of a country's entire range of inhabitants, or at least do not disproportionately benefit one small group at the expense of everyone else. Such policies are those typically considered growth enhancing and necessary for economic prosperity. They include, for instance, low inflation, low taxes, transparent regulation, stable rule of law, free trade, etc.

Policies that serve private interests, in contrast, are those generally aimed at privileging a small class of individuals at the expense of the rest of society. In the absence of a mechanism that punishes them for doing so, politicians prefer to create this kind of policy because doing so serves their own interests. By concentrating benefits on special interest groups and dispersing the costs of these benefits on the rest of society, politicians can benefit themselves in terms of money and votes.

Similarly, by expanding the size and scope of government activities through the introduction of additional regulations, political agents expand their power, increase the number of bureaucratic positions they can offer to connections and friends, and in some cases preserve the rationale for their own positions of political power. Policies that serve private interests are those typically associated with catering to special interest groups. They include, for instance, tariffs, business regulations and state-granted monopoly status. They can also include policies like inflation that benefit incumbent politicians by creating a short run boost in economic activity but harm the economy's longer-term growth. As has been pointed out by others, independent media-provided information increases the transparency of the policy-making process, and accurately reveals to voters which politicians support public-oriented policies and which support private-oriented ones.

By correctly informing citizens about politicians' activities, an independent media makes these activities common knowledge and enables voters to effectively monitor politicians at low cost. This creates an incentive for politicians to adopt policies that serve public rather than private interests, as they are aware that if they do not, voters will find out and punish them accordingly at election time. In short, an independent media provides voters with credible information about the behaviour of politicians that enables them to monitor these agents. On the basis of this information, voters are able to punish politicians who serve private interests and reward those who serve public ones. Where the media is manipulated by the state, however, this mechanism breaks down. The breakdown occurs by affecting the dissemination of credible information.

State manipulated media tends to take two specific forms: (1) information withholding, in which the state prevents media outlets from disseminating unfavourable news, and (2) misinformation, in which the state uses its control to bias news in a way that favours incumbent politicos, or to fabricate untruthful news that will favour these actors. If voters do not receive relevant information about the policy behaviour of politicians, or receive information about this behaviour that is false, then the monitoring capacity of media is compromised and the information it provides cannot be used as the basis for voter punishment. This means two negative things for policy. On the one hand, politicians who refuse to pursue policies in the public's interest will not be effectively weeded out via the election process. Furthermore, if political agents know this, they have an additional incentive to indulge in the creation of policy that serves private rather than public ends.

The harmful effects of media manipulation can be divided into "objective" consequences on the one hand, and "subjective" consequences on the other. The objective consequences of media manipulation are those described above. As a result of state manipulation, less information and/or less accurate information about the behaviour of politicians and political happenings reaches the public, compromising voters' ability to use the media to hold unscrupulous political agents accountable. We call these consequences of media manipulation "objective" because their occurrence is independent of citizens' knowledge about the status of information manipulation in their country.

The subjective consequences of media manipulation, in contrast, are those that depend on citizens' awareness of the extent of media manipulation in their country. The primary subjective consequence we have in mind here is what we call manipulated media's "credibility crisis." Voters who are aware that the information reaching them is filtered may lose their trust in media-provided information, discounting even accurate information that reaches them because they can never be certain of its credibility.

Although the distinction between the objective and subjective consequences of government manipulated media is an important one, it is equally important to appreciate the inextricable connection between the two. Manipulated media's credibility crisis (i.e., its subjective consequences) is a direct effect of the objective consequences of state manipulated media. Without the objective results of media manipulation-less/inaccurate information-there would be no credibility problem for citizens to become aware of (i.e., no subjective consequences).

Credibility Crisis of Media

Citizens simply do not trust their media. For example, Romanians are interested in both the domestic and international, social, political and economic events that affect their lives. Most receive daily information from television, newspapers and radio. Nonetheless, nearly all the subjects we spoke with were highly disappointed with the quality and reliability of the information available to them. Several subjects we interviewed generally considered private media sources more reliable than public sources.

For instance, because Romanians know that government abuses the television and radio licensing procedure to permit entry only to media outlets prepared to do the state's bidding, they generally discount the credibility of these media sources despite the fact that they are privately owned. Citizens are also likely to know the owners of major media outlets as well as their own local outlets. Thus when local politicians, for example, own and operate media sources, citizens know that they cannot believe much of the information these sources provide.

Similarly, citizens discount information from private media sources because they are aware that government uses financial pressure to manipulate these sources. For instance, several subjects we spoke with were aware of the political pressure that government applies to private media outlets that owe back taxes, like ProTV. For these reasons, citizens consider both public and private media sources highly politically dependent. A recent national survey of Romanian citizens corroborates our findings in the field. According to this survey, only 26% of Romanians believe that Romanian mass media is independent.

Media Ownership

Fewer owners have control over more newspapers and their circulation, and most of the media have been absorbed by large conglomerates, 'families' or chains. In addition to ownership concentration of the mass media industry, content provision, packaging and distribution have also 'become a standardised production and marketing process in which the messages communicated are constrained and directed in both quantity and quality to meet the economic imperatives of that process'. Giddens goes even further when he calls for 'the democratising of the democracy'. He criticises the untamed power of media owners:

> The media have a double relation to democracy. On the one hand ... the emergence of a global information society is a powerful democratising force. Yet, television, and the other media, tend to destroy the very public space of dialogue they open up, through relentless trivialising, and personalising of political issues. Moreover, the growth of giant multinational media corporations means that unelected business tycoons can hold enormous power.

The implications of alternative standards are controversial in regulatory circles, in popular public policy debates, as well as in communication and media policy studies. The question for media and communication studies is whether a meaningful contribution to a profound public policy debate can be made on the problem of media ownership and concentration. The first paradox is that very few scholars do research on this issue in a holistic manner.

Few complain about the missing analyses and debates within the scientific community.

As Sterling observes, 'Surprisingly little research has been done—only marginally more than we could draw on two decades ago. Too much is assumed or anecdotal, merely suggesting results from ownership changes'. Compaine and Gomery, editors of *Who Owns the Media* do not agree with this observation about neglect. Gomery argues that 'no research in mass communication can ignore questions of mass media ownership and the economic implications of that control'. Unfortunately, mainstream communication researchers are not very often able, and not very often willing, to analyse the implications of media ownership and concentration.

McQuail argues 'despite the amount and ingenuity of research, it is hard to avoid the conclusion that it has failed to establish clear general effects from monopoly conditions on the balance of cost and benefits, in performance term. Where there is evidence, the effects seem to be quite small'. According to Picard, the primary reasons for the absence of research in this area is the lack of adequate data and funding.

The problem of media ownership and concentration is perceived quite differently from a political economy perspective. The mass media industry is to play a significant role in legitimating inequalities in wealth, power and privilege. When the control of the flow of information, knowledge, values and images is concentrated in the hands of those who share the power of the dominant class, the ruling class will establish what is circulated through the mass media in order to reproduce the structure of class inequalities from which they benefit.

The mass media industry is crucial for the creation of reliable information, knowledge, ideology and propaganda in contemporary capitalist societies. As Strinati argues, its structure of ownership and control are equally crucial.

Marxist 'critical studies' claim that the mass media 'assume an all-encompassing conspiracy by monopolist'. The relationship between ownership and control as an indirect and mediated one. Control is not always exercised in a direct way, nor does the economic structure of media institutions always have an immediate impact on their output. Mainstream communication researchers criticise the conspiracy theories of the media on theoretical as well as on empirical grounds, arguing that political economists' views are supported only by anecdotal evidence.

The most common assumption is that the owners of the media influence the content and form of media content through their decisions to employ certain personnel, by funding special projects, and by providing a media platform for ideological interest groups. In the United Kingdom, Curran and Seaton conclude that the national press generally endorses the basic tenets of the capitalist system—private enterprise, profit, the free market and the rights of property ownership. In the United States, according to some media observers and scholars, a small group of powerful owners of six to ten media conglomerates, control what is read by the population, what people see and hear—or do not read, see and hear. Concerns are expressed about increasing corporate control of mass mediated information flows and about how democracy can function if the information that citizens rely on is tainted by the influence of mega-media.

Overall, the implications of media ownership and concentration on a global scale are as follows. The global interlocking of the media industry and traditional corporate power creates a powerful cartel, which in turn encourages the spread of certain values. There are strong incentives for the displacement of the public sphere with commercial infotainment, reality shows and trivialised news programmes. This strengthens a conservative 'common sense' view of the world, eroding local cultures and communities.

Expansion of Political Power

The economic strength of media conglomerates increases their position in society so that they become powerful institutions with substantial political power. According to Bagdikian the largest media giants have achieved alarming success in writing the media laws and regulations to favour the interests of their corporations rather than the interests of the general public. In Europe and the United States, many cross-media ownership rules have been relaxed or have disappeared with the rise of a laissez-faire ideology within parliaments, governments and regulatory bodies. In the United States, '[w]here the FCC once had stringent ownership controls concerning radio and television stations most are gone and the rest have been liberalised'.

The Federal Communications Commission once believed that programming diversification was necessary to maximise public service. It was argued that the greater the number of independent broadcasters, the greater the chances for achieving the desired diversity. Rules restricting common ownership of broadcast stations, and of broadcast stations in combination with other media forms, were adopted. But media regulators have actually stimulated the ownership concentration process. In the United Kingdom, for example, a law, intended to restrain concentration, was manipulated into a Newspaper Preservation Policy under which in practice preservation meant, not less, but more, concentration of ownership.

As a consequence of the increasing influence of the media conglomerates on public opinion, there is little substantive coverage of the spectacular media deals in terms of the perceived effects of these deals. In most cases, journalists are directly affected but they do not report their own concerns (probably because of internal pressure). Media owners are keen to advertise the advantages of horizontal, vertical, diagonal and international concentration. State agencies play down the potential risks and threats of media conglomeration for the public sphere, in particular, and for democracy, in general.

Regulation and Ownership

One area of concern to media researchers is the regulation of ownership and control of broadcasting institutions. A conundrum has emerged in the contemporaneous relationship between media and political systems in Africa. While it has always been widely accepted that political systems dictate the character of media institutions in Africa, the wind of democratisation at the end of the 20th century was, to a significant extent, a product of the continent's nascent independent media. As nascent media institutions have firmed their presence on the continent's political and social map, a reversal of roles has been discernible, with political systems being consistently defined and redefined by the emerging media.

Indeed, an intriguing relationship is panning out in contemporary Africa polities: previously indomitable state authority is giving way to media institutions wielding formidable influence. The adage, information is power, is finally come true in Africa. Any attempt to explicate this conundrum must begin with recognising that recent paradigm shifts in public policy, coupled with technological advances, have triggered a media revolution around the world.

Paradigm shifts in public policy are characterised by the privatisation of public communications and a radical ideological shift to free market enterprise. Technological advances with major implications for media institutions include digital systems, satellite communications systems and computer-aided communications. The media revolution is evident in Africa, too. In nearly all African countries, sweeping new legislation in communications and broadcasting has been enacted over the past decade alone. The legislation redefines critical issues in the media marketplace such as licensing, signal distribution, and maintenance of broadcasting standards. In a few instances, the legislation may address content generation, public service communications, and control and ownership. The new technologies are omnipresent in Africa; new investments in modern technology are placing the continent closer than ever before to the industrialised West. It is noteworthy that specific effects of each transformational force are difficult to pin down because of the rapidity, simultaneity and interconnectedness of these changes.

The foregoing may not spell out a cause for alarm, but studies of the emerging political economy of public communications in Europe and Asia show disconcerting patterns. New commercial operators have appeared, bringing with them new forms of ownership, economic integration and market strategies. By giving broadcasting a new raison d'etre, the operators have also highlighted a challenge to governments, namely, how to regulate control and ownership.

A Conceptual Framework

The normative justification for regulating media control and ownership is premised upon political and economic considerations. The political dimension posits that media institutions are crucial for political stability and progress. It is generally accepted that, among other functions, media encourage and disseminate diverse opinions and views, and promote national consciousness. Barnett adds that media are instrumental in creating "inclusive" democracies. Murdock sees media institutions as crucial watchdogs and advocates on behalf of the citizenry, and as windows for the comprehension of contemporary issues. McChesney argues that media help citizens to achieve a sense of community, and to participate meaningfully in the political process. These functions give media power to influence public opinion, and justify "control beyond the provisions of the general competition legislation". The traditional government practice of intervening is through regulation.

The economic dimension is less popular, even though equally important. Fleming notes that competition in traditional markets is based upon such factors as consumer choices, availability of good or service, price and quality. However, competition in the broadcast industry is different. The bulk of revenue comes from advertisers and not from sales to media consumers. As such, broadcasting media revenue is not a good indicator of the benefits that viewers and listeners receive. Indeed, as Fleming points out, advertisers choose the broadcasting service, and their interests are not identical with those of the eventual consumers of media output, namely, the audiences. This forms the economic raison d'etre for protecting audience interests externally.

It is noteworthy that media ownership is generally not a danger to democracy; the danger lies in its distorted forms, namely, concentrated and cross-media ownership. Murdock defines media concentration as the tendency by larger media firms to increase their market share by taking over or merging with competitors or by forcing weaker players out. Empirically, concentration is the proportion of the market held by the major media companies. Horizontal concentration, concentration processes within a single media industry sector, often creates highly profitable oligopolistic corporations.

Vertical concentration, tendencies by media enterprises to control some or all steps in the production and distribution of their good or service, allows greater market autonomy, reduced competition and increased market advantage. Cross-media ownership, control of different media products by one media enterprise, allows the firm to benefit from economies of scale and enhances market power. Finally, diagonal (or conglomerate concentration), arising from non-media enterprises taking control of media firms, increases size and market power of a media outfit.

Meier and Trappel argue that cross-media ownership—whether through vertical or diagonal integration — leads to synergies in technology, human capital and marketing. Albarran contends that highly concentrated markets usually lead to strong barriers to entry for new competitors, decline of diversity of public expression, and increased economic power and political influence. Murdock adds that through concentration, few firms decide on the mix of information, expression and debate to be availed to the public. At the same time, he warns that larger media firms have high stakes in other strategic media investments, creating large multimedia corporations with cross-media ownership links.

Either way, he argues, media concentration is a threat to diversity, a crucial tenet of open democracy. Meier and Trappel summarise the impact of media concentration on pluralism, diversity and quality into several observations:

— As economic strength of media conglomerates increases, market power extends to political power;

— Concentration leads to a reduction in the number of information sources and to greater uniformity in content;

— Concentration reduces quantity and quality of local and regional political news;

— Concentration policies favour large, highly integrated media corporations because they are able to take over or drive out smaller competitors;

— In most developed economies, economic explanations dominate political explanations.

Almost always, concentration leads to higher profits for the expanded media enterprise.

Ownership Patterns: A Study of South African Meida Industry

Although South Africa has a robust and fairly sophisticated broadcast media sector, the country's history of racial discrimination has created the most daunting challenge for broadcast regulators. Before 1993, broadcasting in South Africa was generally a state monopoly via the South African Broadcasting Corporation (SABC). The SABC owned 21 radio stations and four television stations. The sole private broadcaster, M-Net, was licensed to the newspaper industry and prohibited from broadcasting news. An intriguing pattern of monomedia, vertical, horizontal, cross-media and concentration characterised the print medis scene, yielding strong oligopolistic market patterns that aided the Apartheid government's initiative to control the press.

After independence in 1994, press ownership patterns changed radically black economic empowerment groups, trade unions and a number of foreign media corporations. Changes in broadcasting were equally far-reaching. The Independent Broadcasting Authority was created in 1993 through the IBA Act negotiated between Nelson Mandela's African National Congress and the white government of F. W. de Klerk. Among other things, the IBA Act was mandated to :

— Open the airwaves to previously disadvantaged groups and opinions;

— Establish viable market conditions for a diverse and independent broadcasting system;

— To establish an authority that will provide for the regulation of broadcasting to promote the provision of a diverse range of sound and television services on a national, regional and local level.

— Encourage ownership of broadcasting services by persons from historically disadvantaged groups;

— Impose limitations on cross-media control of private broadcasting services.

The IBA Act based its commitment to regulation on the premise of furthering democracy, diversity and development. It appreciated that poor regulation of market forces was a threat to the diversity of ownership and opinion, and saw regulation as a prerequisite for the reconstruction of broadcasting as a democratic public sphere. As Barnett posits, the IBA aimed at securing a plurality of independent broadcasters through deconcentration of media industries and separation of media from the state. This endeavour became part of the transformation objectives of the SABC in 1996 when it sold six of its most profitable commercial regional radio stations to black economic empowerment groups.

The IBA also issued eight new regional licenses to applicants with strong black economic empowerment credentials and pledges for diversity in programming. The new media owners included trade unions, women groups, and black-owned empowerment companies. Between 1996 and 2000, the IBA (and its successor, the Independent Communications Authority of South Africa) had issues 65 community radio licences, most of them for four-year periods. The authority also issued the first private free-to-air television licence to Midi, a consortium of trade unions, black empowerment groups and the US media conglomerate AOL Time Warner.

The IBA Act endeavours to regulate most forms of media concentration. It regulates monomedia ownership by requiring that companies may not own more 25 percent shareholding in more than two FM or AM radio stations. It limits cross-media concentration by requiring that broadcast media enterprises may not own control newspapers and radio stations that dominate both the print and broadcast market of the same geographical area. The Act also attempts to regulate international concentration by requiring foreign ownership of media enterprises to remain below 20 percent.

Finally, but of major significance, is the requirement that corporate holders of a broadcasting licence maintain a strong component of black economic empowerment in their ownership structure. It is noteworthy that all four legal provisions purporting to regulate ownership are increasingly under heavy scrutiny and criticism as operatives seek to realign themselves in the moderately competitive media market that has emerged over the past decade. The monomedia concentration regulation has thus far withstood the test, but is constantly challenged by technological advances that elevate the reach of regional stations into subnational status. At the same time, recent proposals for ownership change of Kagiso Media, a cross-media outfit, are expected to either reinforce or crush this legislative provision. The much-awaited review of Nail-Kagiso deal will also have major implications for regulations governing cross-media concentration, considering that Nail already owns the Sowetan, the largest daily newspaper in South Africa by circulation.

Many analysts consider the international concentration legislation to have been ill-advised and have strongly recommended its scrapping. The critics argue that fixing a 20 percent ceiling on foreign ownership of media enterprises contravenes the country's foreign investment code works to limit access to foreign capital for the local companies. AOL Time Warner expressed this frustration after it was unable to increase its shareholding in e.tv beyond the mandated 20 percent. Indeed, Primedia, another cross-media enterprise, is widely believed to have contravened this clause after its foreign shareholder, UK's ActiveShare, increased its stake to 35 percent over the past year. ICASA is yet to rule on the matter.

The regulation requiring the maintenance of a strong empowerment component is probably the most controversial. Many enterprises founded on the premise of black economic empowerment are experiencing serious financial problems, often because the black partners do not inject significant funds. The issue becomes complicated when such enterprises seek to revise their shareholding to attract new capital provide opportunities for present nonempowerment partners to inject funds by increasing their shareholding. Already, Kaya FM and e.tv have found themselves in trouble with ICASA over this predicament. Nail's recent attempt to buy two pseudo-community radio stations was thwarted on the grounds that such a move would harm the empowerment makeup of those stations. While the regulator's intentions are noble in this regard, this provision is unlikely to survive unless specific ways were found to bail out cash-strapped enterprises.

Bibliography

Aarseth, Espen J., *Cybertext: Perspectives on Ergodic Literature,* Johns Hopkins UP, 1997.

Adorno, Theodor and Horkheimer, Max, *The Dialectic of Enlightenment,* "The Culture Industry." Continuum Pub Group, 1976.

Barlow, John Perry, *"The Economy of Ideas: A Framework for Patents and Copyrights in the Digital Age,"* Wired 2.03, March 1994.

Beniger, James R., *The Control Revolution: Technological and Economic Origins of the Information Society.* Cambridge, Mass.: Harvard Univ. Press, 1986.

Berners-Lee, Tim, *Weaving the Web: The Original Design and Ulitmate Desitiny of the World Wide Web,* Harper Business, 2000.

Birkerts, Sven, *The Gutenberg Elegies: The Fate of Reading in an Electronic Age. Boston: Faber and Faber, 1994.*

Bolter, Jay David and Grusin, Richard. *Remediation: Understanding New Media.* MIT Press, 2000.

Castells, Manuel, *The Information Age: Economy, Society and Culture,* 3 vols. Malden, Mass.: Blackwell, 1996-97.

Hayles, Katherine, *How We Became Posthuman : Virtual Bodies in Cybernetics, Literature, and Informatics.* Chicago: Univ. of Chicago Press, 1999.

Landow, George P., *Hypertext: The Convergence of Contemporary Critical Theory and Technology,* Baltimore: Johns Hopkins Univ. Press, 1991.

Laurel, Brenda, *Computers as Theatre. Reading, Mass.: Addison-Wesley, 1993, 1991.*

Manovich, Lev, *The Language of New Media,* Cambridge, Mass: MIT Press, 2001.

McLuhan, Marshall, *Understanding Media: The Extensions of Man,* MIT Press, 1994.

Miscellaneous Topics:

Moulthrop, Stuart, "No War Machine," in Joseph Tabbi and Michael Wutz, eds., *Reading Matters: Narrative in the New Media Ecology*. Cornell UP, 1997: 269-92.

Negroponte, Nicholas, *Being Digital,* Vintage Books, 1996.

Paulson, William R., *The Noise of Culture: Literary Texts in a World of Information,* Cornell UP, 1988.

Poster, Mark, *The Mode of Information: Poststructuralism and Social Context,* Chicago: Univ. of Chicago Press, 1990.

Steur, Jonathan, "Defining Virtual Reality", *Journal of Communication* 42 (1992): 79-90.

Thompson, John B., *The Media and Modernity: A Social Theory of the Media,* Stanford UP, 1996.

Turkle, Sherry, *Life on the Screen: Identity in the Age of the Internet,* New York: Simon & Schuster, 1995.

Index